GCSE/KEY STAGE 4
ENGLISH

GUIDES

Elizabeth A. Cripps

Longman

LONGMAN REVISE GUIDES

SERIES EDITORS:
Geoff Black and Stuart Wall

TITLES AVAILABLE:
Art and Design
Biology
Business Studies
CDT: – Design and Realisation
CDT: – Technology
Chemistry
Computer Studies
Economics
English*
English Literature*
French
Geography
German
Home Economics
Mathematics*
Mathematics: Higher Level and Extension
Music
Physics
Religious Studies
Science*
Sociology
Spanish
World History

* new editions for Key Stage 4

Longman Group
*Longman House, Burnt Mill, Harlow,
Essex CM20 2JE, England
and Associated Companies throughout the world.*

© Longman Group 1988, 1993

First published 1988
2nd Edition 1993
Third Impression 1994

British Library Cataloguing in Publication Data

Cripps, Elizabeth
   English. – (Longman GCSE revise guides).
   1. English Language – Study and teaching
   (Secondary) – England 2. General Certificate of
   Secondary Education – Study guides
   I. Title
   420'.76 LB1631

   ISBN 0–582–22832–8

Set by 17QQ in 10/12pt Century Old Style

Produced by Longman Singapore Publishers Pte Ltd
Printed in Singapore

CONTENTS

EDITORS' PREFACE

Longman Revise Guides for GCSE/Key Stage 4 are written by experienced examiners and teachers, and aim to give you the best possible foundation for success in examinations and other modes of assessment. Much has been said in recent years about declining standards and disappointing examination results. While this may be somewhat exaggerated, examiners are well aware that the performance of many candidates falls well short of their potential. The books encourage thorough study and a full understanding of the concepts involved and should be seen as course companions and study guides to be used throughout the year. Examiners are in no doubt that a structured approach in preparing for examinations and in presenting coursework can, together with hard work and diligent application, substantially improve performance.

The largely self-contained nature of each chapter gives the book a useful degree of flexibility. After starting with Chapters 1 and 2, all other chapters can be read selectively, in any order appropriate to the stage you have reached in your course. As well as the examination-type questions and answers at the end of each chapter, you will also find a 'Review Sheet' to test yourself on the content of that chapter.

We believe that this book, and the series as a whole, will help you establish a solid platform of basic knowledge and examination technique on which to build.

Geoff Black and Stuart Wall

ACKNOWLEDGEMENTS

All the Examination Boards referred to in this book are thanked for their prompt and helpful replies to enquiries. I am particularly grateful to the following for giving permission to reproduce questions from specimen papers: University of London Examinations and Assessment Council; Midland Examining Group; Northern Examinations and Assessment Board, incorporating the Associated Lancashire, Joint Matriculation, North Regional, North West Regional, Yorkshire and Humberside Regional Examination Boards; Northern Ireland Schools Examinations and Assessment Council; Southern Examining Group. Whilst permission has been granted to reproduce their questions, the answers, or hints on answers are solely the responsibility of the author and have not been provided or approved by the Groups.

I should like to thank colleagues and pupils who have helped me in the preparation of this book and especially Miss Jean Hayes, Title Adviser and head teacher of Sir John Cass's Foundation and Red Coat Secondary School, Ms. Anne Clarke and some of the pupils of Stockwell Park School, and Mrs. Zena Maddision of the Marcus Lipton Centre.

Thanks are also due to my husband, R. F. Cripps,who read the manuscript and made many helpful suggestions.

We are grateful to the following for permission to reproduce copyright material:
The Editor for a letter from the *Belfast Telegraph*; the author's agents for an extract from *Native Ground* by Philip Callow. (c) Philip Callow (pub. Heinemann, 1959); William Collins Sons & Co Ltd for an extract from *Intimate Relations* by Jacqui Durrell (pub. Collins, 1976); Guardian Newspapers Ltd for extracts from the article 'Channel Tunnel – playing for high stakes' by Andrew Cornelius in *The Guardian* 17.12.85; the Controller of Her Majesty's Stationery Office for extracts from *Practical Assessment in Oracy at Age 15*; the author's agents for an extract from *If Only They Could Talk* by James Herriot (pub. Michael Jospeh, 1970); the author's agents for an extract from 'Through the Tunnel' in *The Habit of Loving* by Doris Lessing. Copyright 1954 Doris Lessing; The National Trust for extracts from *The National Trust Handbook 1987*; the author's agents for the short story 'The Trout' by Sean O'Faolian; the author's agents on behalf of the Estate of the late Sonia Brownell Orwell & Secker & Warburg Ltd for an extract from *Animal Farm* by George Orwell; the author, Vernon Scannell for his poem 'Growing Pain'.

Elizabeth Cripps

The publishers are grateful to the following schools and colleges for their co-operation:
Bishop Fox's School, Taunton; Chase High School, Malvern; Derby Tertiary College, Mackworth; Impington Village College, Cambridge; Poole Grammar School; Pope Pius Comprehensive School, Rotherham; Queensbury School, Bradford; Rugby School; St Helena School, Chesterfield; St Christopher School, Letchworth; St Mary's High School, Cheshunt; Shildon Sunnydale Comprehensive School; Sir William Perkins's School, Chertsey; South Park Sixth Form College, Middlesbrough; Thrybergh Comprehensive School, Rotherham; Waddesdon Church of England Secondary School, Aylesbury; Wollaston School, Wellingborough.

GETTING STARTED

This chapter outlines the ways in which GCSE is different from earlier examinations in English, indicates what the Examining Groups have in common and where there is scope for choice, and discusses assessment in the examination.

We also look at the impact of the introduction of Key Stage 4 of the National Curriculum on the English course. You will see that *attainment targets* have now been established for English (as for other subjects), i.e. objectives which set out the aspects of knowledge, skills and understanding expected of you. In English these involve speaking and listening, reading, writing and various aspects of presentation of your work.

NATIONAL CRITERIA

A major aspect of the GCSE is the introduction of national criteria. The **General Criteria** lay down certain rules governing the conduct of all GCSE examinations. They provide a framework for teaching and assessment in all subjects.

There are six area GCSE Groups: the University of London Examinations and Assessment Council (**ULEAC**), the Midland Examining Group (**MEG**), the Northern Examinations and Assessment Board (**NEAB**), the Northern Ireland Schools Examinations and Assessment Council (**NISEAC**), the Southern Examining Group (**SEG**) and the Welsh Joint Education Committee (**WJEC**).

The Groups are required to draw up syllabuses which comply with the **National Criteria** for individual subjects. Syllabuses and schemes of assessment will differ, but the Groups will have some things in common, e.g. all will allow a combination of coursework and assessment by written paper. The differences between the Groups are shown in the table on page 6 and are discussed further in the criteria for English later in this chapter.

> Notice that you must be able to 'communicate accurately, appropriately and effectively in speech and writing'.

What does all this mean for you in practice? Well, the **National Criteria** for English will have the most direct effect on your work. They concern the range of things you will be expected to do and how marks will be awarded for your work. Each of these will be discussed below, stressing new emphases which will certainly change the way you study and the way you are taught.

First, though, how is English defined in GCSE? ENGLISH is to be examined as a single subject, including some literary material, although some Groups also offer English Literature as a separate examination subject.

THE RANGE OF THINGS YOU WILL BE EXPECTED TO DO

There are two new things of importance to notice here: the **National Criteria** require students to show that they can 'communicate accurately, appropriately and effectively in speech and writing'.

Reading and **writing** have traditionally been part of English examinations, and this will continue. As well as short pieces for reading comprehension, the *reading of whole works* of literature is advised. As you will see from Chapter 3, studying at least one complete work of literature is compulsory for some Groups. Your reading should cover a range of texts of different kinds, e.g.

- short stories
- novels   LITERARY
- autobiographies   TEXTS
- plays
- poetry

and

- newspaper articles
- advertisements   NON-LITERARY
- brochures   TEXTS
- pamphlets

You will be tested on both 'close' comprehension of a text and more general 'understanding, involving some element of personal response. The multiple-choice type of objective test will still be used – see Chapter 8 for more information on this – but may not account for more than 20% of the whole scheme of assessment. You will also be expected to show that you can read, understand and respond to all types of writing and develop information retrieval techniques when you study.

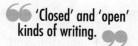

'Closed' and 'open' kinds of writing.

A wide range of *writing* is also required. You should attempt pieces of writing where the subject matter, form and purpose are *given to you* ('closed' kinds of writing), e.g.

- letters
- reports
- instructions
- reviews
- newspaper articles

and where the subject matter, form and purpose are *chosen by you* ('open' kinds of writing), e.g.

- stories
- poems
- personal writing.

Your writing should show that you can use correct grammar and standard English, except where non-standard forms are appropriate, e.g. in dialogue or direct speech in conversation, in a story where the narrator uses a more relaxed style, and so on.

Writing pieces of *different lengths* is also required. The average piece of examination written work is reckoned to be 400–500 words, but much longer pieces of topic work, or sustained narrative, will be encouraged for coursework.

For the first time in examinations in English, **oral communication** is seen to be an essential part of skill in the use of the language. This involves *talking* and *listening*. If you think about it: what you write communicates nothing unless there is a reader, and what you *say* needs a *listener*. An important area of English studies has therefore been officially recognised in the examination.

You have to take an Oral examination.

You will have opportunities to show that you can express yourself clearly and listen responsively, and adapt your style of speech to suit the listener/s and the purpose. The following list gives situations where these skills are needed:

- group discussion
- paired chat
- interview
- debate.

Later chapters will take each of these general areas and explain in detail how you can prepare for the examination, either with the help of your teacher or on your own.

HOW MARKS WILL BE AWARDED FOR YOUR WORK

Assessment in English must match the attainment targets and programmes of study set out in the Key Stage 4 criteria for English.

Schemes of assessment will vary from examining group to examining group, but all must involve the following:

- Assessment must be positive: schemes of assessment should allow candidates to show as fully as possible what they can do, and will either include a variety of papers, or a variety of tasks within papers or coursework.
- Assessment of Oral Communication is compulsory, and a candidate must achieve at least Grade 5 to have a grade in English recorded on the certificate.
- In each scheme of assessment:
  Attainment Target 1 (Speaking and Listening) must be weighted at **20%**.
  Attainment Target 2 (Reading) must be weighted at **40%**.
  Attainment Targets 3–5 (Writing, Spelling and Presentation) must be weighted at **40%**.
- Each scheme of assessment must include a terminal examination. The weighting of the examination must be at least **60%**.

■ Coursework (half Attainment Target 1 and half Attainment Targets 2–3) must be weighted at not more than **40%**.
(NB. The terminal examinations will have at least two levels Foundation and Higher).

Each of these requirements will now be discussed more fully.

For English there are two ways of distinguishing between different abilities, while allowing all candidates to show what they can do. The *first* is to set everyone the same task (e.g. writing about a personal experience or discussing a painting) and then to allow for differences of treatment or approach. The *second* is to set what is called a 'stepped question' with several parts in ascending order of difficulty, each part carrying a separate mark. All candidates should be able to succeed with the early parts of the question.

STEPPED QUESTION

A **stepped question** might be set on a passage concerning the wreck of a passenger liner, and have the following parts:

Q.1 Which three events warned passengers that the ship was in trouble? *(3 marks)*

Q.2 From the statements made by the captain and first mate, how far is there evidence of mistakes made by members of the crew? *(5 marks)*

Q.3 Imagine you were a passenger on board at the time of the disaster. Using only ideas in the passage, write an account (in about 200 words) of your reactions to events as they occurred. *(7 marks)*

Notice that Q.1 only asks you to give facts from the passage; the second part (Q.2) asks you to make a judgement, based on information given; and the third (Q.3), which asks you to write an imaginative yet accurate narrative, gives you the most scope.

The grade descriptions for written English in the **National Criteria** indicate the different demands placed on candidates. A *low* pass grade requires a candidate to show that he or she is capable of 'understanding and conveying information at a straightforward level' and can 'show sufficient control of the written language to communicate effectively, despite some weakness in spelling, punctuation and the construction of complex sentences'. The *middle* grade requires skill in 'understanding and conveying information both at a straightforward and at a more complex level' and 'writing in paragraphs, using sentences of varied kinds and exercising care over punctuation and spelling'.

However, *all* candidates should be given opportunities to show their abilities to

■ understand and convey information clearly
■ understand facts, ideas and opinions and present them in an orderly way
■ consider information and select what is relevant
■ describe what is felt or imagined
■ recognise implied meanings and attitudes
■ understand the ways in which language changes according to circumstances
■ paragraph, spell, punctuate and construct sentences accurately.

Though compulsory, oral English is assessed separately. English is graded by a seven-letter system from A to G (with an 'Ungraded' category), and Oral Communication by numbers from 1 to 5 (with an 'Ungraded' category). If you achieve the lowest grade or better in both, the two grades are shown together on the certificate, e.g.

C3 (Grade C in English and 3 in Oral Communication).

Otherwise, a grade in English or Oral Communication is not shown on the certificate.

The **National Criteria** state what you should be able to do to achieve a pass in Oral Communication. You should be able to

What must I do for a pass in the Oral?

- understand and convey straightforward information
- present facts, ideas and opinions in an orderly sequence
- choose and comment on spoken and written material relevantly
- describe your experience in simple terms, and express what is felt or imagined
- recognise the difference between fact and opinion or attitude in discussion
- vary your way of speaking according to the situation and the listeners
- speak so as to be heard and understood, with an appropriate manner, and at a suitable speed.

3 > ATTAINMENT TARGETS

AT1 Speaking and Listening

You should be able to express a point of view clearly and convey information and ideas to others appropriately, contributing to group discussion.

AT2 Reading

You should show that you can read a variety of literary and non-literary texts drawn from different cultures and times (i.e. some pre-twentieth century writing) and communicate your response as well as show an awareness of style.

ATs3–5 Writing and Presentation

You should be able to write about your experiences and feelings; show that you can discuss factual matters or give your opinions in a suitable style for readers and one which is grammatically correct, with correct paragraphing, sentence structure, punctuation and spelling. Clear and legible handwriting will also be taken into account.

4 > TERMINAL EXAMINATION

The examination will consist of written papers at different levels. There will be at least two levels: Foundation Level; Higher Level. Some boards will also offer an Intermediate Level examination. Your school or college will decide which is the most suitable level for you.

5 > COURSEWORK

It is recommended in the **National Criteria** that there should be a combination of assessment by coursework and by final examination. Some of the work must be done while a teacher is present, and the arrangements under which the work was done, and the time spent, must be noted. This is called working under 'controlled' or supervised conditions.

The requirements mentioned above apply to coursework as well as to written examinations, so you should bear these requirements in mind as you work throughout the year. Your class teacher or tutor will help you to choose the pieces of coursework to submit for assessment (the number will depend on the percentage of coursework being offered). These pieces should normally be handwritten, although some groups allow all but the controlled conditions piece to be done on a word processor. Photocopies, diagrams, etc., may be included, if their source is acknowledged. You may have worked through earlier drafts and at least one of these should be attached to the final effort, along with any comments made by your teacher or tutor.

Working in 'controlled' conditions ...

All the pieces should be put together in order in one folder, with your name and the date the work was done clearly written on each piece. The folder should have

- a front sheet, listing the work it contains
- dividers, separating the creative from the critical work.

It will be marked by your teachers, and your progress throughout the course assessed. Work done by pupils in your school or centre will be considered by your own teachers to make sure that everything is marked to the same standard. Then the assessed work will be compared with work in other centres, to ensure that the standards are comparable and reliable across the whole country.

GROUP	PAPERS	LENGTH/ DESCRIPTION OF PAPERS	COURSE-WORK	% OF MARKS
ULEAC	Paper 1: Coursework Folder	3 sections: Oral, Reading, Writing (1500)	✓	40
	Paper 2: Reading and Response	2hrs	–	30
	Paper 3: Writing (Two Tiers)	2hrs	–	30
MEG	Paper 1: Non-Literary and Media Texts (Reading and Writing)	2 hrs	–	30
	Paper 2: Literature (Reading and Writing) Two Tiers: Standard and Higher	2 hrs	–	30
	Coursework Folder	5 pieces of written work; record of oral work; record of texts studied	✓	40
NEAB	Paper 1: Reading	2hrs	–	30
	Paper 2: Writing (Papers 1 and 2 have two Tiers)	2 hrs	–	30
	Paper 3: Coursework Folder	3 oral pieces; 2–3 written pieces	✓	40
NISEAC	Papers 1 and 2 and Coursework	Two ($1\frac{1}{4}$ hrs, $1\frac{3}{4}$ hrs)	✓	100
SEG	Part 1: Reading	1 hr	–	30
	Part 2: Writing and Presentation (Part 2 has two Tiers: Foundation and Higher)	(1 hr, $1\frac{1}{2}$ hrs) Two versions of Parts 1 and 2: one with pre-released material	–	30
	Coursework	3 parts: i) oral ii) personal writing iii) response to literature	✓	40
WJEC	Paper 1: Reading and Writing: Literary	Tier 1 ($1\frac{1}{2}$ hrs)		
	Paper 2: Reading and Writing: Non-Literary	Tiers 2/3 (2 hrs)		60
	Coursework	Oral Reading (2 units) Writing (2 units)	✓	40

Table 1.1 Comparison of written English GCSE syllabuses

From the above table you can see that the various syllabuses offered by the Groups differ, though all require at least 40% coursework assessment and also examine Oral Communication. We shall consider the distinctive features of each in turn.

Table 1.2 shows you the grading system of *levels* used for GCSE after 1994 and how they relate to the previous system of *letter* grades.

GCSE GRADES USED UP TO AND INCLUDING 1993	GCSE LEVELS USED FROM 1994 ONWARDS
A	10 9
B	8
C D E	7 6
F	5
G	4
U	3 2 1

Table 1.2

In May 1993, however, it was announced that the ten levels would be used for assessing coursework, but that the letter grades A–G would be used for the final GCSE award. There will be an A (a super-A) grading for those achieving the equivalent of a Level 10.

We now look in rather more detail at each GCSE Syllabus.

ULEAC

Paper 1: Coursework Folder
Three sections:
1   Speaking and Listening component, with teacher's record of assessments.
2   Reading and Writing classwork.
3   Candidate's Written work. This should consist of *three* units of writing:
   a) a language-based unit
   b) a literature-based unit
   c) an open unit.
   Folder: 1500 words approximately.

Paper 2: Reading & Response
There will be one or more passages to read and candidates will be given two tasks:
a) response with reference to language;
b) personal response to theme.

Paper 3: Writing
There will be extracts to give candidates' writing context focus and support and they will be given 2 tasks:
a) one will be personal/imaginative/poetic/expressive writing
b) one will be factual/transactional/informative writing.
The two tiers will allow candidates to show abilities at the target levels.

MEG

Paper 1: Non-Literary and Media Texts: Reading and Writing

Two sections:
1 Specific questions on non-literary texts.
2 Tasks to elicit a broader response to texts.

Paper 2: Literature: Reading and Writing

Two sections:
1 Pre-released text for critical/personal evaluation.
2 Broader, thematically-based tasks to elicit a creative imaginative response.
Candidates may take Standard Tier (Levels 4–7) or Higher Tier (Levels 5–10).

Coursework Folder

This must contain:
Five pieces of written work: including one hand-written by student, a record of oral activities attempted during the course. A record of texts studied during the course.

NEAB

Paper 1: Reading

There will be *two* sections:
Section A will require responses to the *close reading of prepared texts* (distributed 6 weeks before the examination). The texts will relate to one theme, *in common with the syllabus for English Literature*.
Section B will require responses to the *close reading of unseen texts*. Questions will be structured to allow candidates in each tier to show appropriate abilities for the target levels. (This paper is common to Paper 1 of English Literature).

Paper 2: Writing, Spelling, Hand Writing and Presentation

There will be *two* sections:
Section A: candidates will be asked to understand, order and present facts, ideas and opinions.
Section B: candidates will be asked to write imaginatively and/or about their own experiences.
The paper will be tiered to provide differentiated stimulus material.
The pieces of writing will be assessed for spelling, grammatical structures, punctuation, hand writing and general presentation.

Coursework

The folder should include *two* sections:
Section A: the Teacher Summary of oral work from three points in the course;
Section B: two to four pieces of written coursework.

NISEAC

There is only **one** syllabus: five pieces of coursework and two written papers.

- Paper 1 – comprehension, based on a literary prose passage.
- Paper 2 – functional or practical writing, and comprehension based on non-literary material.

Oral Communication – assessed coursework. Six tasks, including one formal and one informal situation.

SEG

Written Examination

Version 1: *Part 1:* Reading of pre-released material;
Part 2: Writing and presentation based on the same material.
Version 2: *Part 1:* Reading of unseen material;
Part 2: Writing and presentation based on fresh stimulus material.
There are two tiers for Part 2: Foundation & Higher. Extra reading time will be allowed to candidates taking Version 2.

Coursework: three parts

i) Teacher assessed oral work;
ii) Personal writing;
iii) Writing in response to literature; 1000–1500 words. Candidates should include evidence of skills in information retrieval, in drafting, editing and proofreading and in knowledge of language.

WJEC

Coursework

There will be 3 sections:
Section A: *Speaking & Listening.*
   Here assessment will be based on the best work in a range of situations and with various audiences, including work in pairs, small groups, in larger groups and at least providing evidence of the following:
a) communicating to an audience
b) developing understanding through talk
c) collaborating.

Section B: *Reading.*
Two assignments are involved:
   One will be based on the study of a whole work of literature; the other may be based on literature, or a non-literary or media text.

Section C: *Writing.*
Two pieces should be submitted. One piece should be imaginative writing; the other should be transactional (i.e. an article, leaflet, report, letter).
   There should be *evidence of the overall writing process – planning, drafting and editing.*

Terminal examination:

Paper 1 will have *two* sections:
Section A: reading of literary material will be tested through structured questions.
Section B: writing skills will be tested by two tasks, the first linked to Section A.
Paper 2 will also have *two* sections:
Section A: reading of non-literary material will be tested through structured questions.
Section B: writing skills will be tested by two tasks, the first linked to Section A.
Presentation will be assessed on the evidence of both papers.

EXAMINATION TECHNIQUES

COURSEWORK
READING TECHNIQUES
WRITING TECHNIQUES
TALKING AND LISTENING

WRITTEN PAPERS
RULES TO FOLLOW
COMPREHENSION
CREATIVE WRITING
DIRECTED WRITING

ORAL
GENERAL RULES

GETTING STARTED

This chapter is concerned with general techniques which should help you to succeed in your English examination.

Section A considers techniques which will help you with coursework, Section B techniques for taking written papers, and Section C techniques for the oral examination.

TECHNIQUES TO HELP WITH COURSEWORK

GCSE gives you opportunities to work in ways that have not traditionally been part of English examinations. You will have plenty of scope to try out a variety of ways of reading, writing, talking and listening, but may find yourself in areas that are unfamiliar to you. Many areas will be considered in detail in the following chapters of this book, but there are also certain **general ideas and techniques** to help with coursework.

" **English as an integrated subject ...** *"*

The new stress on English as an integrated subject relates it closely to your experience. What you *write* may grow from what you discuss with friends, or in class, or from a story you have read. What you *read* may be stimulated by what you talk about, e.g. a discussion of the pollution of a river near where you live might raise such questions as: 'What really are the facts of the situation?'; 'Who might help in a campaign to protect the river?'; 'What was the river like twenty years ago?' and you might go on to research the subject in books, or listen to experts in the field or interview older people in the community. You might decide to write up what you had found out as a report, which could be part of your coursework.

Much of our listening and talking is stimulated by media other than books, and there is room for all kinds of stimuli in GCSE English. Students should develop the ability to 'understand and respond imaginatively to what they hear, read and experience in a variety of media'. So, it is hoped that English studies will become more closely related to life, and that some of your coursework will be based on experience of media such as television, films, plays, music and art.

1 ▷ READING TECHNIQUES

Of course, a great deal of your reading will be suggested to you by your teacher or tutor, and for some Groups (e.g. **NISEAC**) a list of literary works – as complete books, rather than extracts – for you to select from and study, will be part of the syllabus. This is a sample list from **NISEAC**, on the theme of *Family*:

Thornton Wilder   *Our Town* *
P. King & F. Cary   *Sailor Beware!*
John van Druten   *I Remember Mama*
Keith Waterhouse   *Billy Liar* *
Anne Frank   *Diary of Anne Frank* *
Carson McCullers   *A Member of the Wedding* *
Honore Morrow   *The Splendid Journey*
John Steinbeck   *East of Eden*
Florence McDowell   *Other Days Around Me*
Alexander Irvine   *My Lady of the Chimney Corner*
Barry Hines   *A Kestrel for a Knave* *
Stan Barstow   *A Kind of Loving*

(* *Available in drama and in prose form.*)

As you can see, these works are very different, but each one has been chosen for its likely appeal to young people.

" **Widen your reading!** *"*

In the last major survey of children's reading interests, fifth form pupils said that they had comparatively little time for reading for pleasure. School work or homework took up so much time. One girl remarked: 'If they made the day longer, we'd all be reading'. Try, however full your time-table, to read widely, both fiction and non-fiction. Think about what you read, and take interesting ideas from it for your work.

USING READING IN COURSEWORK

Here are some of the ways you can make use of your reading in coursework:

- **Continuing a story** – what happened to the characters during the next five years?
- **Alternative ending** – how else would I end the story?
- **Alternative version** – tell the story from the point of view of a different character.
- **Dramatization** – make part of the story into a play.
- **Diary** – keep a diary, as one of the characters in the book.
- **Starting point** – make the book the starting point for a piece of writing of your own, perhaps personal or imaginative.
- **Reader's response** – write down your response to a story and get friends to tell you theirs.
- **Letters** – write a letter to the author, explaining what you like and dislike about the book.
- **Review** – write a 'taster' review to persuade others in your class to read the book.
- **Discussion** – explore issues of plot, character and general significance.

How to 'interrogate the text'.

As well as reading for ideas and creative response, remember also to do plenty of 'close' reading or 'interrogating the text', as it is sometimes called. Few readers bother to use a dictionary, but if you come across a word you don't really understand you should make the effort to find out precisely what it means.

Try reading the following extracts:

'The day passed incredibly slowly. She never knew what to do ... and when, relying on some pert little girl for information, she had started a lesson, she did not know how to go on with it properly. The children were her masters. She deferred to them ... and before this inhuman number of children, she was always at bay. She could not get away from it. There it was, this class of fifty collective children, depending on her for command it hated and resented. It made her feel she could not breathe: she must suffocate, it was so inhuman.'

'In an atmosphere of which the most important constituent is oxygen, it follows that all ordinary examples of combustion are owing to the rapid oxidisation of bodies at a high temperature. It would be wrong, though, to think that the word 'combustion' expressed no other actions. Many substances burn equally well in atmospheres from which oxygen is excluded altogether, and in some cases burn even more readily than they would under similar circumstances in pure oxygen.'

Though both are difficult and need re-reading, I think you'll agree that many would find the second much more difficult. This is chiefly because of the unfamiliar words and ideas. Another reason the second passage seems more difficult is because most people have read many more stories than they have books about science. With a story, we know pretty well what to expect: there will be a beginning, where characters are introduced and the scene set; some development or progress through the middle of the plot or action, perhaps to an exciting climax; and some sort of tying up of matters at the end, unless it is a sophisticated story where the reader is left guessing.

With non-fiction, we are less sure how the work is organised, and it may be worth while to look into this. Consider the following short passages:

a) 'At the museum, we saw the first photograph taken of Queen Victoria. After that we enjoyed looking at the elegant china, before moving on to the display of court regalia. Finally, we looked at the royal portraits in the Queen's Room.'

b) 'At the museum, we saw the first photograph ever taken of Queen Victoria, and then looked at some old china, before moving to a display of court regalia. And finally we looked at the royal portraits in the Queen's Room.'

c) 'At the museum, I was most interested in the royal portraits and the first photograph ever taken of Queen Victoria, then in the displays of court regalia.'

d) 'At the museum, we looked carefully at the displays of old china and court regalia, and at the first photograph ever taken of Queen Victoria, so that we would be able to write a detailed report when we were back at school.'

They are similar, but the first is merely a recital of seeing certain things at a museum, in no particular order. The second shows the order in which things were seen. The third concerns the visitor's reaction to seeing the things, and the fourth gives a motive for looking carefully at them. When you are studying a non-fiction passage, it may be useful to consider how it is organised. Is there a main idea and then a series of minor parts? Are there two contrasted main ideas? Thinking along these lines should help you to understand the passage better.

WAYS OF ENCOURAGING CLOSE READING

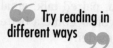
Try reading in different ways

Here are some suggestions for encouraging close reading of texts:

- **Finding the outline** – Discuss, with a friend, the structure of a passage.
- **Predicting what follows** – Cover the latter part of a story. Read the first part, then, on the basis of the clues you have already, predict what is to come. Then read on, to see if you were right.
- **Gap filling** – Take a passage and delete every fifth word. Then discuss in a group what the missing words could be. You'll have to look very closely at the text to do this well.
- **Group comprehension** – Take a passage, and write a set of questions about it for another group in your class. Get them to write or record their answers, and to write a set of questions for you. Compare the responses.

More about close reading can be found in Chapter 9.

---

2 > WRITING TECHNIQUES

Coursework gives opportunities for kinds of writing that could not be included in all traditional examinations because of the limited time available. Now in GCSE you can be examined on a much wider range of written work. Some of these types of writing are:

- topic work – handling information and ideas on a particular subject
- extended personal writing, e.g. autobiography
- writing stimulated by research carried out by the writer
- creative responses to literature, e.g. dramatisation of a story
- writing preceded by a period of reflection, e.g. on an earlier visit to a historic house
- writing that goes through a series of drafts and revisions.

In the traditional written paper the choice of essay seemed wide: you could choose between descriptive, narrative, personal, discursive or dramatic writing, but would only be required to write one or at most two pieces. The Government Assessment of Performance Unit Report, *Language Performance*, HMSO (1979), identified various kinds of writing task, as follows:

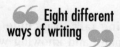
Eight different ways of writing

- **Narrative/descriptive**, e.g. written response to a picture as a story or description.
- **Reflective/analytical**, e.g. discussion of motives of characters in a play you are studying.
- **Task controlled by examiner,** e.g. written comprehension paper.
- **Task controlled by writer**, e.g. piece of individual topic work.
- **Task based on first-hand experience**, e.g. personal writing.
- **Task related to knowledge from a second-hand source**, e.g. writing up an interview you had recorded.
- **Literary writing**, e.g. a story or poem.
- **Functional writing**, e.g. a report or an article, etc.

Your coursework folder should also show that you can write for *different purposes and readers*, and in *different modes and styles*. The above list and scheme will help you to make sure that you will have a wide selection of pieces.

3 ▷ TALKING AND LISTENING

These skills are discussed *together* because the National Criteria stresses the importance of their 'interactive' nature. Some oral work that you do for the examination may not require a listener, or at least a listener who reacts to what you say. There is a place for including some speech of this kind, e.g.

- reading aloud
- a prepared talk
- a formal speech.

But mostly, though, you will speak *and* listen and will be assessed for both. This may well be a new area of experience for both teachers and pupils, who may be used to many kinds of talk in the classroom – directed discussion, paired talk, small group discussions, etc. – but *not* to its being assessed. How can you become a better talker and listener? With any kind of speech it will be helpful to consider

- its purpose
- who the listeners are
- where it occurs.

Let us look at each in turn.

a) SPEAKING TO THE PURPOSE

'Product' and 'process' type talking ...

First of all, think positively about oral work. It is not a test of accent. Your main aim should be to *communicate something clearly*, so as to interest the listener.

Speaking can be an end in itself (known as *product*-type speaking), or can grow from some other activity (known as *process*-type speaking). Examples of the first kind are:

- reading a poem aloud
- giving a prepared talk
- telling a story
- making a speech of thanks.

When you are doing any of these, even as an exercise, you will tend to be conscious of how well you are performing, but you will find it improves matters if you concentrate hard on what you are saying. It will often be helpful to practise beforehand with a tape recorder, or have a series of cards listing the points you wish to make, but finally you should remember you are trying to interest or persuade your listeners, and should attend to them and what you are saying, and forget yourself.

Examples of the second kind, where speaking grows from some other activity, are:

- 'brainstorming' in a group
- having a group discussion
- problem-solving in pairs
- interviewing someone
- discussing a poem.

All of these involve considerable skill as a listener; using talk to include shy or reluctant speakers and to quieten those who try to dominate; and knowing when to take charge and when to let another speaker put forward a point of view. Take turns in group work to be listener and speaker, and to take the lead in talk as well as to support other speakers. Playing back a tape recording of a group discussion with friends, assessing your own performances informally as a group, can teach you a great deal. Group orals are considered at length in Chapter 6 below.

b) THE NATURE OF THE AUDIENCE

Your talk will naturally be affected by *who* the listeners are. Try to forget that your talk is being assessed – most of the time it will not be. Try to talk with one other person, in a small group of friends and in a large group or the whole class. You will react very differently as a speaker each time. Notice how your speech becomes slower, more formal and careful as the size of the group increases.

Your audience will not usually be passive: even if they remain silent, there may be fidgeting, smiles of support, or interested or bored looks. You should take notice of all this and respond appropriately. If finally you must talk to an assessor, try not to be overawed!

c) PLACE WHERE TALK OCCURS

Physical conditions around us affect our responses as speakers and listeners. Imagine telling something to a friend, while hugging a radiator in the corner of a small room, during a chilly break, and then having to make an announcement about the same matter to an assembly of the whole school. If you have a choice, find a *place* you like and invite listeners to sit in a way that makes them and you comfortable. Ask your teacher or tutor if you need help in such matters, too.

TECHNIQUES FOR TAKING WRITTEN PAPERS

RULES TO FOLLOW

Follow the rules!

In this section, we shall look at the general rules for taking any written paper, and then describe three types of GCSE paper. You should go through the rules carefully first, then think how they may be applied to each type.

a) Read the general instructions to the paper very carefully.
b) Read the questions very carefully.
c) Decide on the questions you wish to answer, if there is a choice.
d) Decide on the best order of answering questions.
e) Decide how much time you should allow for each question.
f) Plan your answers.
g) Make sure you answer relevantly.
h) Leave time for checking your work.

a) READ THE GENERAL INSTRUCTIONS VERY CAREFULLY

There are always some candidates who answer more than the number of questions required. Even though you will be assessed on your best answers, this is a dreadful waste of time. There are also candidates who ignore 'turn over' and do not read every page of a question. If you are asked to present your work in a particular way, do so. If you are given a word limit, do not exceed it.

b) READ THE THE QUESTIONS VERY CAREFULLY

Great care is taken by those setting questions to make the wording as clear as possible, so that you will not be confused or misled. But quite a few candidates give themselves problems by careless reading, because they are in a hurry to begin. It is worth spending a little extra time to make sure you have understood the question. For example, if you are asked to give the advantages and disadvantages of an issue, do not give only one side; if you are asked to write an account based on ideas in a set passage, do not depart from it and introduce ideas of your own.

c) DECIDE ON THE QUESTIONS YOU WISH TO ANSWER, IF THERE IS A CHOICE

Most English papers of an 'Understanding and Response' type will not give you a choice of question. There are, however, still some examination groups setting essay-writing options, and here the title you choose may be very important. Know your own strengths and weaknesses and do not choose to write a play, or a story that needs a great deal of conversation if you know your punctuation is weak! Choose to show your strong points.

d) DECIDE ON THE BEST ORDER OF ANSWERING QUESTIONS

If you tend to have difficulty in timing your paper correctly, choose to do questions which carry most marks first.

e) DECIDE HOW MUCH TIME YOU SHOULD ALLOW FOR EACH QUESTION

Do not get carried away in an examination and write at very great length. You will probably make a lot of mistakes and will finally run short of time.

f) PLAN YOUR ANSWERS

A few minutes spent planning an answer is time well spent. Either, think the answer through, or make a flow-chart, a scheme or list of points, or a rough draft. Cross through all rough work when it is finished. It is worth knowing that if you fail to complete your final draft, examiners will look at your rough work to see if they can find the conclusion there. If they do, they will give you credit for it.

g) MAKE SURE YOU ANSWER RELEVANTLY

This is easier said than done. If you have read the question carefully and spent time thinking about it, you will have a better chance of seeing what is required and keeping to it. Avoid any temptation to be wildly original or over-subtle in examination answers.

h) LEAVE TIME FOR CHECKING YOUR WORK

You should leave five minutes or so for reading your answers and looking out for mistakes that you may have made. You may be surprised how many slips there are when you are working in examination conditions. See Chapter 19 for detailed advice on how to correct your work.

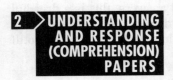

This type of English paper will be set by all groups and is variously called 'Understanding and Response', 'Aural', 'Understanding and Appreciation", and so on. It consists of a general instruction, e.g. Part 1 of this examination consists of two extracts about which you will be asked to do some writing in Part 2. Fifteen minutes are allowed for reading the extracts and for making any notes you wish, after which you will be given Part 2, with the questions based on the extracts, and a passage or pair of passages for you to read (or listen to on a tape, while you follow the text).

A series of 'stepped' questions follows (see page 4 of this book), with the maximum marks to be awarded in brackets at the end.

All the general rules above apply (except (c)) and before you begin you should, of course, read the passages themselves very carefully and think about what is required for each answer.

Examples of typical passages and questions can be found in Chapter 9.

These will variously be called 'Continuous Writing', 'Personal and Expressive Writing' (MEG), etc.

You will be invited to write on one or two (from a set of seven or eight) essay titles, covering the whole range of narrative, descriptive, discursive, imaginative, personal and dramatic writing. A picture will often be included to which you will be expected to respond. The normal length of the essay is 450 words, but this will be specified in the instructions to candidates, as will any other requirements, e.g.

■ Write on ONE of the following … You should write between 350 and 600 words (**MEG**).

■ Write approximately two sides on one of the following subjects. If, however, your handwriting is unusually large or unusually small, you should make some adjustments in the amount you write … (**NEAB**).

All the general rules above apply, and (a), (b), (f), and (g) are particularly important. Examples of typical essay topics for you to try can be found in Chapters 12–17.

> ## 4 DIRECTED WRITING PAPERS

These will be set by **MEG**, **NISEAC**, **SEG** and **WJEC**. You will be given one or two passages about something factual – e.g. the Channel Tunnel Project – and asked to respond to a series of about four or five questions. You may be required to give a simple, factual answer, or your response may involve inference from evidence in the text or evaluation of opinion, summarising, etc.

All the general rules above (except (c)) apply, and typical passages and questions of this kind are to be found in Chapters 11 and 14.

TECHNIQUES FOR THE ORAL EXAMINATION

> ## 1 GENERAL RULES

Most of your oral work will be assessed by your teacher or tutor, but there may be occasions when an external examiner is directly involved.

a) Plan what you have to do beforehand.
b) Be polite and friendly to your audience.
c) Concentrate on what you have to say rather than the way you are saying it.
d) Try to speak as clearly as possible.
e) Speak a little more slowly than usual.
f) Try not to lose your audience's attention.

Rules for the Oral …

a) PLAN WHAT YOU HAVE TO DO BEFOREHAND

This is, of course, essential, but the extent to which it is possible varies. If you are giving an unscripted talk or are taking part in a discussion, think out in advance points that you would like to make. Some cards with reminder headings on them help to make you feel more confident, but do not read the headings out, and do look at your audience as you are speaking, not down at your notes.

b) BE POLITE AND FRIENDLY TO YOUR AUDIENCE

However nervous you may be feeling, be pleasant, saying 'Good morning' or 'Good afternoon'. If your audience is enjoying the occasion it will help you to relax and do your best. If you are not sure about any instructions, ask politely for them to be repeated.

c) CONCENTRATE ON WHAT YOU HAVE TO SAY RATHER THAN THE WAY YOU ARE SAYING IT

You will be assessed for effective and appropriate speech: this includes clarity of speech but also how you interact with others, and the content of what you say. The best advice is to try to enter into the experience as freely and naturally as you can.

d) TRY TO SPEAK AS CLEARLY AS POSSIBLE

You must be audible and intelligible, so remember that you may be speaking to someone who is not used to your manner of speech. Take care to speak out fairly loudly and clearly.

e) SPEAK A LITTLE MORE SLOWLY THAN USUAL

The normal tendency of a student in an oral examination is to speed up, because he or she feels nervous and wants to get it over. This is a mistake. Try to remember that rapid speech is likely to be difficult to understand.

f) TRY NOT TO LOSE YOUR AUDIENCE'S ATTENTION

You are most likely to do this if you have not prepared yourself properly in the first place; see rule (a) above. Visual aids, e.g. diagrams, may help make your points clear and fix attention. Watch out for signs of inattention, e.g. whispering, or even yawning! Remember that successful communication is a two-way process.

IMPORTANCE OF THE TOPIC AREAS

ULEAC

MEG

NEAB

NISEAC

SEG

WJEC

GETTING STARTED

The remaining chapters of the book, after the present one, deal with fifteen special topics relating to GCSE written English and Oral Communication. All the topics have some relevance, whatever course you are taking, and some are especially important. The purpose of the present chapter is to help you decide *which* chapters and topics are most useful for the papers you personally will be taking, and the coursework you will be submitting.

CHAPTERS, TOPICS AND EXAMINATIONS

The table gives an overview:

Chapter and topic	Examinations					
	London	Midland	Northern	Northern Ireland	Southern	Welsh
4 'Correct' English	✓✓	✓✓	✓✓	✓✓	✓✓	✓✓
5 Individual Oral	✓✓	✓✓	✓✓	✓✓	✓✓	✓✓
6 Group Oral	✓✓	✓✓	✓✓	✓✓	✓✓	✓✓
7 Researching and Writing up a Topic	✓	✓	✓	✓	✓	✓
8 Case Study – Preparing an Assignment	✓	✓	✓	✓	✓	✓
9 Reading Comprehension	✓✓	✓✓	✓✓	✓✓	✓✓	✓✓
10 From Reading to Writing	✓	✓✓	✓✓	✓✓	✓✓	✓✓
11 Summarizing from a Particular Point of View	✓	✓✓	✓✓	✓✓	✓✓	✓✓
12 Writing Narrative	✓	✓	✓	✓	✓✓	✓
13 Writing Dialogue	✓	✓	✓	✓	✓	✓
14 Argumentative and Persuasive Writing	✓	✓	✓✓	✓	✓	✓✓
15 Descriptive Writing	✓	✓	✓	✓	✓✓	✓
16 Responding to a Stimulus	✓	✓	✓	✓	✓	✓
17 Personal Writing	✓	✓	✓	✓	✓	
18 A Sample Coursework Folder	✓	✓	✓	✓	✓	✓
19 Checking and Correcting	✓✓	✓✓	✓✓	✓✓	✓✓	✓✓

(✓✓ = mentioned as compulsory, or of special significance in syllabus)

Table 3.1. Which chapters and topics are relevant for which examinations

Some chapters obviously apply to *any* examination you may take: all require a range of examination techniques, such as careful reading, note-taking, planning your time, and many more matters that have been discussed in Chapter 2. Also, it is always important to write in an appropriate style, paying some attention to accuracy of expression: Chapter 4 is concerned with this. In written examinations it is wise to leave time to check and correct your work. How does this apply to written coursework, though? Should you submit work for the examination which has been corrected by your teacher or tutor? Chapter 19 looks at these matters.

Three other chapters also deal with topics that are important because they are part of the syllabus for all Groups and courses. You will be assessed for your speaking and listening abilities as one of a group and, most likely, individually and as one of a pair, therefore Chapters 5 and 6 will be important to you. Researching and writing up an assignment is a key part of coursework activity and Chapters 7 and 8 will help you with this, as will Chapter 18. All courses require candidates to read and understand a passage and respond in writing – so Chapter 10 will also be important.

To explain Table 3.1 further, and give some more information, each Group's syllabus will now be looked at briefly. Details of the options offered by the Groups are given at the end of Chapter 1.

EXAMINATION GROUP SYLLABUSES

1 > ULEAC PAPER 1 – COURSEWORK FOLDER

There are *three* components of the Coursework folder. **(40%)**

- Section 1 is the *Speaking and Listening* component. **(20%)**
  The teacher's record of your assessments throughout the Course will be included here. You should have done work which shows that you can
  a) express what you have felt and imagined
  b) understand facts, ideas and opinions;
  c) show an awareness of listeners and choose an appropriate style
  d) communicate a personal response to something heard or read;
  e) discuss and consider others' written or spoken language.

- Section 2 is a *Reading and Writing* component. **(10%)**
  This will show a list of the assignments or tasks you have undertaken and the standard you have reached in reading and responding to literary and non-literary texts of the present, as well as some pre-twentieth century texts, including Shakespeare. You should show an awareness of how language varies in style to convey meanings.

- Section 3 is your *own choice of Written Work*. **(10%)**
  There should be *three* units here:
  a) A *language-based unit*. This should be a study exploring one or more of the following: the language of school, work, advertisements, children's books, text books, gender, race, class, politics, sport, accent and dialect, jargon, slang. Both written and spoken sources may be used here, including drama and media texts.
  b) A *literature-based unit*. This unit should include reading response and writing resulting from it. There should be evidence of your having read some pre-twentieth century literature, including Shakespeare. There may be writing in role, personal writing or critical work.
  c) An *'open' unit*. Here you have an opportunity to show skills not demonstrated elsewhere in the folder, after discussion with your teacher or tutor. It might, for example, include a review and assessment of your own work during the Course.

PAPER 2 – TERMINAL EXAMINATION PAPER **(30%)**

Reading and Response

The paper will be in *two* tiers: *Foundation* and *Higher*. Each paper will give one or more passages, varied in style, and you will be asked to read them, then attempt two tasks. Each task will be based on the passages, and they will have equal marks. The first task will ask you to respond to the material with reference to its language – *how* it is expressed. The second task will ask you for a personal response to the passage or its theme – *what* it is all about.

PAPER 3 – TERMINAL EXAMINATION PAPER (30%)

Writing

The paper will be in *two* tiers – *Foundation* and *Higher*. Each paper will contain a passage (or passages) as a starting point for your own writing. They may be from literary or non-literary sources. Again, you will be asked to attempt two tasks. The first will be to write personally, poetically, imaginatively or expressively. The second will be to write factually or informatively.

For Paper 2 and Paper 3 there will be assessment of your spelling, punctuation and presentation (5%) on each.

2 > MEG

PAPER 1 – NON-LITERARY AND MEDIA TEXTS: Reading and Writing (30%)

This paper is of 2 hours' duration and will be in *two* tiers: *Standard* and *Higher*. Candidates will be given tasks based on non-literary texts and asked specific questions about linguistic effects, style, sense of audience and presentation. Also there will be an opportunity for a broader response: a sustained piece of creative writing.

PAPER 2 – LITERATURE: Reading and Writing (30%)

A booklet with pre-release extracts will be sent to schools by the beginning of the Summer Term. Tasks will be based on this material – both critical and imaginative/creative.

At the Higher Tier, candidates should show an awareness of attitudes towards language, show a wide range of suitable vocabulary and a personal style, and good level of accuracy.

COURSEWORK FOLDER (40%)

Your folder must contain:

Up to five pieces of your best written work, including one handwritten by you, a record of the oral activities on the Course and the assessment; a record of the texts you have studied throughout the Course.

3 > NEAB

The **TERMINAL EXAMINATION** will consist of two 2-hour papers.

PAPER 1: Reading (30%)

This will be in *two sections:*

Section A

Here you will be asked *to respond to questions on an anthology of prepared texts* which will be given to centres about six weeks before the examination. The texts, which will cover different periods and styles of writing, will relate to one theme (e.g. Experience of School), changing each year of the examination. You will have chances to read and discuss the material but you will not know what the questions are until the examination date. (15%)

Section B

Here you will be asked *to respond to questions on an anthology of unprepared texts*.

(15%)

This paper is the same as Paper 1 NEAB English Literature.

PAPER 2: Writing, Spelling, Handwriting and Presentation (30%)

This will be in *two* sections:

Section A

Here you will be asked to write about some factual matter, giving your ideas and opinions. **(10%)**

Section B

Here you will be asked to write imaginatively about your experiences. There will also be assessment of spelling, handwriting and presentation. **(20%)**

Both papers will be set in three tiers, and you will be entered for one at the appropriate level, either:

Levels 4–6 (equivalent to grades D–G GCSE pre-1994)

Levels 5–9 (equivalent to grades A–F GCSE pre-1994)

Levels 8–10 (equivalent to grades A–B GCSE pre-1994)

COURSEWORK (40%)

Your folder will show evidence of work of *two* kinds:

a) *Oral Work:* This will give a description of your work in speaking and listening, and samples from *three points* in the Course. **(20%)**

b) *Written Work:* There should be two to four pieces of your written work, depending on length, of your own choice. **(20%)**

The examination consists of *two* compulsory papers and written coursework.

PAPER 1

This is a comprehension test, set on a prose passage from a work of literature.

PAPER 2

This has two questions, one needing functional or practical writing, and the other a comprehension test on non-literary material.

COURSEWORK

The **coursework** (five pieces) should cover three elements:

■ response to reading on one of the following themes – family, love, nature, conflict
■ creative or imaginative writing
■ functional or transactional writing.

Oral coursework will be assessed on a candidate's ability to listen and speak in a variety of formal and informal situations, preferably where more than one pupil is involved. The following six kinds of talk should be attempted:

- describing and/or expressing feelings about a place, person or experience
- relaying information
- persuasive argument – recognizing and expressing opinions
- collaborating – starting a discussion, stating a problem, commenting on how a discussion is going and reaching an agreed conclusion
- speculating – putting forward ideas about what might happen
- role play.

5 > SEG WRITTEN PAPERS

There are *two* versions of written papers:

Version 1

This is based on an anthology of material sent to candidates about eight weeks before the examination. The anthology will have a theme e.g. 'Outsiders' and be a collection of passages from plays, poems, graphics and so on. Candidates will have an opportunity to discuss the material but will not know the questions until the examination.

Part 1: Reading response to the material. (30%)

Part 2: Direct questions and other written response, which may involve directed writing such as a pamphlet, advertisement, newspaper article. (30%)

Version 2

As above, except that the material will be unseen. Candidates will have fifteen minutes' extra reading time at Foundation Level and half an hour extra time at Higher Level on these papers.

COURSEWORK: three sections

i) A selection of teacher assessed work in speaking and writing which should include some of the following: a response to reading a work of fiction; an individually planned activity of your own choice; a collaborative group activity; a task involving pairs interacting; a task focusing upon talk about language use and appropriateness.
ii) Personal writing including description, narration, based on experience etc.
iii) Response to Literature including more than one genre and whole works of literature. Candidates taking levels 7–10 should include some pre-twentieth century works.

Include some of your drafts, and edited or proof-read work (you may include drafting done on a word-processor), as well as something to show your skills in information retrieval and your knowledge about language. The latter could be something on the development of language in children, the language of persuasion and argument, language in the media, bilingualism, the historical development of language and language in the classroom or workplace. (40%)

6 > WJEC COURSEWORK (40%)

There will be *three* sections:

Section A: Speaking and Listening

Here samples of oral work that you have done during the Course should be included, with your teacher's evaluation. There should be an example of your work in a pair, e.g. problem solving; in a small group e.g. discussing a topic, and in a larger group e.g. addressing the class. Your work should show that you can speak effectively to an audience; collaborate with a fellow student in discussion, and develop ideas through talking them over. (20%)

Section B: Reading

There will be *two assignments* here: one based on the study of a complete work of literature; the other may also be literary but may be a non-literary or media text.

(10%)

Section C: Writing

There should be two pieces of work here: one an imaginative piece e.g. a story, a drama script, a poem or group of poems, and one a transactional piece e.g. an article, a report, a leaflet or a formal letter. You should include some material to show the writing process e.g. a draft which has been edited.   **(10%)**

TERMINAL EXAMINATION   (60%)

There will be *two written papers*, each 1½ hours long at Tier 1, but 2 hours long for Tiers 2 and 3.

Paper 1: Reading and Writing:

Section A: Reading literary material, e.g. a story, drama or poetry, and answering set questions.   **(25%)**
Section B: Two writing tasks, one linked to the material in A above; the other with freer choice.

Paper 2: Reading and Writing:

Section A: Reading non-literary material e.g. an advertisement, newspaper report and answering set questions.
Section B: Two writing tasks, one linked to the material in A above; the other of freer choice, but probably directed to a particular type of reader and for a particular purpose.   **(25%)**

On each paper 5% of marks will be devoted to presentation aspects.

4

'CORRECT' ENGLISH

WRITING STYLE

SPEECH

'CORRECT' GRAMMAR

PARAGRAPHING

PUNCTUATION

SPELLING

GETTING STARTED

For the purposes of GCSE, 'correct' English should not be defined too narrowly. This chapter is as much about appropriate expression as correct grammar, spelling and punctuation. Most of us have a range of forms of English we are able to use and our 'linguistic manners' unconsciously suggest to us which is the right form; there would be considerable difference between a report of an accident you might make in court as an eye-witness and how you would describe it among friends and family.

Among the many forms of English there is one form that is generally considered to be the most 'correct'. This is 'Standard English'. It is important for all who speak or write in English to be able to use this form, when appropriate. This is because it is universally used for official communications. In the examination you will be expected to show that you can adopt different styles, and this will certainly include expressing yourself in Standard English.

The word 'correct' is not used in the **National Criteria**, but among the skills to be assessed are included the ability to

■ show a sense of audience, and an awareness of style in both formal and informal situations

and

■ exercise control of appropriate grammatical structures, conventions of paragraphing, sentence structure, punctuation and spelling in writing.

ESSENTIAL PRINCIPLES

1 > ADOPTING AN APPROPRIATE STYLE OF WRITING

You would probably be surprised to read in an essay on 'Visiting Friends' part of a telephone conversation like this:

'Good afternoon, John. I was hoping I might visit you this afternoon, at three o'clock.'

'Good afternoon, Bill. Yes, it will be quite convenient for you to call at the time you suggest.'

You would feel it was very stilted, and that people don't really talk like that. Bill and John would be more likely to say something like this:

'Oh, hello John, it's Bill. Look, I'd like to pop round for a while this afternoon, all right? About three?'

'O.K., Bill. I'll see you then.'

On the other hand, you would be equally surprised to read in a pamphlet 'Succeeding in an Interview' these sentences:

'You must let them know you are well up in things that are going on. Don't get in a flap and go on about how much money you will be paid.'

Something like this would be more appropriate:

'Try to show that you are interested in current affairs. Keep calm, and avoid asking about the salary.'

 Develop a sense of style   It is very important for the examination that you should be able to write in different and appropriate styles. But how is a sense of style to be developed? Only by wide reading and practice in writing.

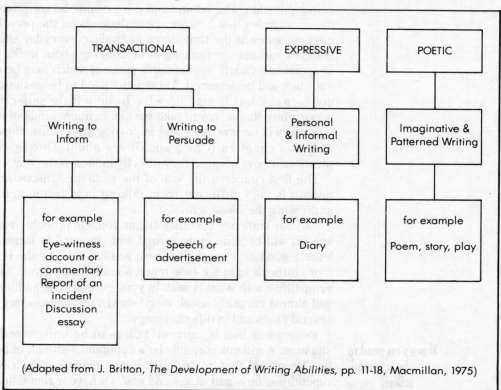

(Adapted from J. Britton, *The Development of Writing Abilities*, pp. 11-18, Macmillan, 1975)

Fig.4.1. Categories of writing

There have been many attempts to describe and classify different types of writing. One model, given in a simplified version in Fig. 4.1, describes a range of styles in written English from the most informal *Expressive writing* (the sort of writing you might do if you kept a diary, or wrote down an incident from your own life) to the more formal *Transactional writing* (reports, essays, summaries, and so on). There is also another very important kind of writing, *Poetic writing* (imaginative writing that has a definite pattern or way of being organised, as in stories and poems).

In school, you will almost certainly have plenty of opportunity in different subjects to do transactional writing but much less to do poetic writing. English coursework will give you the opportunity to do both.

Take your writing seriously as a craft at which you can get better. Sometimes, try out your own ideas very roughly at first, in draft form, and then work at the draft, rewriting, reshaping and improving your first attempt until you are more satisfied with it. You can put both the draft, or drafts, and the finished piece in your coursework folder, so that the *way* your story, poem, description, report – whatever it is – has grown is clear. Most authors of published works make several drafts and revisions of their first attempt. The chapter you are reading now has been through this process! More advice on different kinds of writing is given in Chapters 11–17, too.

| 2 ▷ | **ADOPTING AN APPROPRIATE KIND OF SPEECH** |

'Correct' speech, like 'correct' writing, is not something fixed. Consider the following remarks made by someone within the space of an hour to his employer, a colleague, and his wife:

> 'All right, Mr Hammond, I'll collect it on my way home. I know Richard Hobbs & Co.'

> 'Got to run an errand for N.H., and pick up a parcel from Dirty Dick's.'

> 'I got landed with collecting a parcel from Hobbs' for Old Nick.'

The remarks are in different styles, but each is an example of effective communication. The second and third cannot be considered incorrect. It is clear from these examples that how we speak depends on the person we are addressing and the circumstances at the time. Even in familiar, everyday situations, our way of speaking changes without our noticing it, or thinking about it. But at school, you will be asked to speak in a variety of situations, some of which may be new to you. Also, samples of your talk will be assessed. There is no need to be anxious or self-conscious about oral coursework but it may be wise to be a little self–critical and also to take any opportunity that arises to take part in as many kinds of oral work as you can. In this way you will be practising and improving your skills. How to do this is really what the next two chapters (Chs 5 and 6) are about. One or two general matters will be mentioned now, because they directly influence the way we talk.

The first concerns the size of the audience. Discussing something with *one* other person is very different from talking in a *group*, and even more different from addressing the *whole* school.

As your audience becomes larger you will probably feel less confident and so your speech will become more formal and standard in form. Talking to a friend you can leave a good deal unsaid, because you know he or she is likely to respond. It is much more difficult to judge how much a really large group will be able to understand and sympathise with what is said. In your efforts to be audible and clearly understood you will almost certainly speak more slowly, put points more simply or even repeat them several times and in different ways.

> 66 There's no need to be a smooth talker! 99

Remember that if 'correct' talk is to be understood as talk appropriate to the situation, it will not normally be a continuous stream of perfectly formed sentences. It has been said that 'to "er" is human': natural speech is full of hesitations, pauses, repetitions, ums and ahs – and ers! To have a reputation as a 'smooth talker' is not enviable because the talk sounds too perfect to be sincere. In a prepared short talk you may well speak more carefully and formally than in a group discussion, but each way of speaking will be 'correct', in the sense that each is natural and suits the occasion.

3 > 'CORRECT' GRAMMAR

'Correct' grammar, then, is all part of the 'good linguistic manners' referred to. In fact, most of us have a very good knowledge of the English grammatical structures used in speech, acquired through long practice from our first use of words in infancy. It is possible to make occasional mistakes, but for those with English as a first language it is not so very usual. The grammatical structures of speech and writing, though, are not the same. To help us when we speak we have *non-verbal* aids, such as gestures or changes of expression. We can also change our *tone of voice*, speak *more quickly or more slowly*. Finally, we have *someone to interact with*: if what we are trying to communicate is not being understood by the listener, we can rephrase, try another arrangement of words, and so on. None of these things is normal in written English. The grammar of written English tends to be more formal and disciplined. If you write just as you speak you will find that this can be inappropriate and therefore considered 'incorrect'.

Below are some of the **common mistakes** made by pupils in written English examinations.

INCOMPLETE SENTENCES

When writing quickly it is easy to leave out an essential part of the sentence, which often includes the verb. There are some occasions when this would be perfectly appropriate: an example (known as 'elliptical sentence') would be in a dramatic scene, where tension was being built up, e.g.

'He paused and strained to listen. An intruder!'

 Basic errors to avoid

You could easily justify the exclusion of a verb in the second sentence. It speeds up the action and makes the situation seem more tense. But, take the following example: the omission of the verb forces us to go back, re-read and still feel unsatisfied:

'I hate getting up on Monday mornings. It is not so bad in summer but in winter, when temperatures end up at extremely low levels and there is ice on the window panes and swirling mist outside. The alarm clock rings at about half-past seven and I sleepily stop it.'

CONFUSED USE OF TENSES

This is particularly common in very long sentences where the writer forgets his or her original intention and keeps changing the tense of the verb, e.g.
'Every Sunday we would get up early, shower and have our breakfasts, do the washing up, get out the car and then we rush to the local market where we look at all the antique stalls. We bought all the paintings we liked and we used to bring them home and brushed them off with a soft brush.'

WRONG IDIOM

The fault often involves a muddle over a misheard phrase, not usually seen written down, e.g.

'You should *of* known about it'

instead of

'You should *have* known about it.'

Sometimes, the muddle can be quite amusing!

'My mother came in and cleared out all my clutter in one *foul* swoop'

instead of

'My mother came in and cleared out all my clutter in one *fell* swoop.'

FALSE AGREEMENT

Here a singular verb is often used with a plural subject – or the other way round – and pronouns get muddled too, e.g.

'It was a raw evening. No-one seemed to be about. Everyone was huddled up inside their homes by the fireplace.'

instead of

'It was a raw evening. No-one seemed to be about. People were huddled up inside their homes by their fireplaces.'

Here is another example:

'At an interview one should always be punctual and they should look presentable.'

which should read as follows

'At an interview one should always be punctual and one should look presentable.'

MISRELATED PARTICIPLE

In this case, a participle, intended to qualify one noun, is placed beside another noun in the same sentence. This leads to confusion, e.g.

'I could hear music coming from a transistor floating out from the shore'

would be better as

'I could hear music floating out from the shore, coming from a transistor.'

4 > PARAGRAPHING

There is no rule of thumb here: paragraphs should relate to the organisation of what is being communicated. Each new idea or stage of development needs a new paragraph. One paragraph, extending over dozens of pages has been known, as in James Joyce's novel *Ulysses*, but this was appropriate because it was used for the flow of a woman's thoughts, as she lay in bed.

Young writers sometimes have the uneasy feeling that new paragraphs should occur every ten lines or so. This may often be a convenient way of breaking up the text but it is not a rule. Paragraphing should be logical.

Compare the following examples from a pamphlet 'Succeeding at an interview':

Young people are often criticised for being slow and unenthusiastic. The first impression is the most important impression you give to the interviewer. Check your appearance. Is your hair in place? Are your shoes as clean as you can get them? Are your finger-nails clean and tidy? The smallest detail is an important detail. Watch how you put your attitude across.

Interviews can take anything from ten minutes to half an hour. The longer interviews are designed to get to know the real you!

You must let them know you are well up in things in the real world. You know what's going on in current affairs.

Tell them about your interests and hobbies incorporating that you get on well with people, so getting to know the other staff shouldn't be too difficult. Let them know you will be committed to your job.

Having a mind of your own matters – do not copy what parents and friends have told you to say. Speak your mind, but do not be rude.

There are five paragraphs. The first paragraph concerns first impressions; the second, the likely length of an interview; the third advises you to show that you can keep up with current affairs. So far, the arrangement may seem rather 'bitty' – too many short paragraphs for comfortable reading – but it *is* logical. The last two paragraphs are less well arranged, though: ideas about hobbies, staff relationships and work commitments jostle for attention. The final paragraph 'tails off' with after-thoughts.

A better version might run as follows:

Paragraph 1
'Young people are often criticised for being slow and unenthusiastic. The first impression is the most important impression you give to the interviewer. Check your appearance. Is your hair in place? Are your shoes as clean as you can get them? Are your finger-nails clean and tidy? The smallest detail is an important detail. Watch how you put your attitude across.'

Paragraph 2
'Interviews can take anything from ten minutes to half an hour. The longer interviews are designed to get to know the real you!'

Paragraph 3
'You must let them know you are well informed about the real world, and know what is going on in current affairs. Also, tell them about your interests and hobbies, indicating that you get on well with people, so getting to know the other staff shouldn't be too difficult.'

Paragraph 4
'Make it clear that you have a mind of your own, and are not just repeating what your parents and friends have told you to say. Speak out, but don't be too assertive. Show that you have thought about this particular job for yourself, and will be committed to it.'

5 > PUNCTUATION

"Putting in the right stops."

Punctuation in the twentieth century has become less heavily used in writing than it used to be a hundred years ago, chiefly because of the growth of modern business technology, and the need for speed in communication. Even so, some punctuation is basic and essential, and your ability to punctuate will be assessed in the GCSE examinations.

The use of full stops to mark the ends of sentences is essential but examination candidates have been known to write whole stories of four or five pages without any stops to pace their work, apart from an occasional comma. The reader of the story then has to work very hard to make sense of it, e.g.

'That evening I was working late, it must have been about seven-thirty when I finally walked out through the office doors, it was a dark wet dreary winter's night the sky was overcast and snow was already falling, the view before me was very grim and bare the car park was empty and so was the street beyond nobody was about there was not even anyone waiting at the bus stop they must all have gone home by now I thought.'

Putting in normal punctuation marks makes a great difference here:

'That evening, I was working late. It must have been about seven-thirty when I finally walked out through the office doors. It was a dark, wet, dreary winter's night; the sky was overcast and snow was already falling. The view before me was very grim and bare: the car park was empty, and so was the street beyond. Nobody was about. There was not even anyone waiting at the bus stop. "They must all have gone home by now," I thought.'

Apart from failing to put basic stops in punctuation, the error most commonly made is confusion over setting out direct speech, and what to do when writing dialogue in a play. The rule to remember about the layout of *direct speech* is that *each speaker's words begin on a new line*, e.g.

'Hello!' – a cheerful voice brought me back to the present. 'May I give you a lift?'

'Oh, yes please. I was just wondering whether there would be any public transport on such a dreadful night.' I had never been more relieved to see my next door neighbour as when I climbed into the car.

The simplest procedure to adopt, if this were *dialogue in a play*, would be to *dispense with quotation marks altogether*, e.g.

Neighbour: Hello! May I give you a lift?

Girl (*relieved*): Oh, yes please. I was just wondering whether there would be any public transport on such a dreadful night.
(*She climbs quickly into the car.*)

Always try to be consistent in setting out dialogue.

If you have more problems with punctuation there are some helpful textbooks – see 'A Step Further' below.

6 > SPELLING

Spelling hints.

English is not a regularly phonetic language and such rules as can be given for spelling are not practically very useful for most people with major spelling difficulties. The process by which we learn to spell is a complex one. People have different ways of remembering spellings: some have strong visual memories and can 'see' the word vividly in the mind, or write it down to check whether it 'looks right'; others rely more on the sound of the word. One thing that has been definitely established is that attempts to learn lists of words by heart out of context is unproductive for most spellers. It is better to concentrate on words you mis-spell in your own writing. A simple technique has been suggested for improving spelling and it can be adopted by anyone. You look up the word in a dictionary, then turn the book over and try to reproduce the word. If you cannot find it in the dictionary, ask someone who knows the word to write it down on a piece of paper for you. Look again if you are doubtful, until you are sure you have remembered it correctly, but never copy it. Once you have written a version you feel is right, make a final check in the dictionary, or on the piece of paper. This process can be remembered by the simple expression – LOOK – COVER – WRITE – CHECK.

A STEP FURTHER

The following list gives a few titles of books which will help you to learn more about some of the matters discussed in this chapter:

Close, R. A., 1975, *A Reference Grammar for Students of English* , Longman.

Cripps, C., 1986, *Catchwords: Ideas for Teaching Spelling*, Harcourt Brace.

Crystal, D., 1988, *Rediscover Grammar*, Longman.

Dunsbee, T. & Ford, T., 1980, *Mark My Words*, Ward Lock.

Sutton, C., 1981, *Communicating in the Classroom*, Hodder and Stoughton.

REVIEW SHEET

✎ Verbs are *doing* words. They are concerned with what people and things do and what happens to them. Look at the paragraph below and underline all the verbs in it.

When Hannibal led an army with 37 elephants across the Alps to invade Rome 2200 years ago, he created a reputation for daring that lives on today. As well as the elephants, Hannibal's army consisted of some 50,000 men and 8,000 horses. They took 15 days to battle their way about 121 kilometres through difficult terrain and over snowy heights - it was October and winter was approaching - while being harried by hostile tribesmen. Their average speed of about 14 kilometres a day on a climb to over 2750 metres was a remarkable feat.

✎ Verbs are used in different forms depending on whether you are talking about the past, the present or the future. The different forms of the verb, which relate to the different times of past, present and future, are called tenses. 'I do' or 'He is doing' for instance, are present tenses. 'She did' or 'They were doing' are past tenses. The most common future forms are 'I shall do' and 'I am going to do'.

Now look again at the verbs in the passage about Hannibal.

1 Are they mostly past, present or future forms? _____

2 There is one exception. What is it? _____

✎ In the following paragraphs there are some verbs which are in the wrong tense. Underline the wrong verbs in each case and then write them in their correct forms.

1 This is how you play 'Jack, where are you?' You blindfold two people and everyone else stood in a circle. One of the two blindfolded people is called 'Jack'. The other one shouts out 'Jack, where are you?' Jack replied 'Here I am'. The other one then tries to move towards Jack and to catch him but Jack tried to escape from him and quickly runs in a different direction. It was a very good game.

_____

_____

_____

2 Last week we went to town. We wanted to buy some clothes. We waited ages for the bus and it is very late coming. Then it broke down on the way to town and it takes the driver two hours to repair it. Then we started off again but we have to go very slowly as the driver was afraid the engine would break down again. When we eventually arrive in town the shops were already closed and we could not find anything we wanted to buy.

✎ Idiomatic expressions are often used in everyday conversation.

Complete the sentences below by explaining what the idiomatic expressions mean.

They were really *pulling his leg.* _____

They were really *only joking/teasing him* _____

1 The mischievous boy often managed to *get out of hand.* _____

The mischievous boy often managed to _____

2 The boy was told if he wanted to remain he would have to *pull his weight.* _____

The boy was told if he wanted to remain he would have to _____

3 The family only go there *once in a blue moon.* _____

The family only go there _____

4 They agreed when they realised that it was *the lesser of two evils.* _____

They agreed when they realised that it was _____

5 The young boy *let the cat out of the bag.* _____

The young boy _____

6 He always seems *to rub her up the wrong way.* _____

He always seems _____

7 She didn't expect the girl to help her as she was only a *fair weather friend.* _____

She didn't expect the girl to help her as she was only a _____

8 I am always astonished at how some people *live beyond their means.* _____

I am always astonished at how some people _____

9 He was unable to *make head or tail of* the instructions that had been left.

He was unable to _____

10 The boy heard the news *on the grapevine.* _____

The boy heard the news _____

✎ False agreements are a common mistake, i.e. pupils often use a singular verb with a plural subject, or vice versa.

Change the following sentences from the plural into the singular. This, of course, involves changing not only the verb but also the subjects and sometimes some other things as well. The first one has been done for you.

1 The girls wear blue dresses.
The girl wears a blue dress.

2 The women sit on those seats.

_____

3 The men rush to their work.

_____

4 Policemen watch the border.

_____

5 Wives do a lot of housework.

_____

6 The children pass the post office every day.

_____

7 Parents worry about their children.

_____

8 The ducks go down to the pond.

_____

9 The students hurry down the stairs.

_____

10 Let us have a look at your teeth.

_____

For the next two exercises use a piece of paper or notebook of your own.

_____

✎ Write out the following passage, this time using the correct punctuation.

can any bus service rival the elchester to drayford route in england in may 1992 it was reported in the daily echo that the buses no longer stopped for passengers this had come to light when one of them mrs jane smithson reported that buses regularly sailed past queues of up to thirty people when questioned about this situation councillor wilfred wilson said if these buses stop to pick up passengers theyll disrupt the timetable its a disgrace said mrs smithson im going to buy a bicycle tomorrow

Put in all the necessary punctuation in the following paragraph. Remember that you will need to begin with a new line for each new speaker.

The market was crowded as the man pushed his way forward can I help you asked the stall holder yes please replied the man I want to buy some vegetables as the stall holder was weighing the carrots the man glanced round suspiciously suddenly he ran off at full speed oh no cried a woman nearby my purse is missing she was clearly very upset call the police the stall holder shouted I can give a good description of the thief

INDIVIDUAL ORAL

AUDIBLE AND INTELLIGIBLE SPEECH

RESPONSE TO OTHERS

WELL-ORGANISED TALK

READING ALOUD

HOLDING A CONVERSATION

GIVING A TALK

GIVING INSTRUCTIONS

RELAYING INFORMATION FROM A TAPE

DESCRIBING A PROCESS FROM A TAPE

GETTING STARTED

Assessment in Oral Communication will now be compulsory for all GCSE candidates. According to the **National Criteria** (5.2) 'the interactive nature of listening and speaking cannot be demonstrated solely by reading aloud or delivering a talk'. However these do have 'a useful role to play in the assessment of the spoken language' by providing 'contexts for the interview and/or discussion in which both listening and speaking are to be assessed'.

EXAM GROUPS AND ORAL COMMUNICATION

There is considerable diversity in the approaches of the different Groups. **ULEAC's** syllabus, for example, assesses competence in *four* areas:

■ content
■ interpersonal skills (i.e. relationship between speaker and listener)
■ language style and structure
■ clarity of expression.

These areas of competence may be shown in coursework and a compulsory Group Oral Test.

For **SEG** assessment will be through coursework, but each candidate must attempt work in

■ a paired situation in which both participants collaborate in a specific task
■ an open-ended group discussion
■ an exposition given by the candidate to an audience of one or more persons.

As his or her exposition, a candidate might

■ introduce a topic for group discussion
■ report back on a group discussion
■ give instructions on the use of a piece of equipment, or the carrying out of a process
■ explain an operation or a phenomenon
■ narrate a story
■ relate an experience
■ present an argument
■ propose a motion for debate.

> **What is 'interactive' talk?**

For **NISEAC** assessment will be by observation of the candidate's ability both to listen and speak in a variety of situations, ranging from the formal (e.g. a prepared talk) to the informal (e.g. a group discussion of a book). A range of tasks is offered for the examination in the form of a list, from which candidates choose six:

■ formal interview
■ formal presentation of information; description, relaying information, persuasive argument
■ formal role play (e.g. as news reader)
■ small group discussion of a particular subject
■ problem solving in small groups
■ informal role play (e.g. as a narrator)
■ hypothesising and speculation.

MEG has a variation on this – five activities are expected from a similar list, including additionally

■ play reading and reading aloud
■ pupil in conversation with a teacher
■ giving instructions to others for a task
■ giving a description or information about something seen or heard.

SEG adds

■ introducing a topic for group discussion
■ reporting back on a group discussion
■ giving instructions, e.g. on the use of a piece of equipment
■ relating a story or experience
■ presenting an argument
■ preparing a motion for debate.

As you can see from these lists of suggestions, there is a very wide range of oral work that can be offered as part of the examination. This chapter will be concerned, then, chiefly with **Individual Oral Work** and the next will concentrate on **Group Oral** situations.

ESSENTIAL PRINCIPLES

Whatever form of *individual oral work* you are engaged in, there are certain basic principles to bear in mind.

1 ▷ AUDIBLE AND INTELLIGIBLE

Firstly, you must be **audible** and **intelligible**: no talk is successful unless it can be clearly heard and understood. Speak fairly loudly and a little more slowly than usual. Suppose, for example, you are asked to read aloud something which is given to you. You will have time to read through the material quickly, if it is unseen. It may however be something you have prepared. In the first case, try to read as if reading to someone you know well, using your voice to make the meaning as clear as you can. In the second case, bear the following advice in mind. Choose a passage

- of an appropriate length (usually between 250 and 500 words but check with the syllabus to make sure)
- that you think will interest the listener
- that has a shape, i.e. is complete in itself, e.g. an episode from a story or an article from a newspaper.

Can they hear you at the back?

If you feel you can handle it, you could consider choosing something with emotional impact – amusing or tense. Avoid a lengthy introductory stretch of narrative; you can always give a brief explanation yourself to start with. Whatever you choose, discuss it with your teacher or tutor.

When you have found something you are comfortable with, you can practise reading it to a friend. Don't do this too often, or your reading will have an over-rehearsed, unnatural effect.

2 ▷ RESPOND TO THE OTHER PEOPLE PRESENT

The **second** principle to remember is that, whether you are talking with your teacher, an external assessor or among a group of people, a vital part of communication is that you **respond to the other people present**. Of course, it is easiest to do this well if you are relaxed and can behave naturally. This may not always be possible, especially if you are talking about something fairly formally, e.g. giving a talk you have prepared beforehand to someone you aren't very familiar with. Whatever the situation, it is essential to appear friendly but polite. Show that you are engaging in the activity with a sense of its importance but not so stiffly that the talk becomes what is sometimes described as 'frozen'. Given the opportunity, begin by introducing yourself and what it is you are going to talk about. Even if someone else is involved, in an individual oral it is *your* talk that is being assessed and you will need to show that you can sustain a conversation or a lecturette and not 'dry up'. If you do, don't worry. The assessor or others present will want to put you at your ease and start you off again.

Avoid using simple 'yes', 'no' answers; try to interest the listener and genuinely want to tell or teach him or her something. You are responsible for how the talk goes. If you think in this way, you will be careful to interest and involve the listener.

If you are giving a *prepared* talk, try to have plenty of material ready and know it well. You can then answer any questions that are put to you. As long as you keep to the main area of discussion there is no reason why you should not talk about your own experience of whatever is the topic of conversation. You will talk with more warmth and fluency if you are personally involved.

WELL-ORGANISED TALK

3

66 **Planning matters.** 99

A **third** important matter (and another aspect of intelligibility) is that a prepared talk should be **well organised**. This is particularly important if you are, say, giving a lecturette or relating information about something seen or heard.

In the case of a lecturette, you can choose to talk about something you feel you know quite well, or can research effectively, and will enjoy. You will then be more likely to hold the attention of the listener. Also choose a topic which has some breadth or depth and then decide how you can plan it clearly. A good plan involves thinking of five or six main points that you would like to make. This will probably be sufficient for the average length of a formal talk – about five minutes. Do not write out the whole talk as a continuous piece and then read it aloud. This will result in a much duller performance.

Remember that you need to interact with your listener and to do this you must address him or her directly. It is a good idea to have a set of cards and make brief notes such as a heading and one or two details, e.g. date, statistics – small things that you may not feel confident you will remember. Keep these very brief – just enough to see at a glance. You may want to illustrate the points you make with more visual or aural aids. You may want to show a map or diagram – if so, make them big and clear.

If you are going to do some sort of practical demonstration, practise beforehand until you are confident that you don't make mistakes that will worry you and your audience. When you have finished your talk, don't just relax. Keep your attention on any questions asked and try to answer as fully as you can. Remember, you will almost certainly know a good deal more about the topic than the listener!

Again you could consider choosing something with emotional impact – amusing or tense for example – provided you feel you can cope with the topic and situation. Avoid a lengthy introductory stretch of narrative (you can always give a brief explanation yourself to start with). Whatever you choose, discuss it with your teacher or tutor. The right choice of passage is, of course, very important, if your oral work is to be a success.

USEFUL PRACTICAL APPROACHES

The following speech situations are some of those which will be used for assessing individual oral work:

1 Reading aloud
2 Holding a conversation
3 Giving a talk
4 Giving instructions.

READING ALOUD

1

As you read new stories or non-fiction material throughout the year you could keep a note of any passages which you like and think would be suitable for *reading aloud*. Then you will have plenty to choose from.

Consider the following passage from George Orwell's *Animal Farm*:

'June came and the hay was almost ready for cutting. On Midsummer's Eve, which was a Saturday, Mr Jones went into Willingdon and got so drunk at the Red Lion that he did not come back till mid-day on Sunday. The men milked the cows in the early morning and then had gone out rabbiting, without bothering to feed the animals. When Mr Jones got back he immediately went to sleep on the drawing-room sofa, with the *News of the World* over his face, so that when evening came, the animals were still unfed. At last they could stand it no longer. One of the cows broke in the door of the store-shed with her horns and all the animals began to help themselves from the bins. It was just then that Mr Jones woke up. The next moment he and his four men were in the store-shed with whips in their hands, lashing out in all directions. This was more than the hungry animals could bear. With one accord, though nothing of the kind had been planned beforehand, they flung themselves upon their tormentors. Jones and his men suddenly found themselves being butted and kicked from all sides. The situation was quite out of their control; they had never seen animals behave like this before, and this sudden uprising of creatures whom they were used to thrashing and maltreating just as they chose, frightened them almost out of their wits. After only a moment or two they gave up trying to defend themselves and took to their heels. A minute later all five of them were in full flight down the cart-track that led to the main road, with the animals pursuing them in triumph.

'Mrs Jones looked out of the bedroom window, saw what was happening, hurriedly flung a few possessions into a carpet bag, and slipped out of the farm by another way ... Meanwhile the animals had chased Jones and his men out on to the road and slammed the five-barred gate behind them. And so, almost before they knew what was happening, the Rebellion had been successfully carried through: Jones was expelled, and the Manor Farm was theirs.

'For the first few minutes the animals could hardly believe in their good fortune. Their first act was to gallop in a body right round the boundaries of the farm, as though to make quite sure that no human being was hiding anywhere upon it; then they raced back to wipe out the last traces of Jones's hated reign ...

'Then they filed back to the farm buildings and halted in silence outside the door of the farmhouse. That was theirs too, but they were frightened to go inside. After a moment, however, Snowball and Napoleon butted the door open with their shoulders and the animals entered in single file, walking with the utmost care for fear of disturbing anything. They tiptoed from room to room, afraid to speak above a whisper and gazing with a kind of awe at the unbelievable luxury, at the beds with their feather mattresses, the looking-glasses, the horsehair sofa, the Brussels carpet, the lithograph of Queen Victoria over the drawing-room mantelpiece. They were just coming down the stairs when Mollie was discovered to be missing. Going back, the others found that she had remained behind in the best bedroom. She had taken a piece of blue ribbon from Mrs Jones' dressing table, and was holding it against her shoulder and admiring herself in the glass in a very foolish manner. The others reproached her sharply, and they went outside. Some hams hanging in the kitchen were taken out for burial, and the barrel of beer in the scullery was stove in with a kick from Boxer's hoof, otherwise nothing in the house was touched. A unanimous resolution was passed on the spot that the farmhouse would be preserved as a museum. All were agreed that no animal must ever live there.'

(George Orwell, *Animal Farm*)

The passage is of a suitable length, interesting, with a definite beginning and end and concerns a rather dramatic episode in the book: the capture of Manor Farm. There are points where the *pace* of the narrative changes and as a reader you would want to go *faster* and *louder* – for example, 'The next moment he and his four men were in the store-shed with whips in their hands, lashing out in all directions' – and *stress the verbs* which show the furious reaction of the animals – 'flung themselves', 'butted', 'kicked' – working up to a crescendo with the flight of the men and the animals 'pursuing them in triumph'.

Another major change in mood – and as a reader you would want to try to bring this out by reading more slowly and quietly – occurs with the entry by the animals into the farm buildings: 'Then they filed back to the farm buildings and halted in silence outside the door of the farmhouse. That was theirs too, but they were frightened to go inside.' Another place where a slower more emphatic reading would help to stress meaning might be the last two sentences of the extract.

Certainly, it would help to have read the whole novel to know that this is not just an animal story, but a fable, with something ironic to say about human beings and society. To know this would help you to read the extract with the right tone, perhaps showing the indignation of the animals. You could also answer questions. Suppose you were asked why you thought George Orwell had written this story, or how you could explain the animals' action in burying the hams? This extract would be a good passage for reading aloud.

HOLDING A CONVERSATION

This is probably the easiest part of the oral test to prepare, because it is what we do all the time. You might list topics that you would like to talk about to the assessor, who will be your teacher or an examiner. The following list of suggestions offers a starting point – you should certainly be able to talk about most of them:

- Yourself and your interests
- Your family and home
- Your school or work
- What you do in your leisure time
- Books you have read
- Films and TV you enjoy
- Hobbies
- Travel
- Sport
- Music
- Fashion
- Food you enjoy
- People you know
- Your local town or village
- Items in the news.

3 GIVING A TALK

There are as many subjects for a prepared talk as there are readers of this book, of course. Turn back to the list in the previous section and write down topics you would like to research. Next, break down your topics into five or six short headings, e.g.

FASHION
Making my own clothes (*Title*)
Where I get ideas/Choosing patterns and materials/Stages in making/Reactions when garment is first worn (*Sections of Talk*)

ANIMALS
Keeping tropical fish
How to get going/Choosing fish/Keeping the tank healthy/Feeding/Breeding

SPORT
Long-distance running
How I became interested/Training/Sports events/Where I go from here

MUSIC
Playing the drums
How I became interested/Basic skills/Practice/Playing with others

Of course, this is only one way of arriving at a title and plan for your talk, and there are many others. Whatever approach you use, it is very important that the talk is well planned. Note that you will only be allowed a limited time to speak – say five minutes, usually.

4 GIVING INSTRUCTIONS

Passing on information to a friend.

It is surprising how hard it can be to explain something that you think you know how to do, to someone else who has had no experience of it, in a way that makes it really clear to them. If you have not attempted this before, try an experiment. Explain to a friend how to operate a simple appliance, e.g. to make a cup of coffee with an electric percolator. You will find out how easy it is to overlook basic steps and get the stages of the process in the wrong order.

Alternatively, you could give instructions for doing a job you are familiar with, e.g. issuing books in the school or college library. However well you know the task, it is best to check the instructions very carefully.

EXAMPLES OF INDIVIDUAL ORAL WORK

The following are examples of the kinds of task that you might embark upon for individual oral work:

You listen to an educational or informative tape, and while doing so make notes on a note-sheet given you. Then you tell some other pupils what you have learned about the subject of the tape. What you say is recorded, for example:

a) Here is a transcript of a topic about spiders:

There are over 23,000 different kinds of spiders and over 600 of these are found in Britain.

Spiders are not insects. All insects have six legs but spiders have eight. Also, insects have three parts to their bodies: the head, thorax and abdomen. Spiders have only two parts. The head and the thorax are merged into one part to which the legs are attached. Another difference between insects and spiders is that the young of spiders emerge from their eggs as slightly smaller versions of their parents. As they grow, they split their skins and shed them. Insects on the other hand pass trough a number of different stages of development before attaining their adult form. One final difference between insects and spiders is that a spider has no wings or feelers and there is always a pair of poison claws in front of the mouth.

Most spiders rely mainly on their senses of smell and touch. Spiders are very short-sighted, they detect their prey by smell and not sight. They have smelling bristles on various parts of their bodies, but the sense that counts for most is that of touch. A spider does not usually, for example, see a fly that gets caught in its web. It feels the vibration caused by its struggles.

With most kinds of spiders the female is able to spin silk. Spiders' silk consists of numerous strands which are woven together like rope or cable. Spiders have glands capable of making several different kinds of silk. The pattern of the silk strands is changed to suit the purpose for which the spider is spinning the silk. For example, there's one kind of silk for trapping insects, another for use as a cable along which the spider can run to catch its prey, another for use as parachutes or balloons on which the spider may go sailing through the air, and so on.

Nearly all spiders make webs. The most obvious use that the spider makes of the web is to catch prey. There are many different kinds of webs. Some upright and others horizontal, some like tents and others like domes. The orb web of the garden spider is one which is particularly attractive.

In the next part of the exercise you will hear of how the garden spider builds her web.

b) These are notes made by a fifteen-year-old pupil:

These sub-headings relate to the main points on the tape.

1 *The numbers of spiders*
    over 23,000
    600 in GB

2 *How spiders differ from insects*
    insects 6 legs – 3 parts for body
    s. 8 legs – 2 parts (merged)
    no metamorphosis – split skins
    insects have stages of development
    no wings, feelers but poison claws

3   *The spider's sense of smell and touch*
      s. sighted
      relies on touch
      smelling bristles on parts of body
      feels insect on web

4   *The spider's silk*
      female spins
      like rope
      glands make different kinds
      trapping, a cable
      parachutes

5   *The spider's web*
      to catch prey
      vertical, domes, tents
      orb-web of garden spider

c) This is a transcript of the pupil's report:

Assessor: O.K.

Pupil: There're over twenty-three thousand types of spiders in the world, and six hundred of those are found in …Great Britain. Spiders *aren't* insects there're several differences, insects have six legs, whereas spiders have eight legs and spiders only have two parts of the body. The first two par … the first part is merged, to the second part. Insects have three parts of the body the head the thorax and the abdomen. And spiders go …, don't go through a metamorphosis. They em … are born a *small* image of their parents and they … as they grow they split their skins, whereas insects go through definite stages of development. In …, insects have wings, but spiders don't and spiders do …, do not have feelers either but in front of their mouth they have poisoned fangs. Spiders are very short sighted and they rely a great deal on their sense of touch. For instance, if there's an insect who's on a spider's web, the spider would not *see* it but would feel it, feel the s…, the insect moving on the web. They have, also smelling bristles on various parts of their body. Only the females spin silk and, silk is made up of different materials spun together like rope. And the spiders' glands make various different kinds of s…, silk for trapping., t…, to make parachutes so they travel, or, or cable for instance so they can slide down on their webs. A spider's web is primarily used to catch prey, but it is many different shapes vertical, domes, tent, horizontal. The prettiest webs are probably those of the garden spider, which is an orb web.

Assessor: O.K., Thank you.

2 ▶ DESCRIBING A PROCESS FROM A TAPE

You listen to a taped account of the process, and while doing so look at a series of illustrations or diagrams. Then you describe the process to some other pupils, who are also shown the illustrations. What you say is recorded, for example:

a) This is an account of the web-building process:

This is how the garden spider spins her web.

1   First of all, the spider carries a thread of silk between two supports, though sometimes the thread can be blown across by the wind.

2   After the first thread has been fastened, the spider spins another thread down from the middle of this thread and fastens it to a third support.

3   Then the spider runs backwards and forwards, adding more spokes to the web, and reinforcing the edges of the frame of the web, to make it stronger.

4   Next the spider starts to join all the spokes together. First of all it spins a spiral of widely-spaced threads, starting at the centre of the web and working outwards to the edge.

5 When the spider reaches the edge of the web, it turns around and comes back, spinning the threads more closely. These threads replace the first spiral, which the spider eats on its way back to the middle of the web.

6 When the web is finished, the spider will hide in its lair, ready to dash out and catch its prey when it feels a tug on the web.

b) The illustrations are shown below.

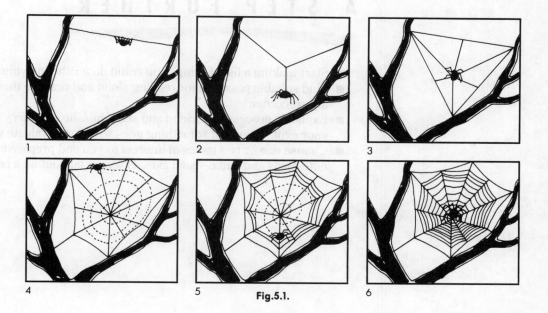

Fig.5.1.

c) This is a transcript of the pupil's description:

Pupil: Well, for a start, the spider puts one thread across the support, the supports, like that. And then from that she drops one down the middle to make a third support, and then moves in and out of these three, to make the web, well you know, make more supports, for the web. And then she starts from the middle and goes outwards in a spiral shape until she gets to the edge. Then she turns round and starts going back in. An' while she's going back in she eats the first lot, the, the spiral what she put out to start with. An' then once she gets to the middle, of all …, after going back in, she goes to the lair and waits for the prey.

Assessor: Fine, right, thank you very much.

A TUTOR'S COMMENTS

1 The pupil's notes were good: brief and organised under sub-headings. She could see at a glance the information she needed to keep going when giving her talk. Normally, there should be an introduction, e.g. 'I'm a pupil at school, in the fifth form, and I'm going to give you some general information about spiders.'

This is very fluent – the small hesitations and repetitions are normal in speech – and it is very well organised. She followed the order of the stages of the tape exactly, and the information given was clear and comprehensive.

2 The pupil spoke fluently, with only a few hesitations and corrections. He had understood the process, and he mentioned all six stages, but his descriptions of four of them are unsatisfactory: such phrases as 'like that', 'from that', 'these three' are vague and he could have been more explicit. He was not altogether clear when he said 'she eats the first lot', but quickly added a bit more explanation. This is rather short. His descriptions of the process as a whole would not be intelligible without the drawings.

A STEP FURTHER

- Start making a list of things you could do for the individual oral.
- Find suitable passages for reading aloud and practise them with a friend with a tape-recorder.
- Explain a process to a friend and see if he/she can carry it out successfully from your explanations. If something goes wrong, re-evaluate your instructions.
- Choose one or two topics of interest to you and prepare a short talk, with a set of note-cards and audio-visual aids. Try your talk out on a receptive adult or friend.

R E V I E W   S H E E T

✎ What basic practical points of advice would you give to someone who asked you how best to deliver a speech to an audience?

1 _____

2 _____

3 _____

4 _____

5 _____

6 _____

✎ Which of the following pieces of advice are in general helpful for someone who has to make a speech of some kind? Underline the helpful points.

1 Start by addressing your audience.
2 Give them an outline of what you are going to say before you say it.
3 Use plenty of hand gestures.
4 Illustrate points you are making with examples.
5 Make the structure of what you are saying explicit.
6 It's better to talk for too long than for not long enough.
7 Use long words and sentences to show that you are an authority.
8 Tell the occasional joke.
9 Summarise the main points you have made at the end.
10 Write out what you are going to say in full beforehand.

✎ Read the following sentence aloud.

> I think you're right.

Now read it in these different ways:

a   as if you are not quite sure about it.
b   as if you are absolutely sure.
c   as if others may not believe it although you yourself are convinced.
d   as if a lot of different people have put forward other ideas.

✎ Now say this sentence aloud.

> I'm in love.

Now say it as if you were in different moods:

a   very happy.
b   very sad.
c   confused.
d   bored.
e   relieved.
f   afraid.

✎ Now say this sentence aloud.

> I want to go home.

Now say it as if you felt:

a   tired.
b   doubtful.
c   angry.
d   nervous.
e   excited.
f   enthusiastic.

Now say this sentence aloud.

> He has found out the truth.

Now say it as if you were in these different moods:

a   content.
b   alarmed.
c   puzzled.
d   amazed.
e   thrilled.
f   amused.

 Prepare a short talk, with a set of note-cards and visual aids on any *four* of the following. Try your talk out on a friend or relative and ask for their comments.

1   Give a speech of welcome to some students from a different school who have come to play sports with your school's team.
2   Give a speech to a teacher who is retiring thanking him or her for all they have done for you and your classmates.
3   Make a speech proposing to your class that homework is unnecessary.
4   Give a talk introducing your area to a group of foreign visitors to the place where you live.
5   Introduce your school to a group of visiting teachers from abroad.
6   Give a five-minute talk on someone who is your hero or heroine. Describe the person and explain the reasons why you chose him or her.
7   Explain to someone how to play a game of your own choice.
8   Explain to an employer why you think they ought to give you a particular job which you very much want.
9   Argue the case that more time at school should be spent on physical education.
10   Discuss a particular issue in the news at the moment. Give your point of view and your reasons for it.

_____
_____
_____
_____
_____
_____
_____
_____
_____
_____
_____
_____
_____
_____
_____
_____
_____
_____
_____
_____
_____
_____

GROUP ORAL

SKILLS

METHODS OF PREPARATION

GROUP ORAL WORK

GETTING STARTED

As has been said, all examining Groups will expect you to submit evidence of *group* oral activities. Boards do not specify exact tasks, but here is a list of the kind of activities you might choose from:

1 In pairs

- consider a problem and suggest a solution
- produce a piece of work jointly
- plan an event
- interview each other
- instruct another pupil in a task.

2 As a group

- discuss a text or audio or video recording
- talk about a topic of current interest
- discuss a theme explored in literature
- discuss possible ways of ending a play or story
- compare two poems
- play different roles in turn
- record a mock trial
- plan a TV or radio programme and record it
- hold a formal debate
- work on scripted drama, or at improvisation.

ESSENTIAL PRINCIPLES

1 ▷ SKILLS INVOLVED

Group oral work may be unsupervised – pupils talking on their own – or partly directed by an assessor or teacher. Work may range from the formal (e.g. debating) to the informal (e.g. undirected group discussion). Whichever approach you choose, marks will be awarded for skills in several areas. It could be said broadly that you will need to be able to

- speak clearly and with appropriate pace, volume and intonation
- speak directly and involve a listener
- organize ideas effectively
- communicate thought and feeling with expression
- develop, illustrate and explain ideas, opinions and feelings
- respond to changes in the direction of a conversation or discussion
- react intelligently to new ideas and defend or modify a position, as needed.

Four rules for oral work

There are various essentials to bear in mind when taking part in a group discussion:

1 You cannot discuss anything capably unless you are well informed. This means having some facts, as well as opinions, ready. Research the subject well first.

2 You should show that you are able to lead the discussion, perhaps act as chairperson and direct others, as well as take your place in the group, listen to others and be receptive to their ideas.

3 You must be good humoured and courteous, and show toleration for others who may disagree with your views.

4 You should take care to speak in an appropriate manner for the occasion.

2 ▷ METHODS OF PREPARATION

Group discussion will almost certainly be part of your normal classroom work. Every opportunity that you have to work in a group, discussing, for example, a story, a poem or some topic of current interest, gives you a chance to practise your skills. In any group discussion it is not the person who speaks most frequently and most emphatically who gains the respect of the group, but the one who knows what he or she is talking about. So, if you have been told in advance what is going to be discussed, it is a good idea to make a few preparations. This may mean no more than thinking about the subject, to see what you remember about it. On the other hand, if a topic in the news is going to be discussed, you might read it up in the newspapers, or talk about it to your friends and family. Remember, too, that the reference sections of libraries contain books which give up-to-date information about a huge range of subjects, and that library assistants are normally very helpful. If you are going to be the discussion leader, it is more or less essential for you to be well prepared, so that you can help things along by occasionally asking questions, by encouraging and stimulating remarks, and by summarizing points for the rest of the group.

Audio and video recordings can provide a valuable record of your group oral work, as they give those taking part the opportunity to evaluate their performances. They do introduce difficulties of their own, however. Both make you behave rather self-consciously: you may not be used to them. Audio recordings, of course, do not show your gestures and facial expressions, which can be a very important part of communication – but tape recorders are easy to come by and to use. Video equipment is expensive and requires special skill to operate if a good recording is to result. Its use in schools and colleges is increasing, however, and you may well find that you have access to it.

3 ▷ EXAMPLES OF GROUP ORAL WORK

The range of possibilities for group oral work is large, and at different times you will probably narrate, describe, expound, argue, persuade, speculate, act, and do many other things. Here are some of the activities you might be engaged in:

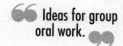 **Ideas for group oral work.**

1 Discuss, in a small group, first reactions to a novel, play or poem you have read.

2 Record your own version of an established soap opera, or an invented one.

3 Set up your own 'Any Questions?' panel, and ask and respond to questions on topical issues.

4 Hold a formal debate on a proposition of interest to the group, e.g. 'School would be better if there were half-day attendance'

or

'Sixth form pupils should be given a maintenance grant, like that awarded to students in higher education.'

5 Set up a mock trial.

6 In pairs, improvise short conversations between people in a situation where they have time on their hands, e.g. in a waiting-room, at the bus stop, in a queue.

7 In pairs work together, first as interviewer and then as the person interviewed (e.g. a famous person in history).

8 Chair a group discussion on a topic of current interest.

9 In a group do a prediction exercise on a text you are all reading.

10 In a group, work at a cloze (deletion exercise, i.e. blank filling) activity on a text you are all reading.

SAMPLE DISCUSSIONS

1 The following is a transcript of the beginning of a discussion by pupils who had read Alan Garner's *Red Shift*, for the first time.

B1: 'Well, we have decided to talk about this book by Alan Garner. Keith, what did you think?'

B2: 'I read up to page twenty … I read to the end of the Tom and Jan section and thought "I can't take this any more!" I just put it down and I didn't start it again until yesterday night. Then I read a bit more of the next part and I carried on and really … I really didn't enjoy it.'

G1: 'I liked the characters on the first page. They amused me. I wasn't very sure about all the short sentences, though … I … I got to the second part. Then I was trying to think "Were they Romans? Were they in the future, or what?" I don't think I'd have gone on from there if I'd been reading it just for myself.'

G2: 'Well, I enjoyed it. I thought though the fact that I liked it … it had something to do with seeing it on television, some time ago. I could remember the plot and realised that it was happening in three different times and that there was a link between them. I think that did help a lot.'

B1: 'That would be like a second experience of the book, because you'd been over it once on the television.'

G2: 'Yes, it was.'

B1: 'When you said you were trying to find a link, did you think there was like a key, and if you could just find it, it would all fall into place?'

G2: 'Well, yes! But I never did find it!' (*Laughter and general agreement.*)

B2: 'But I didn't, either. I only read on because I couldn't understand it. I thought "I'm going to understand this the more I read", but I didn't.' (*Laughter.*)

B1: 'When you were reading, what was happening if no meaning was coming through?' (*Laughter*.)

B2: 'I thought "It's going to come clear in a minute. Keep on! Keep on!" I wanted to know what was going to happen to Tom and Jan. That's what I wanted.' (*Murmur of agreement.*)

G1: 'I thought "It must be worth doing because we've been asked to read it." I thought "Great! A story to read" but when I started it, I thought, "Wow!" (*Laughter.*)

B1: "What about Tom's Mum and Dad? Do you think they were like people in real life, or not?'

G1: 'Um, yes, especially his Mum, grumbling at him to keep his things tidy, all the time … Yes, that was all right, but I was put off by the first piece about Roman times. You could tell from certain clues that it was Roman times, but the language they were using sort of clashed. They kept saying things like "Come on, kid" and "Don't push it" – more like the army today talking.'

B2: 'I …' (*pause*)

G2: 'Perhaps what it was saying is that ways don't change all that much – like only on the surface it changes. Wars are the same. War's always war'

2 Here is a transcript of two pupils role playing as housewives, talking to pass time while waiting for a bus:

G1: (*cheerfully*): 'Hello, Eve. How are you today?'

G2: (*surprised*): 'Hello, Dawn. Haven't seen you for ages.'

G1: 'I know I've been a bit ill, really.'

G2: 'Oh – nothing nasty?'

G1: 'No … not really. It's my knee, and Fred has been getting a bit – a bit on my nerves, you know.'

G2: 'Oh-h-h?'

G1: 'Um.'

G2: 'Well, what are you doing with yourself now?'

G1: 'Oh, well, I'm getting ready for my sister-in-law coming down. I still haven't told Fred yet; I don't think that he's going to be very pleased, you know. Doesn't like things like that.'

G2: 'Oh, doesn't he get on well with his sister, then?'

G1: (*laughing*): 'We-e-e-ll. I don't know. She's a funny old dear, she really is. She … you know … she comes over and she sort of goes in all the rooms. She has a good nose round. It's so bad – you have to lock all the drawers up. It's awful'

G2: 'You haven't seen her for a while have you? You've never mentioned her to me before.'

G1: 'No – we don't like to mention her very much. No, poor thing. She'll get over it one day.'

G2: 'She coming far?'

G1: 'Um – yes. Um … Liverpool. So, you see …'

G2: 'How's she getting here?'

G1: 'On the train.'

G2: 'You'll have to meet her, then?'

G1 (*emphatically*): 'No. I can't meet her, not with my leg. I'll have to get Fred to go. Yes. He'll have to have a day off work; he won't like that, either.'

G2: 'No, I see. No, we don't have much trouble with relations. All ours live nearby, so they're for ever popping in and out. We never worry about them …'

G1: 'Oh, I wouldn't like that! Well, ought to go now – no use waiting here all day.'

G2: 'I'll wait a bit longer.'

G1: 'See you later, then. Bye.'

3 Here is a transcript of two pupils working at a simple sequencing task. The speakers are trying to put in the right order instructions for planting a bulb in a pot.

G1: 'Oh, we've got to sort this out. What do you think?'

G2: (*reading slowly from a slip of paper*): ' "Cover the bottom of the pot with the mixture".'

G1: 'That must be the first one.'

G2 (*continues reading*): ' "Leave the shoulders of the bulb above the surface" – Oh, that's wrong. We haven't even got the bulb yet!'

G1 (*continues reading*): ' "Place the pot in a sunny position" – What … where shall I put this?'

G2: ' "Fill the pot …" Fill the pot!'

G1: 'Oh, yes, I see. That must come next, after "Cover the bottom of the pot".'

G2: ' "When the first growth appears …" Oh, no; not yet!'

G1 (*thinking aloud*): 'Cover the shoulders of the bulb, then fill the pot with the remaining mixture … that must be right.'

G2: 'That "When the plant is growing …" bit must come near the end, don't you think?'

G1 (*still thinking aloud*): 'How about having "Fill the pot with the remainder of the mixture", then "Place the pot …" '

G2 (*irritated*): 'Look! We haven't even got the bulb in yet!' (*Hysterical giggles from both girls.*)

G1: 'Oh, I've got it. Look "Place the bulb in a central position", etc., then "When the buds appear, water more often …".'

G2 (*excited*): 'Yes, then "When the plant is growing, support it with a cane or stick" – that goes right at the end. Yes?'

G1: 'Yes! right! Let's try it in order, now.'

G1 and G2 (*together*): ' "Soak the potting mixture thoroughly and squeeze out the surplus mixture. Cover the bottom of the pot with the mixture. Place the bulb in a central position. Fill the pot with the remainder of the mixture, pushing it down firmly, so that the shoulders of the bulb are just above the surface. Place the pot in a sunny position and water sparingly. When the first growth appears, water freely from time to time. When the buds appear water more often, probably every day. Then, support it with a stick or cane." '

G2: 'Good. Yes, I think that'll grow!'

A TUTOR'S COMMENTS

1 There are quite a lot of good points to notice here. Let's work through a short check-list of the kind that would be used by an assessor. We shall consider the following for the speakers:

- Delivery
- Content and appropriateness
- Ability to respond to others' remarks
- Ability to convey ideas, feelings and experiences
- Asking and answering questions
- Presenting and backing up a point of view.

Delivery

Although you can't tell this from the transcript, all of those taking part spoke loudly and clearly and could be heard easily. The laughter shows that members of the group were relaxed about the discussion.

Content and appropriateness

All four speakers contributed to make this quite an interesting discussion, as regards content, though they had different evaluations and opinions of the book they had read. There is a good balance kept between details from the book and opinions about it. Appropriateness, here keeping to the point, was chiefly the responsibility of Boy 1. As leader of the discussion he introduced the subject and invited Boy 2 to start. When he thought the group was getting a bit stuck in the groove of what to decide about the meaning of the story he turned to something else by asking 'What about Tom's Mum and Dad ...?' This enabled Girl 1 to carry on. His question about the 'clash' of language in the Roman sections of the book helped Girl 2 to articulate a really profound idea. Boy 1's role in this would be rated highly.

Leading a discussion

Ability to respond to others' remarks

All four speakers are fairly good listeners. They took in what the others said and picked up the thread of the discussion as it unwound. Follow Girl 2. She disagreed with Girl 1, and liked the novel, even though she didn't really understand it. She went quiet for a while, but, by listening to the others, was able to contribute the final idea in this extract.

Ability to convey ideas, feelings and experiences

The members (excluding Boy 1, the leader) are good at conveying ideas and experiences and are honest about their feelings. Boy 2: 'I thought "I can't take any more!" '; Girl 1: 'I don't think I'd have gone on from there if I'd been reading it just for myself', and later 'I thought "Great! A story to read!", but when I started it, I thought "Wow!".'

Asking and answering questions

Boy 1, quite suitably in his role as leader, was good at asking questions to draw out the other speakers, or keep the discussion going, and move it forward, e.g. 'Did you think there was any reason for that?' The other three responded readily, though sometimes in a way that brought that line of investigation to an end, e.g. Girl 2: 'Yes, it was', and 'Well, yes! But I never did find it.'

Presenting and backing up a point of view

It is not enough just to have opinions about what you read, you need evidence to support them. Boy 2 explained that he gave the book a fair chance ('I read up to page twenty ... I read to the end of the Tom and Jan section') before he gave up and decided he didn't enjoy it. Girl 1 thought Tom's Mum was like a person in real life 'grumbling at him to keep his things tidy, all the time'. She also gave good examples she had remembered from the text of the odd language, which she couldn't see the reason for, as she read.

Altogether this was a lively and interesting discussion, in which all four participants took part ably.

2 This is an attractive short dialogue, in which each girl sustains her role convincingly.

Delivery

On the tape it is clear that both girls are 'in character'. Girl 1 speaks clearly but, after her cheerful opening greeting, in a tone of tired resignation, the pitch of her voice dropping at the end of each remark. Girl 2, in the role of the sympathetic friend, speaks in gentler tones, often of enquiry, with a rising note at the end of her contributions. Both show the hesitations and repetitions that are natural to relaxed speech. Both girls speak in an informal idiom, just as two housewives might, e.g. 'Fred has been getting a bit – a bit on my nerves' or 'She's a funny old dear, she really is.'

Content and appropriateness

Both speakers talk about nothing very significant, as suits an idle chat at the bus stop, but they do manage to develop the chief topic – the sister-in-law's unwelcome visit – quite well.

Ability to respond to others' remarks

Each follows on from what the other says remarkably well, considering that this was spontaneous role play. At one point Girl 2 interrupts her friend, when she hesitates, in a way that anticipates what she was probably going on to say next – at least it is a very convincing continuation: Girl 1: 'Um – yes. Um … Liverpool. So you see …' Girl 2 breaks in with 'How's she getting here?'

Ability to convey ideas, feelings and experiences

Girl 1 conveys her situation and its problems partly by stretches of narration: 'She's a funny old dear, she really is … She … you know … she comes over and she sort of goes in all the rooms. She has a good nose round. It's so bad – you have to lock all the drawers up. It's awful!' and partly by dark hints, which are equally effective, e.g. 'No – we don't like to mention her very much' or 'I still haven't told Fred yet; I don't think that he's going to be very pleased, you know.' The role of Girl 2 is that of steady confidant, and appropriately she shows no surprise at the revelations of her friend.

Asking and answering questions

Here, it is only necessary to do this in order to sustain the dialogue. Girl 2 asks most of the questions to draw out Girl 1 and get details of what has been happening to her. Both girls are very consistent in keeping to their questioner and respondent roles.

This is a well-shaped, convincing short dialogue, and both girls took their part commendably.

3 The girls obviously had a little difficulty working out the correct sequence of instructions. They had some fun while they were attempting it, but they could have collaborated more effectively, especially in the early stages.

Delivery

Girl 2 was the dominant partner and spoke more loudly, and at one point, aggressively: 'Look! We haven't even got the bulb in yet!' Girl 1, who spent some time in thinking aloud, tended to mutter her ideas quietly.

Content and appropriateness

Insofar as the task was set for them, the content of the girls' talk was partly predetermined – there was a fair amount of reading aloud to remind themselves of the different instructions. They did concentrate on the task in hand, though this was over a fairly short stretch of time. Their speech was appropriate for the problem-solving activity they were engaged in.

Ability to respond to others' remarks

Girl 1 was not very good at responding to her partner. Girl 2 attempted to move things along but sometimes her attempts were ignored, e.g. Girl 2: 'That "When the plant is growing …" bit must come near the end, don't you think?' Girl 1 continued thinking

'How about having "Fill the pot with the remainder of the mixture" then "Place the pot …" ' This resulted in Girl 2 interrupting in exasperation 'Look! We haven't even got the bulb in yet!' After the release of laughter they got down to helping each other to sort things out quite quickly.

Ability to convey ideas, feelings and experience

Rather surprisingly, the girls did not translate the stages of the instructions into their own words to help them decide on an order. Their explicit thinking was confined to remarks such as 'Not yet' or 'That bit must come near the end'. Quite a lot of their thinking was not communicated to each other. If Girl 1 had explained the lines along which she was thinking in the middle of this exchange the pair might have got on more quickly.

Asking and answering questions

Each girl asked at least one question but they tended to work out the problem independently: their questions were sometimes just to reassure themselves that they had established something that was acceptable, e.g. Girl 2: 'That "When the plant is growing …" bit must come near the end, don't you think?'

Presenting and backing up a point of view

They began better than they went on, in this respect: Girl 2's statement about where to start ' "Cover the bottom of the pot with the mixture" ' was adopted by Girl 1 as reasonable: 'That must be the first one.' They tended to assert their views, rather than explain them or back them up, e.g. Girl 2: ' "Fill the pot …" Fill the pot!' If they had offered reasons for their decisions, the breakdown in communication at one point would probably not have occurred.

This was only partly successful: the girls had more difficulty with the task than they should have had, and this was because they did not tell each other what they were thinking sufficiently often.

BEYOND THE COURSEWORK

Watch television programmes and notice in particular how the persons introducing the discussions handle things. How well do the speakers measure up to the standards indicated in 'Essential Principles' above? You might also have an opportunity to attend a live discussion, e.g. of a local issue.

Role play is best produced from spontaneous drama situations. Get involved in as much school or college drama as you can, or even consider joining a local drama group, if there is one in your area.

R E V I E W   S H E E T

✎ Here is a useful exercise for working in *pairs* with a friend.

i) You and your friend are both going for an interview for a job. You both very much want the job. Take it in turns to be the interviewer and the interviewee.

After the interviews, discuss the following questions: Which of you do you think would get the position? Why? How could you have presented yourselves even better?

_____

_____

_____

ii) Discuss with your friend about whether it is better to go to college or university after leaving school or whether it is better to find a job as quickly as possible. One of you should argue for further study and the other should argue for work.

When you have finished your discussion, consider how effective each of you were in the points that you made and the ways that you made them. How could you each have been more effective?

_____

_____

_____

iii) With your partner, compare the most frightening and the most exciting experiences that each of you has had.

When you have finished, discuss the ways in which you each told the stories you had to tell. Do you think that you could have told them in a more effective way? If so how?

_____

_____

_____

_____

iv) Imagine that your friend is trying to sell you something. You would like what he or she is offering but cannot really afford the price suggested. What conversation do you have?

After you have had the conversation discuss how your friend tried to persuade you to buy. Was he or she successful? How could you both have been more effective in the conversation?

_____

_____

_____

_____

My Room

Suppose you are the person sitting at the table in the picture overleaf. Use suitable prepositions of place and other expressions to describe your position and your surroundings to a friend. Ask your friend to draw a picture as you speak.

   You could use some of the following expressions.

- opposite
- near (to)
- beside
- next to
- on or to the left
- on or to the right
- on or to the left-hand side
- on or to the right-hand side
- on top of
- under
- above
- in the corner

- in the middle
- between
- about a metre from
- in front of
- at one end
- at the other end
- in the foreground
- in the background
- in the distance
- in the top right-hand corner
- in the bottom left-hand corner

Check how close the picture that your friend has drawn is to the room above.

 Using the pictures as a guide instruct a friend on how to use a coffee maker. Write down what you are to say below the pictures, as clearly as you can, and then present your instructions to a friend.

_____

_____

_____

_____

_____

_____

CHAPTER 7

RESEARCHING AND WRITING UP

GETTING STARTED

It is probable that you will at some time have been given the task of investigating a subject, and then writing an essay or extended report based on what you discovered. A piece of work of this kind may be a very suitable choice to put in your coursework folder for GCSE assessment.

The original stimulus for the work may come from your own interests, a group project, a suggestion from your teacher or tutor or an examination question. Whatever your starting point, the essential approaches are the same. This chapter will discuss these approaches in detail.

ESSENTIAL PRINCIPLES

This section deals with the general techniques of researching and writing up a topic. There are seven main areas to be considered, and they will be looked at in turn:

66 Seven rules for topic work 99

- Choosing a topic
- Deciding what you need to find out
- Locating the resources
- Organising and planning your work
- Using the resources
- Evaluating the materials
- Writing up the topic.

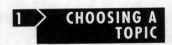

1 > CHOOSING A TOPIC

Part of the justification for examinations by coursework is that they give the opportunity for an individual choice of work, so do talk about things that are really important to you. After all, in the world outside school or college, writing and talking are invariably related to a purpose: if you are a police constable, you will write an account of a traffic accident because it has to go into the records and may be needed in court; as a journalist you would interview a person in the news to inform or entertain the public. Most writers have an idea of their readers, and try to satisfy them as well as to express themselves. There is no need for coursework pieces to be a series of dreary exercises. If you choose something which really interests you and which you want to tell others about, then you have taken a first step towards communicating successfully, and are likely to be better motivated during the hard-slogging phases of bringing the work to completion.

When you are doing your coursework folder, be open to ideas from all quarters, not just school. Read as widely as you can, get involved in debate with fellow-students and keep up to date on current affairs and on developments in the arts and sciences. And don't forget those most popular of media – television, radio and films. At least one of the Groups (ULEAC) recommends these as sources of promising stimuli for oral coursework.

2 > SELECTING AND REFINING IDEAS FOR TOPICS

BRAINSTORMING

You may have quite a few ideas for writing or talking in mind but not know how to develop them. One of the best ways of doing this, apart from a discussion with your tutor or teacher, is 'brainstorming' with fellow-pupils. In this process, key words or ideas are suggested by the members of the group, as many as possible being thought of. One member of the group notes them down as they occur – there is no need to classify them; that can come later. This is a useful stage in any project – following the maxim 'two heads are better than one'. Several persons can come up with angles and questions that you hadn't thought of by yourself, either adding to your original idea, refining it or even changing it radically. Collaboration at this stage is quite legitimate, provided the finished pieces are your own work.

66 Putting heads together 99

Suppose that an item in the news about football hooliganism had caught your attention and set you thinking in general about its causes and cures. A quick brainstorming session with friends might come up with the following:

group violence	European ban
macho image	police patrols
drink and drugs	youth clubs needed
TV influence	sports idols should set example
frustration at losing game	special trains
more police needed	'No drink' enforcement
unemployment	surveillance in the stands
bad facilities at grounds	video cameras
ticket touts	heavy fines
police provocation	imprisonment
crowd control	counselling
identity cards	international co-operation

I think you will agree that these are more ideas than you would be likely to think of by yourself. The next stage would be to classify these ideas as causes or cures.

■ Try for yourself

For each of the following topics try, preferably in a group, to produce a list of ideas by brainstorming:
  the Council Tax
  GCSE
  private health care
  Youth Employment Schemes
  school trips
  international exchange visits
  AIDS
  animal rights
  pollution
  wildlife preservation

RELATED PIECES OF WORK

If you are interested in a topic, it may well be worthwhile to attempt more than one piece of work on it and submit the related pieces as one unit. Suppose the topic were 'The Argument'. You might write a poem, concentrating on the emotions of the people involved, and the suppressed violence of the situation, and you might also write a story in which a man and his wife had an argument when the man came home late.

 Try two different approaches

Compare the treatment of the same piece of material in a poem and in an extract from a novel in the example below:

POEM

Discord in Childhood

Outside the house an ash-tree hung its terrible whips
And at night when the wind rose, the lash of the tree
Shrieked and slashed the wind as a ship's
Weird rigging in a storm shrieks hideously.

Within the house two voices arose, a slender lash
Whistling she-delirious rage, and the dreadful sound
Of a male thong booming and bruising, until it had drowned
The other voice in a silence of blood, 'neath the noise of the ash.
  (D. H. Lawrence, *Collected Poems*)

EXTRACT FROM NOVEL

'In front of the house was a huge old ash-tree. The west wind, sweeping from Derbyshire, caught the houses with full force, and the tree shrieked again. Morel liked it. 'It's music,' he said. 'It sends me to sleep.' But Paul and Arthur and Annie hated it. To Paul it became almost a demoniacal noise. The winter of their first year in the new house their father was very bad. The children played in the street, on the brim of the wide, dark valley, until eight o'clock. Then they went to bed. Their mother sat sewing below. Having such a great space in front of the house gave the children a feeling of night, of vastness, and of terror. This terror came in from the shrieking of the tree and the anguish of the home discord. Often Paul would wake up, after he had been asleep a long time, aware of thuds downstairs. Instantly he was wide awake. Then he heard the booming shouts of his father, come home nearly drunk, then the sharp replies of his mother, then the bang, bang of his father's fist on the table, and the nasty snarling shout as the man's voice got higher. And then the whole was drowned in a piercing medley of shrieks and cries from the great, windswept ash-tree. The children lay silent in suspense, waiting for a lull in the wind to hear what their father was doing. He might hit their mother again. There was a feeling of horror, a kind of bristling in the darkness, and a sense of blood. They lay with their hearts in the grip of an intense anguish. The wind came through the tree fiercer and fiercer. All the cords of the great harp hummed, whistled, and shrieked. And then came the horror of the sudden silence, silence everywhere, outside and downstairs. What was it? Was it a silence of blood? What had he done?

(D. H. Lawrence, *Sons and Lovers*)

To take a second example, something you have prepared for oral assessment may also be shaped into a piece of writing. Compare these two pieces by a student, first talking then writing about an experience recalled from childhood:

ORAL (TALKING)

```
My name is Stephen - the earliest thing I can remember is
standing on the door-step waving my brother good-bye as he
went off to school - well he went to school and what I did
was fall down the stairs afterwards and the next day I can
remember as well because I was playing with a model plane
and what happened was I thought I was a pilot and I
stepped forward which was deadly because - because well
there was no more space to walk forward see and I fell
down the stairs - and I had a bit of a headache afterwards
- and the plane was a bit smashed up too so what I did was
I went in the garden and I buried it and got out my
soldiers - yes it did die actually - and I smashed up
another plane and used that and buried that as well you
see - got my soldiers out and played with them and the two
planes as if they had fought each other and blown each
other up - it was quite a good game really because it was
just like it was real.
```

WRITTEN WORK

```
The earliest thing I can remember is standing on the front
door step, waving good-bye to my brother. When he had gone
I slipped and fell; I didn't break anything, but I fell
heavily. The next day I can remember well too, because I
was playing with my planes on the top of the stairs and
what happened was I thought that I was a pilot. So I was
walking round and round, then I took a step forward, but
that was silly because there was no more space to walk
forward, and I fell down. When I reached the floor I had a
headache, but worse, the plane was broken to pieces.
  What I did next was go into the garden, crying and bury
it. Then I got another old one and broke that up and
buried that too. I got my soldiers to make a procession
for the funeral. It was a great game. I pretended that the
planes had collided and crashed in the mud, with no
survivors.
```

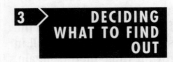

3 › DECIDING WHAT TO FIND OUT

You will probably know something about the topic already, and a good way of making a start is to list what you know. Then, if possible, discuss it with friends and borrow one or two books from the school or public library which treat the area generally. You should consult your teacher or tutor, too, to make sure that the subject is a suitable one, and consider any suggestions offered at this stage. After these steps, you should be able to make a first list of things you definitely need to find out and to do.

4 LOCATING THE RESOURCES

When you have decided what you need to find out, you will have to discover suitable sources of information. This may not be very easy, and it may help to consult again your friends and teacher or tutor. Library staff are usually very helpful, too; and it is also just possible that you might be able to do a computer search.

Suppose that you were researching the following topic: 'Acting in the Seventeenth-Century Theatre.' After a period of thinking, discussion and general reading you may make two lists along these lines:

What I know already

a) Some seventeenth-century actors are famous, e.g. Richard Burbage, Edward Alleyn, Shakespeare himself.
b) Boys played women's parts.
c) Stages were often in the open.
d) There were few costumes and props.
e) Audiences were from a wide cross-section of the public.
f) Puritans were opposed to the theatres and players.

What I need to find out

a) What evidence is available of early theatres and players? Is there much good source material?
b) Were there theatres outside London?
c) Which were the most popular plays and players?
d) What status did acting have as a profession?
e) Why were the Puritans so hostile to theatres and acting?

Many of these questions could probably be answered by visiting the local library and consulting literary reference books (e.g. *The Oxford Companion to the Theatre*), dictionaries of biography, and the section of the library on theatre history. As the period is in the past, there would be comparatively little non-book material available. You might be lucky enough to have a theatre museum within visiting distance; there is, for instance in London, at Southwark, a small museum on the site of the Globe Theatre, where Shakespeare acted, and also a National Theatre Museum, near Covent Garden.

Alternatively, a local museum might have a section devoted to the theatre.

In contrast, consider a contemporary topic: 'Drug-Taking as a Threat to Young People Today.' Possibly, after thinking, discussing and reading, your lists of ideas might look something like this:

What I know already

a) There are TV films and videos warning young people against drugs.
b) Some young people have been prosecuted for drug-handling.
c) People in the news sometimes set a bad example to the young.
d) Drugs can kill.
e) Some dangerous drugs are fairly easily obtained.
f) Drug-taking can lead to crime to finance the habit.
g) Some powerful drugs are used as medicines.

What I need to find out

a) What organizations help and advise young people about drug-taking?
b) What laws are there about obtaining and using drugs?
c) What proportion of young people today take drugs?
d) How much money does the average drug-taker spend on the habit?
e) What are the names of the dangerous drugs?
f) What cures are there for drug dependency?

There may be comparatively few books on the subject, so other resources come to mind: a social studies textbook or video; current news items or documentary programmes on television; centres in your area, offering information and help; stories and articles in the local and national newspapers; HMSO publications; information gained from friends; posters or photographs, and so on.

These two projects would require a totally different range of resources.

Now let us look at three further assignments and try to identify the range of resources needed for each.

ASSIGNMENT A

Returning to the topic of football hooliganism, you will remember that brainstorming produced a long list of relevant ideas, and it was suggested that you classified these as 'causes' and 'cures'. You can now delete any that seem unimportant, or that it would take you too far afield to discuss.

Your 'cures', i.e. ways of diminishing the hooliganism, may have been:

crowd control
European ban
police patrols
more police
youth clubs
surveillance in the stands
sports idols setting an example
special campaign
special trains
'No drink' enforcement
video cameras
heavy fines
imprisonment
counselling
international co-operation

You might start by noting down the sources of information you already know about, e.g. a TV documentary, recent articles in the press about measures taken against supporters of a team who got out of hand. Perhaps you also have a fair amount of general knowledge about this topic, being a soccer enthusiast yourself. Visits to the school library and the public library should also be worthwhile: they often have collections of non-book materials – articles or photographs – which would be helpful, and you may find something useful under 'Sociology'. If you are going to refer to particular incidents that you remember vaguely, and to the steps that were taken by the police and club officials, it will be best to make sure that you have the facts right. However, a topic of this kind may be one you can embark on fairly quickly, without any need for detailed investigation.

■ Try for yourself

Choose two of the above topics and decide what would be the best sources of further information about them.

ASSIGNMENT B

At your teacher's suggestion, you are going to write a chapter of an autobiography for inclusion in your coursework folder. After further thought, you decide to make it a chapter comparing your expectations of the future with those of your grandmother or grandfather at your age.

The sources of information needed would be rather different from those for Assignment A. Your grandfather or grandmother would be the first source of information. He or she might well speak of leaving school at fourteen, without any qualifications, because very few school pupils took public examinations then. He or she might mention the threat of war, which in the late thirties affected everyone's expectations, or talk about what it was like during the War.

This talk with your grandfather or grandmother could lead you to the school library and the public library. What could you find out about the thirties and forties, about the pre-War and War periods generally, to supplement their reminiscences?

You have already investigated the non-book information for Assignment A and found out where it is filed. Look through it again for any old newspapers or photographs of the thirties. Also, some Sociology packs have useful information. Next, make use of the catalogues: subject first, then author index and find the right classification numbers (most likely they will be the Dewey system). Note down titles of likely books to look into further. Remember that your grandfather's memory might not correspond exactly with what the prospects really were. For a fuller picture you will need to consult the other sources. Don't forget fiction too – this is another valuable source of interesting information in a very readable form.

And now, what about your own expectations? No doubt you have discussed the future endlessly with your friends and found it difficult to be certain about the chances for yourself and your contemporaries. It might be best to ask the careers teacher about latest employment possibilities and perhaps to look at various publications by HMSO (Her Majesty's Stationery Office) and by the local authority.

Once you have all this information, your chapter would have a chance of capturing the vividness of real-life experience, and at the same time might be able to achieve a balance based on its well-researched social background.

■ Try for yourself

Find out about one of the following, noting what resources you would need:
- school memories of someone you know;
- first job experiences of different people.

ASSIGNMENT C

Suppose the complete text you have been studying is William Golding's *Lord of the Flies*. You have been asked by your teacher or tutor to chair a discussion on how the boys in the novel seem to compare with their present-day counterparts.

Your first resource is the novel itself. You should re-read as much of it as you can very carefully, especially incidents which seem to reveal character and to determine the boys' behaviour on the Island, e.g. electing a leader; the death of Simon; Jack's revolt; the end of the novel.

A search in the library reveals a book about William Golding. You find out that he worked as a schoolmaster for part of his life and so knew about boys at first hand. You have heard in a literature lesson a recording from the radio where a group of critics discussed *Lord of the Flies* and gave their opinions of the characters. It has stayed in your mind and seems to you to give a good range of views with which to lead the discussion and to supplement your own reading of the text. You arrange to hear this again. Now you have enough information to enable you to undertake the role of chairperson, confident that if the discussion dries up you can get it going again: for instance, if it gets stuck in a rut you can help it to change direction. You can also open and close the occasion skilfully, giving a clear lead at the beginning and a helpful summary of the contributions at the end.

■ **Try for yourself**

Choose a novel or play you have worked on, and find out more about some aspect of it for group discussion.

ORGANISING YOUR WORK

It would be a great pity if coursework became a burden to the learner, the stress of taking several written papers being replaced by anxiety about keeping up with your work and making sure that you have produced enough pieces at an acceptable standard. To try to prevent this, think about getting your work organised at the start of the course. Some of the organisation has already been done for you, as you are timetabled for English at school or college. Within those sessions, though, and more particularly in homework or study time on your own, you need to think about making the best use of your time. Here is some advice about getting organised.

■ **Work steadily throughout the course.** If you postpone work and it keeps piling up you will feel worried, and possibly not do your best.

■ **Keep a balance between study and relaxation.** You will work better if you feel fit and refreshed. Much of your work in English is creative, needing a lively, enquiring attitude of mind, so keep alert for good ideas.

■ **Make the best use of your time.** It is easy to think you have spent an hour and a half studying, when you have actually spent about half of that panicking about what you should be doing, and wandering about making coffee and telephoning friends to see if they are panicking, too. This sort of behaviour is known as displacement activity, i.e. a way of avoiding getting down to what you should be doing. It is better to work hard for a stretch and then to have a break, knowing you have earned it. It is important to have a clear idea of what you want to do, e.g. in a weekend read four chapters of a novel; write a narrative; make notes for a project. Estimate how much time you will need, at your normal working pace, before you start.

■ **Find working habits that suit you.** There are many different ways of studying. Despite the remarks above, you may work better with the reassurance of friends, so time spent telephoning them occasionally may in fact be time well spent. You may work better if you can discuss your task with your family. Alternatively, you may find it better if you shut yourself away in your room at home, or go to the public library's reading-room. Whatever you feel comfortable with, establish that as a working habit early on.

■ **Cultivate business-like working habits.** It wastes time if your notes are unreadable or consist of a jumble of scraps of paper. Have a working-folder, and date what you do, even your draft pieces of work.

■ **Understand your task.** Find out from your teacher or tutor exactly what you have to do and learn to make choices quickly. Time can be wasted making false starts. If you have a large piece of work to complete, e.g. a project, subdivide it into manageable portions.

■ **Make use of helpful study methods.** You may be able to learn to read faster and more efficiently, to make better notes, to plan an essay more confidently. Advice about all these matters will be found later in this chapter.

■ **Complete work as you go along.** It is an uncomfortable feeling to know that you have left several pieces of work half-done, and so you should finish everything to your satisfaction as you go along. If you have been given poor grades for your work by your teacher or tutor, ask if you are allowed to attempt another piece of work of a similar kind. Remember, though, that you must not include something corrected or changed after it has been marked. This is not allowed.

■ **Review what has been achieved.** There may be more work ahead, but try to finish each study session by checking what you have achieved. Did you complete the task? Did you understand what the author was getting at? If not, decide what to do about it next time. Some people even like to make a note of where to start when they sit down again.

PLANNING YOUR WORK

Planning your work can be done in different ways. Let's consider the following:
- an outline timetable;
- a flow-chart;
- a topic tree;
- an outline plan for writing or talking.

AN OUTLINE TIMETABLE

Some pupils prefer to carry this in their heads, but it can be reassuring to map out the task to be completed in the time available. Going back to the three assignments mentioned in this chapter, the timetable might look like this:

Assignment A (4 weeks)

Ways of curbing football hooliganism

■ **CLASS-TIME**

- Brainstorm in a group for ideas.
- Organise the list of points in the best order.
- Consult teacher or tutor.

- Visit school or college library, looking especially for non-book material.
- Make essential notes and work on rough draft.

- **SPARE TIME**
  - Write to/visit local football club for information.
  - Watch a relevant video, if available.
  - Go through newspapers for up-to-date information.
  - Talk to friends and football enthusiasts.

- **HOMEWORK TIME**
  - Visit the public library, especially the reference section, and consult staff there.
  - Make further notes and write first draft.
  - Write up final version.

Assignment B (6 weeks)

Write a chapter of your autobiography in which you compare your expectations now with those of your grandmother or grandfather at your age.

- **CLASS-TIME**
  - Make a flow-chart of ideas as they occur to you.
  - Consult your teacher or tutor.
  - Visit the school or college library for useful background books.
  - Make essential notes and start work on a rough draft.

- **SPARE TIME**
  - Talk to (and if possible record) grandparents, and collect reminiscences of their life at your age.
  - Sort through family photographs and documents.
  - Write to HMSO for latest figures on youth unemployment.

- **HOMEWORK TIME**
  - Visit public library and consult the History section for background information on the 1930s.
  - Make notes and write first draft.
  - Write up final version.

Assignment C (2 weeks)

Prepare an introduction as chairperson of group discussion on characters in William Golding's *Lord of the Flies*.

- **CLASS-TIME**
  - Re-read the novel and note page references to relevant places in the text.
  - Consult teacher or tutor.
  - Visit school or college library and get any information on Golding or the novel.
  - Enquire about the radio recording heard in class.
  - Make outline notes of key ideas, ideally on a card index.

- **HOMEWORK TIME**
  - Check through your cards and get them in the best order.
  - Run through your introduction and if possible record yourself. Play back recording and listen to it critically.

A FLOW-CHART

A *flow-chart* shows the main relationships of the ideas involved in a topic but leaves the final choice and order of ideas open. You take a fairly large piece of paper, and write the topic in the centre. The main ideas are arranged around it, then subordinate ideas written under the main ones. The relationships of the main ideas are shown by putting arrows from one group to the next. You can experiment with various links and cross-connections, until you are satisfied that you have the best arrangement. Fig. 7.1 shows an example, by a student, of a flow-chart for Assignment B.

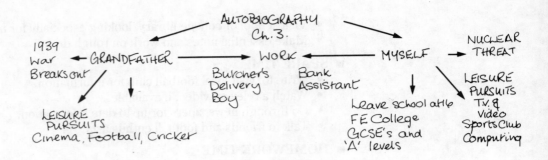

Fig. 7.1 A Flow-chart

A TOPIC TREE

This is a helpful way of planning a piece of work which requires a logical structure. You draw a tree, the trunk corresponding to the topic, the branches to the main related ideas, and extensions to subordinate ideas. By this means you can see immediately the whole outline of your thinking from the main theme, through the major branches of the argument, to the subsidiary parts. It would be a good approach to take for Assignment A, after you had made a list of ways of curbing football hooliganism. It might look something like the following:

Fig. 7.2 A Topic Tree

AN OUTLINE PLAN

You will be invited to do a wide range of kinds of writing and talking for GCSE English coursework, and each type of work – summaries, reports, persuasive speeches, advertisements, poems, stories, plays – will have its own structure. Whatever you attempt, spend some time before you start, thinking of how you hope to:

- BEGIN;
- DEVELOP THE WORK THROUGH STAGES;
- CONCLUDE.

6 USING THE RESOURCES

By now you will have decided on your topic area and will probably have a list of questions to which you want to find answers. You will have decided too the most likely sources of information. The next important principle is to be as business-like as possible in using your resources. Even if you find yourself facing a mountain of potential material, streamline your enquiries so that you collect a manageable amount of data, but try not to sacrifice balance and accuracy in doing so.

When gathering information from books, there are different styles of reading for different purposes. Make sure that you can vary your reading pace, and the way you read, for maximum efficiency (techniques for doing this will be explained in the section on 'Useful Practical Approaches' below). In order to remember what you have read you will need to make meaningful notes that will reconstruct the material for you when you return to them later; this will also be explained in the next section.

Information gathering from non-book sources uses a variety of skills, including listening carefully, observing and responding, asking well-focused questions, and so on. You may make notes from these experiences, but in a different way from the notes you make when you read. The following section also contains advice about making notes, formulating questionnaires and conducting interviews.

Seeing someone else's point of view

In your encounters with print, film and people you should remember that the facts you are looking for will often be presented to you subjectively. You have to allow for another's point of view, or bias, and take that into account. Of course, you yourself have biases, and these may get in the way of your fully understanding the material. It is a good idea to talk over your topic with as many people as possible: this is where several heads can be better than one. On the other hand, your own personal involvement can be an advantage: if you are sincerely concerned about an issue it will be clear to readers, and they will find what you write or say more convincing and persuasive.

Gathering information can be very rewarding, though often it is time-consuming and hard work. If you are to do justice to the efforts you have put in you should remember the following advice:

DON'T ...
a) rely chiefly on your memory
b) forget to record titles of books, authors' names, page references, etc.
c) write notes on scraps of paper
d) leave notes incomplete
e) leave it to the last minute to find photographs or other visual aids to fill out your topic
f) forget to list sources of information, or do so in random order.

DO ...
a) collect information and make notes accurately
b) date each of your pieces of work and keep them in order
c) record full details, especially author, title and date of publication, for books you use
d) finish each piece of work, if possible, before going on to the next
e) keep notes in one folder
f) collect photographs and other non-book material as you go along
g) make a list of all sources of information and check to see that it has been worked through.

7 EVALUATING YOUR MATERIALS

When you feel you have obtained enough information to answer the questions on your list, you will have built up a body of material that will have to be structured and evaluated.

Let us look at an example 'A proposal to install speed humps in Bridge Lane, and local reactions.'

Here is a simple time-table for a project to be completed within three weeks:

A proposal to install speed humps in Bridge Lane, and local reactions.

CLASS TIME
a) List what you know
b) Consult teacher or tutor and discuss with friends.
c) Visit school or college library, choose relevant book and non-book material.
d) Distribute questionnaire, if necessary
e) Make essential notes or flow-chart and work on first draft.

HOMEWORK TIME
a) Write to local council and other associations involved.
b) Visit public library, especially the reference section, and consult staff there.
c) Make further notes and start writing up first draft.
d) Write up your final version.

SPARE TIME

a) Visit site and take photographs.
b) Obtain and consult map of the area.
c) Contact local newspaper office for the latest developments.
d) Talk to local residents.

Your materials might now include the following:

- notes based on a guide to the area, and other notes based on a book about house-holders' rights
- three questionnaires completed by school friends
- some notes on documents you were shown at the Council offices
- three photocopies of parts of books on local authority administration
- two letters from local residents
- notes on interviews with local residents
- a photocopy of a map of the area.

You now decide to review your original list of things you had to find out, supplement it with other questions, and put all the questions in order, ready for writing. The revised list might look like this:

- What is the general character of the area around Bridge Lane?
- What are the traffic problems affecting Bridge Lane?
- What is the case for installing speed humps?
- What are the objections to installing them?
- Who and what is the highway authority?
- Does it have the power to install the humps, despite any objections?
- What do local people think?
- How do matters stand at present?

You indicate which of your materials give information relating to each of these questions, e.g. Question 1 – map, books, photographs; Question 2 – questionnaire, Council documents, interviews, maps, and so on.

Finally, you decide to give some attention, before getting down to writing, to how reliable your materials and sources of information are. The guide to your area and the book on householders' rights are presumably all right, although the latter is several years old. Your notes on the Council documents will have to be used, but you may not be sure how well you really understood the documents. Most of the people you interviewed clearly favoured the humps in Bridge Lane, although one or two overstated their case.

Now you are ready for the final stages:

- Prepare a final plan, with each of your sections or paragraphs decided upon.
- Reorganize the contents of your folder, so that material relating to each part comes in order. (If your topic is small-scale, you can number pieces of material instead.)
- Write the first draft of the topic.

It doesn't seem so formidable, does it, now that you have broken it down into stages?

8   WRITING UP THE TOPIC

You should now be in a position to write up. Begin with the introductory paragraph. Go on with a series of sections, corresponding to the questions on your final list, referring to your materials as necessary. End with a concluding paragraph. The result will probably not satisfy you when you read it through, and you may have to revise it more than once before reaching a final version. Add any items, such as charts or maps you wish to include, a title page, and perhaps a contents page and a book list. Put the work in a clean folder or plastic envelope, with your name on it.

Here are some notes which may help you:

a) PRESENTATION

Your work will make a favourable first impression if it is neatly written, well spaced out, and has diagrams that are well drawn and positioned. The work should be kept in a clean folder or plastic envelope.

b) STYLE

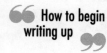
How to begin
writing up

Try to write the project in an appropriate style – probably Standard English – but there may be a choice; if you are writing for a special audience, that will influence the way you express your ideas, e.g. information on drug addiction as a general article, in contrast to a pamphlet for young people.

c) SECTION HEADINGS

Unless the project is very short, it will help the reader to find what he or she is interested in if you begin each section with a sub-heading. The sub-headings can be based on the questions in your final list: the road humps project might have sections headed 'Introduction', 'Bridge Lane and the surrounding area', 'The problem of speeding in Bridge Lane', 'The case for installing road humps', and so on.

d) TITLE PAGE

This should give not only your title, but (unless you are given other instructions by your teacher) the course for which the work is being submitted, and the date of completion.

e) CONTENTS PAGE

It is easy to look through a short piece to find any part one wants, but a contents page can be helpful with a longer project.

f) BOOK LIST

If you refer to several books in your project it is a good idea to list them alphabetically by author at the end. Give the author's name, the title, and the place and date of publication. A book list can also be called a 'bibliography', and this is the word to use if you want to include items which are not books, such as newspaper articles.

Let us now look in more detail at the various stages involved in writing up your work. Here are some examples of student work on the various stages.

BEGINNINGS

These can be difficult. Beginnings should catch the attention and interest of the reader, and take him or her to a point from which the work can grow. Consider the following openings by pupils in their coursework:

66 Some examples of student project work **99**

■ a) One Inch High in the Bathroom

One day I was sitting in the bath when a strange feeling came over me and the water suddenly hit me in the face..... I had shrunk!

I certainly had because the bath seemed like a gigantic shiny white mountain, with me drowning in the lake in the middle. I was bobbing up and down swallowing great mouthfulls of soapy water, although of course they can't have been that big when I was only 1 inch high. I was not a very good swimmer, so by the time I reached the plug chain I was quite out of breath.

Now I was faced with another problem: how was I going to climb the plug chain? Because the chain was made of silver balls joined together. I scrambled up the first few balls with some difficulty but the next lot seemed easy. I must have developed a certain 'knack', but I don't think I could do it again.

■ b) Why I intend to stay on at school

The temptation of leaving school to earn some money is very great in my case. Nearly all the friends I have got have left school, and are earning fairly good wages for people who have just left school. My parents give me as much pocket money as I could expect, but I am still restricted in some ways. If I go out to a disco, that soaks up quite a bit of money, and if I need, say, a shirt I have to save up for a couple of weeks to get it. This is a prominent reason in my mind against staying on.

■ c) Our unpredictable weather

Summer is always a time of year when it is the warmest in Britain. The lovely lush meadows with bright coloured flowers covering the fields like a patched quilt. The humid air makes the movement of all life slow as the gleaming sun burns down on you. The delicate winds sway the grass like a swinging pendulum, rippling across the meadows, and the smell of the wonderful vegetation all around acts like a soothing drug, relaxing you completely.

Examiner's comments

- Opening a) This is a very successful opening because it makes you read on. You want to know whether the plug chain is scaled and what happens next. The writer has sustained the one-inch-high idea well, with comparisons of the mountainous bath and the bathwater lake and the huge silver balls of the plug chain. All this is very compact, taking only two short paragraphs.
- Opening b) The writer here seems to have difficulty starting. The style is repetitive and a bit awkward. One objection to staying on at school is raised and several illustrations given. It is not clear where the argument will lead, as it seems to be marking time.
- Opening c) The opening of this descriptive piece is promising. There are some well-observed details, 'the delicate winds swayed the grass like a swinging pendulum' as well as some rather well-worn phrases, e.g. 'fields like a patched quilt'. The pace is very slow. It could be argued that this is appropriate, as the writer says the humidity made 'the movement of all life slow'. You wonder, though, if the description will continue like this and become too static and therefore dull.

DEVELOPMENT

The stages of *development* in a piece of work depend largely on the type of coursework it is. It is often worthwhile to experiment: the order you first thought of may not necessarily be the best. Let's consider ways of developing material for three different purposes:

1 PLANNING AN ARGUMENTATIVE PIECE

You may intend on the one hand to offer a balanced discussion of an issue, or on the other hand to argue all out for one particular side. You could proceed on the basis of a set of headings, as in the following:

a) This discussion is about …
b) Some people think that …/There is some evidence that …
c) But others think …/However evidence can be shown to prove that …
d) You yourself may feel that both …
e) And I am offering evidence for both/I should like to persuade you that …

You could use these actual phrases or similar ones at the openings of paragraphs, in a piece of written work. If it were a talk, you could make a set of cards with the phrases written on them to help you keep track of where you were going, and any facts or figures that you thought you might forget – but keep your notes brief. No one speaks effectively with his or her head buried in notes!

Here is an example of a piece of student's work; it is in fact the continuation of opening b) above.

Perhaps people would say to me after making this statement "Why don't you get a Saturday job?" I answer this by giving the reason that Sunday is nearly always taken up by my main hobby Angling, week nights by homework and evenings out, and I like Saturdays to have a long rest in bed, and a leisurely day. But I would sacrifice my Saturdays if making money really made me feel I had to leave school.

Of course, the main reason for staying on is more exam. passes, bringing a better job and more wages. But my main reason is my hoped for career as a chartered surveyor. The chartered surveyor profession demands five years' training. There is a training scheme of five years, and you must have one 'A' level and four G.C.S.E's at the least to start it. This is my target if I fail to succeed in my greatest objective. That is the main reason for staying on. If I obtain two 'A' levels, instead of one I can start a different training scheme with a B.Sc. degree as the target which, of course, is much better. The latter scheme only involves three years' training. The other two years I would have to wait, until I had completed the five years necessary, could be taken up by a temporary job with an estate agents (which is also counted as training but in fact is not).

In both case at the end of five years I would obtain membership of the Chartered Surveyors Royal Institute and could get a job as a surveyor almost anywhere.

To obtain my hoped for career, I must stay on, and so I have definitely decided against leaving now.

Examiner's comments

After raising in the opening paragraph the question of whether to leave school, the student goes on to give reasons against that course of action. He deals with what turns out to be a point of lesser importance (more money now), and goes on to give his main reasons for staying on – his hoped-for career in surveying and the steps needed to realise it. The final one-sentence paragraph is all that is needed to demonstrate that a clear decision has been reached. The piece is matter-of-fact, but effectively argued.

2 PLANNING A SUMMARY

Your starting-point for a summary will usually be a body of information or a collection of data which you have to re-present succinctly from a particular point of view and for a specified audience. Although there is scope for individuality in a summary, there are always a number of key ideas you need to include, as well as some minor supporting ones. The main thing to do is to reproduce the appropriate part of the material briefly in your own words, without distorting the original. It is well worth experimenting with different ways of organising the piece until you are satisfied that you have explained all relevant aspects of the topic clearly and effectively.

■ **Try for yourself**
Read the passage below, and then follow the instructions, using different material for each part:

Suggestions have been made occasionally that the age of admission to school should be raised to six, and the infant teacher shortage in some parts of the country may soon make such a course of action necessary.

Staff shortages recently compelled one local authority to arrange that children becoming five during a term were accepted for half-time education only. How did the hundred parents involved in this scheme react to the arrangements? A questionnaire was sent to them asking whether they thought that half-time education in the first term for their child had been a) advantageous; b) harmful; c) neither. There was a hundred per cent response and only two parents felt that the arrangement had been harmful. Twenty-one thought that it was not really either advantageous or harmful; the rest said that there were considerable advantages in the arrangement.

Typical of the majority were the following comments from parents: 'I think having to attend just the mornings may have been a contributing factor to her easy acceptance of school. It helped her to get used to a routine and gave her confidence in herself.' 'He has enjoyed school from the start and I think this is because of half-time education at the beginning of his school life.' 'Most children have never been away from their mothers before and it is a very big thing for them. I hope this arrangement will continue so that they get used to returning home after only a few hours at first ...' 'I believe half-time education is a very good thing for a five year old who has been used to freedom. A long school day is tiring for them when they begin.' The head teachers of the schools at which this scheme was tried out were enthusiastic about it. One of them reported a high rate of attendance for children in the reception class, above average for children in their first term. Another mentioned that the children always appeared bright and lively.

Here is a possible solution to some of the problems that beset education. Staffing would be easier, and part-time teachers could also be used to greater effect: by working with the same group of children half the day only, they could give their pupils the security of one teacher. Most important, there are clear signs that the children would benefit from a more gradual introduction to full-time schooling.

■ **NOW**

Write a letter from the head teacher of one school adopting this system to the parents of the children concerned, stating the decision that has been taken and reasons for it, and saying that they will be invited to respond to a questionnaire on the matter after the end of term. The letter (excluding address, etc.) should not contain more than 85 words, should be in an appropriate style and should begin as follows:

```
                                    Church Street Infants' School,
                                    Wolchester,
                                    Bucks.
                                    6 June, 19--

Dear Parents,

and should end:

                                    Yours sincerely,
                                    H. A. Smith (Head teacher)
```

■ **ALSO**

The head teacher reported to the Parents' Association on the results of the questionnaire. Write two paragraphs from the report stating a) the advantages parents found in the scheme and b) the advantages the head teacher found. Your report should not contain more than 100 words.

Student answer

Here is a student's attempt at this piece of work.

Church Street Infants' School
Wolchester
Bucks.

6 June 19__

Dear Parents,

This coming term we are starting mornings only schooling for our rising fives and this will affect your child.

As you may know we are still suffering staff shortages and this arrangement will enable your child to have the security of the same teacher throughout the term. We feel also that it will be beneficial for your child to be introduced gradually to school life. After this term normal schooling will continue and we will invite your response through a questionaire.

Yours sincerely,

Extract from head teacher's report:

As many as 77% of the parents said that the scheme had been beneficial, with a further 21% expressing neither approval nor disapproval. Only 2% were against. A typical comment from parents pointed out that their child had more confidence, got less tired and enjoyed school more. The majority of parents, then, approved of the scheme.

I, myself, in company with the staff, also found it worked well: the children involved seemed always bright and lively and we had a higher attendance rate than is normal in the Reception Class, though there may be difficulties next term when the children face full time school attendance.

Examiner's comments

In the *letter*, notice that the student has started with the head's main point, then given detailed reasons for it, whereas in the *report* the opposite approach has been taken: the head teacher first gives the findings of the questionnaire, then the general judgement: 'The majority of parents, then, approved of the scheme.' He goes on to offer a *balanced* view of the scheme, from the point of view of himself and the school staff. The summary is slightly over the required word-limit, but the main points have been included without confusion or changing the emphasis of the original information. The style of the piece is formal, it is appropriately paragraphed and accurately expressed.

3 PLANNING A NARRATIVE PIECE

Narrative, by definition, follows chronological order, because that is the way our everyday experience happens to us. Think of how you tell your family what sort of day you had. You do not give every detail, but unless you tell it in an orderly sequence no one will be able to follow.

The same applies to the narrative parts of the stories you write, but a story does not have to begin at the beginning and work through to the end. It may be more effective to vary the time sequence. Consider the following possibilities:

- Flashback – interrupting the main narrative to go back to significant earlier incidents.
- Prediction – looking forward to future happenings.
- Two sides of the truth – describing the same events from the point of view of two different characters.
- Repeated sequence - ending as you began, sometimes with a slight variation, to stress some aspect of the story.

Student answer

Here is the continuation of the opening a) on page 70 above. It is an example of simple narrative, although, of course, a very imaginative piece.

Once at the top of the bath mountain I looked down at the soapy water which seemed miles away. It made me feel quite dizzy so I decided to have a rest on the sponge. But this was very difficult as it was three times my height. I eventually got up there but just as I looked up, I nearly fell off again when I saw a great yellow, hard thing peering down at me. It was the duck scrubbing brush. It must have been, but it seemed to have white trees for legs. I scrambled up the trees onto the duck's back with difficulty when it fell down into the bath with an almighty thundering splash!

I climbed slowly up the chain again and sat down to think. What if I would always be like this from now on? What had made me so small? Was it something I ate? Let me see, what did I have for dinner — ham and salad. No! I'd eaten that hundreds of times. But what about that new paté Mum had bought? Yes — that must be it!

I was really very worried, on the verge of tears. So would you have been if you had been in my place at that moment. I got up, consoling myself by saying, "I expect it is just a dream".

But it wasn't....

Here is an example of a piece where the time order is more complex.

The child screamed on, face contorted and scarlet under its sun-hat, in the blazing heat.

'She's frightened. She's frightened of the water'. Around her the golden ocean of sand shimmered and heaved, treacherous, while eager hands tried to tug her from her haven and force her to place one foot on the uncertain ground.....

'Lynn!' her mother hissed. 'You're next. Go on up.' The heat in the concert hall smothered her, like a hand over the mouth.

She was frightened, so frightened. Before her the golden linoleum-covered steps to the rostrum shone and heaved as she sat, unable to move a foot.

This is a convenient point to mention the distinction between *literal writing*, where the words have their usual meaning, and *figurative writing*, where imagery and poetic devices are used. Here is the continuation of opening c) on page 70 above.

Time passes quickly as you are taken aback by the sheer effect of great outstanding beauty, like turning on a light in a dark sinister room and suddenly seeing the true room, with an elegant picture of a loving relative mounted proudly on the wall, and a vase of golden daffodils on a table beneath. The time had edged on and the light was being dimmed. The warmth around me had gone and the wind started to pick up. The sky above had turned a lighter grey and herds of bulging blackened clouds were moving in above.

Suddenly, the sky was darkened as clouds closed over the sun. The warmth and brightness had gone and the dull coldness had come. It was as if it was the turn of the dark evil to have his say. The clouds in the sky were gathering rapidly, bunching up, filling any holes of light. The black army of clouds seemed to march slowly across the sky, looking down, with the chance to let out and attack. The light was poor and the valley had gone dark. Only silhouettes of buildings could be seen with darkened trees, as though life had been taken from them....

Examiner's comments

The first extract uses a simple narrative technique and does so rather amusingly. The second begins with a vivid flashback to the writer's childhood, and the third uses careful detail as part of the description, but also uses figurative expression, developing very well the idea of darkness and evil in the scene. This adds a dramatic element and prevents the rather monotonous developments we might have predicted from the opening.

- **Try for yourself**

  Choose a theme for a narrative and write it in two different ways, using a literal approach on the one hand, and a more figurative approach on the other. See which you prefer.

4 ENDINGS

Endings can be as problematic as beginnings! Sometimes students exhaust their invention before the end, and, feeling that they must conclude in some way or another, repeat in a sentence what they have explained much more fully already. This is a fault common in argument and summary. Try to keep for the conclusion an idea that you haven't used before, preferably one that makes a comment on the whole issue.

Let us look at the endings of the three pieces a), b) and c).

■ **Ending a)**

The writer of a) did not take an easy way out. Her story ended as follows:

> 'I expect it is just a dream'. But it wasn't.....
> I hauled myself over the edge of the jar and fell 'splish!' into some cold cream. It was awful. Never in my life have I experienced such a messy incident. As I scrambled to the edge of the bowl and fell headlong into the bath again I felt strange. I couldn't see my legs. It had been VANISHING CREAM! But dimly a blurred outline returned and... yes... it was a BIG outline. I was actually NORMAL again.
> At that moment my elder sister came in and told me off for using her cream. She said I was a stupid girl when I told her what had happened but then I don't expect anyone will believe me, do you?

This keeps the mystery going right up to the end and leaves it unresolved. The reader is invited to participate by the final question, and the ending is left open.

■ **Ending b)**

> To obtain my hoped for career, I must stay on, and so I have definitely decided against leaving now.

This conclusion is short and to the point. It tells you for the first time that a firm decision has been made.

When writing narrative, the thing to avoid is developing the plot to a point where you see no way out. An ending like 'Then I heard Mum's foot on the stairs and she called "When are you going to get up to go to school?" I realised it had only been a dream!' will irritate most readers and leave them feeling let down. Before you start, think how you can resolve your story in a satisfying way.

■ **Ending c)**

Concluding descriptive writing can be just as difficult. Sometimes writers just stop, and finish with a short personal comment e.g. 'Dusk was coming on and we wearily made our way home.'

The writer of extract c) does adopt this approach, but with a difference:

At last I trudged home, wet as a drowned rat and in an awful mood. Opening the soaked wooden gate I saw that all the flowers had dropped in the storm and there was a stream of water running down the path. As I stood on the grass my foot became embedded in the ground - the earth was water-logged and my foot was submerging.

Once indoors I changed my saturated clothes and sat by my bedroom window, looking out at the dark silhouette of the hills against the grey storm clouds. I was warming up now and in a dry place at last, out of the soaking wet.

The storm had ruined a lovely day and I was beginning to wonder whether it was summer after all.

9 ▷ PRELIMINARY DRAFTS AND FINAL VERSION	So far we have looked at the various stages of beginning, developing and ending a piece of coursework. Here we look at the progression from a first, preliminary draft to a final draft of your coursework project.

Preliminary drafts

66 Try drafting 99

When you have gathered your ideas, collected your information, brainstormed and/or tried a flow-chart or topic tree, you'll be ready to write fluently. Sometimes it is necessary to ask students to complete a piece of written work 'straight off' in class or for homework, but this is rather uncommon. Recent thinking about the writing process suggests that good writing usually evolves through one or more stages. If you are writing in rough, letting your ideas flow freely, you can go back and improve the arrangement of working and check spelling and punctuation. You may be using a word-processor, and all this can then be done quickly and easily. When you have written a draft, try to set it aside for a few days, and then read it critically, as editor rather than as author. If you are able to consult your friends, teacher or tutor this should be done while the work is still at the draft stage. You can then incorporate suggestions from others. Once the work is finished and assessed, though, you must not alter it. You may include drafts of work with the final version in your coursework folder.

Mandy had just received her exam. results and after reading them she was disappointed that she had failed all of them. She was not so bright, but her school record was good and she always worked hard. Just before the exams. she was under pressure and she had problems which made her fail her exams. Now Mandy

Here is the beginning of a pupil's first draft of a story:

had to return to school and redo her exams in six subjects which would be taken in January.

First day of term in the Lower Sixth Mandy went to see the Head Mistress who was disappointed that she had not even got one pass. She encouraged her to work harder and concentrate very hard. Unfortunately, Mandy did not take one word in, it just came out the other ear. She was not interested in studying and just felt like relaxing.

Compare the final version

It was the first day of term in the Lower Sixth year. Mandy hardly had time to say hello to her friends and talk about the holidays before she had an appointment with Miss Temple the head mistress, that she didn't look forward to at all.

In the holidays she had received her examination results and had been disappointed to find that she had failed all the exams. She did not think of herself as very clever, but her school record had always been good and she had always worked hard. What more could she have done? Just before the exams, too, she had been under pressure with personal problems and that had not helped. She felt really discouraged.

She tapped on Miss Temple's door and in response to a quiet 'The door is open' walked in. Miss Temple began talking in an encouraging way: 'Work harder ... make up your mind ... try to concentrate hard ... put that behind you ... ' It was what she had expected, but she found that she was not listening; she was distracted by two girls laughing outside the window. No, she was no longer interested in studying; she just felt like relaxing.

Examiner's comment

As you can see, the content within the paragraphs has been re-arranged, and extra detail has been added to bring the scene in the head mistress's office to life, and we are given Mandy's thoughts directly. The time sequence moves from the present to the past, and back. Some errors have been edited out. Altogether, this is a more interesting and more accurate opening.

When you are checking your own work, underline words whose spelling you are unsure about and use a dictionary. A rough guide to punctuation is to read through what you have written aloud. Punctuation should help to pace the work: a full stop for a long pause, commas or semi-colons for shorter pauses. Your teacher or tutor should help you with other forms of punctuation. Paragraphing should be logical and follow the development of the piece. There is no rule which says you must start a new paragraph every ten lines or so!

The final version

You will want your *final version* to be as accurate and readable as possible, so bear the following points in mind:

- The work should be written clearly, or typed where allowed.
- It should be dated and, of course, have a title.
- It may be easier to follow if it is divided into sections with sub-headings.
- Illustrations and diagrams should be clear and neat.
- Titles of books should be underlined.
- Quotations should be displayed or in inverted commas, with the source given at the end.
- If a list of references or books used is included, it should be complete, accurate and in alphabetical order.

These rules are mostly easy to understand, but something extra might be said about *quotations*.

- *Long quotations* should be *displayed*, that is, *set apart from* your own text. For example:

> Simon seems to be different from the other boys, on a more spiritual plane. He likes to go off to the jungle by himself to reflect:
>
>> Simon dropped the screen of leaves back into place. The slope of the bars of honey-coloured sunlight decreased; they slipped up the bushes, passed over the pale candle-like buds, moved up towards the canopy and darkness thickened under the trees. Within the failing of the light the riotous colours died and the heat and urgency faded away. The candle-buds stirred – their green sepals drew back a little and the white tips of the flowers rose delicately to meet the open air.
>>
>> (William Golding, *Lord of the Flies*, p. 155).

A displayed quotation can also be given inverted commas.

- A *short quotation* may be incorporated in your own sentences in *inverted commas*, the source being then put in brackets. For example:

> The set of rules established is challenged by Jack in his bid to become leader: ' "The rules!" shouted Ralph, "You're forgetting the rules." ' (*Lord of the Flies*, p. 87).

■ When quoting poetry, you should reproduce the line arrangement exactly as it is in the original, e.g.:

Button to chin
Till May be in;
Cast not a clout
Till May be out
(*Traditional*)

USEFUL PRACTICAL APPROACHES

There are several skills, referred to in the earlier sections of this chapter, that will be explained here. Their use should help to make the task of researching, planning and writing a piece of topic work quicker and easier.

1   READING FOR RESEARCH

The first is **reading for research purposes**. You can read in different ways for different purposes, and some ways are quicker than others:

(a) **Skimming:** a quick look through a book to get a general impression and decide whether it is likely to be useful. The title page, contents, blurb, pictures or diagrams, and a few pages might be looked at.

(b) **Scanning:** a quick look along certain sections of the text to find particular details or blocks of information, e.g. to find all the names of seventeenth-century actors.

(c) **Intensive reading:** a slower, sometimes a word-for-word read, where you concentrate on the meaning of the text, and perhaps pause to question or think about it.

(d) **Reflective reading:** a reading where you respond fully in thought and feeling to the general content.

How to size up a book.

If you are about to use a book for the first time, you should not plunge straight into the middle of it, but do a little preliminary 'sizing up'. The blurb should not be trusted. The date of publication should always be noticed. (Is the book out of date? When was it last revised?) How is the author described on the title page and cover? How well known is the publisher? An author's preface should never be entirely ignored: it will tell you something about the book, and often something about the author, too. How detailed is the index? Does the bibliography contain some books you didn't know about?

One special area of reading is worth mentioning separately: interpreting tables or charts, and, in general, statistics. Here you are given facts and have to interpret them yourself, remembering to take into account all the factors which are relevant. For example, in a report on children's reading, the statistic was given that 40% of boys aged fourteen-plus said that they did not read books for pleasure. This caused alarmist headlines to some reviews. Yet the next table given stressed that nearly 50% of the same group said that they read between one and three comics and periodicals a week. It is a matter of interpretation what difference you feel the second table makes to your views of boys' reading. Is it less valuable to read periodicals or comics than to read books? Are books read in school for study purposes never pleasurable? You should question what you read, not just take it on trust, and preferably modify your ideas in the light of each new piece of information.

2 > MAKING USEFUL NOTES

The second important technique is **making useful notes**. Making notes is an individual matter, but some general advice can be offered:

(a) **Be orderly:** don't get your notes in a muddle.

Be orderly! Be brief! Be flexible!

(b) **Be brief:** there is no point in rewriting the information in your own words (paraphrase): this is time-consuming, and liable to lead to error. It is better to quote anything important exactly, and note lesser matters by a phrase or two.

(c) **Be flexible:** you may find it convenient to add something to a note later, e.g. a further fact, a cross-reference or a comment. If this is likely to be so, leave plenty of space for additions.

Making notes from films, television or radio is less easy. If you are trying to write you may be distracted from what is being shown, or from following the finer points of argument. It is better to involve yourself in the experience first, and write up your impressions immediately afterwards. Alternatively, jot down quick points as the programme proceeds, and go over them, expanding and correcting them as soon as you can afterwards, preferably in consultation with someone else who has also been listening or viewing. They will almost certainly have noticed things you haven't.

3 > PLANNING A QUESTIONNAIRE

The third technique is **planning a questionnaire**. A questionnaire can be a useful means of gathering information from a group of people. Questionnaires take time and care to construct, so before writing one it may be worth asking yourself whether there is a better way of getting the information you want. An ideal questionnaire has to give you information that is clear and correct, in a form you can use; and, to assist the people filling it in, there should be no questions that will cause them to hesitate and wonder what is meant. Also, you should avoid loaded questions, which show bias, e.g. 'Do you honestly prefer school lunches to sandwiches?', and long, complicated questions, e.g. 'Would you prefer a two-course hot meal to sandwiches or a bag of crisps and an apple for lunch?' Don't try the patience and good-will of those you hope to answer your questionnaire by making it extremely long.

Here are a few basic ideas to bear in mind when drawing up a questionnaire:

a) Keep the questionnaire short.
b) Keep the questions short.
c) Make the wording of instructions simple.
d) Make questions specific, not vague.
e) Make sure that the meaning of each question is clear (not ambiguous).
f) Place the questions in the best order.

4 > CONDUCTING AN INTERVIEW

A fourth technique concerns how to set about **interviewing** somebody. There are three stages to consider:

a) BEFORE THE INTERVIEW

Ask permission of the person or persons concerned well ahead. Let them suggest a convenient time. Give them some idea of what you are trying to find out, so that they will have time to think about it. Plan a list of basic questions that you really want to ask and make them as specific as possible.

b) DURING THE INTERVIEW

Improving your interviewing technique

Take a partner who can jot down notes, leaving you free to ask questions and devote your attention to the person being interviewed. You can also both discuss what happened, later. If you want to make a tape-recording of the interview, ask permission first, and remember that it may make the person you are talking to self-conscious and less spontaneous. Make sure that any electrical equipment you use is in working order! Take your prepared questions with you and start with them. You will probably get a good deal of extra information, too, so try to keep a balance between what you want to learn and what the interviewee wants to tell you. Thank the person concerned and offer to let him/her see a copy of your project when it is finished.

c) AFTER THE INTERVIEW

Discuss what took place with your partner. Write it up while it is still fresh in your memory. If you have made a recording, transcribe the parts of it you think you definitely want to use. Acknowledge the help of the interviewee in your project, and send a brief letter of thanks.

Suppose you were interviewing a very old lady about what she remembers of your locality from her childhood. You may have a list of basic questions, something like the following: 'Where were you born?', 'What was the local school like, when you went there?', 'Who lived in the old cottages in Mill Lane?', 'What do you remember about the tradespeople here?', 'What sort of things did you do in your spare time, before there was television?', 'What jobs were there for boys and girls, when they left school?' Almost certainly, you would get a great deal of fascinating information in answer to these few questions if you were friendly, tactful and patient.

EXAMPLES OF TOPICS FOR COURSEWORK

Topic work will obviously vary enormously. However, all Examining Groups require some evidence of non-literary as well as literary study. Some specify that one whole work of literature should be studied. (Work that results from reading literary texts will be considered fully in Chapter 10.) Most Groups ask that some work should be in an 'open' situation, i.e. where the form, readership and purpose of the writing are chosen by the candidates, expecting that some of this will lead to several kinds of informative writing – reporting, persuading and expressing opinions.

This gives an opportunity to include topic work.

Here is a selection of suitable topics:

1 Write a pamphlet informing members of your class of the dangers of taking drugs.
2 Plan the curriculum of your ideal school.
3 Trace your family tree and tell something of the history of your ancestors.
4 Compare transport in your area as it must have been in the late nineteenth century to how it is today.
5 Discuss the difference between job prospects now and in your parents' youth.
6 What is good and what is not-so-good about commercial television?
7 Find out what kind of Youth Club teenagers in your area would prefer, and plan a suitable scheme to provide one.
8 Investigate the history of some well-known building or landmark in your locality.
9 Plan a field trip to investigate the environment in a part of the country that you know well.
10 Investigate a conservation project in your area.

SAMPLE QUESTIONS AND ANSWERS

Before reading further you should choose one or two of the topics above and spend a short while outlining your own plan for an answer, in each case. Most of the topics offer scope for quite small-scale pieces of writing, as well as extended and researched pieces of work.

QUESTION 1

Write a pamphlet informing members of your class of the dangers of taking drugs.
     Here is a pupil's answer.

ANSWER 1

DRUGS

'I am here today to tell you all about drugs, well some facts about them. Drugs are various things; some of their names are cocaine, heroin, cannabis, crack, speed and ecstasy, and there's others as well. Some times doctors prescribe drugs when you're not well, but these drugs are medicines which make you well again.

'Once you take drugs you can get addicted to them. You would do anything just to get drugs; you would do things which you wouldn't have even dreamed about like leave your family, steal, or even kill a person.

'People who drink tea or coffee can also be addicted to it (tea/coffee). Although drugs like cocaine, heroin and cannabis are illegal, people smuggle them into countries for greed, because for a small amount of drug, you get a high price.

'People that take drugs are usually in the age group of about thirteen to forty-five. They take drugs if they are depressed or under pressure. This could be because they are unemployed, they have no security, family, etc....

'At first you think you'll just have a taste to be like some of your friends, but that taste leads you to become a drug addict. You think you can control yourself but gradually it takes over your life. Drugs cost you your health and looks. Remember in the end the drug is the one that gains by killing YOU!'

Tutor's comments

This piece of writing is informative and persuasive. The information given is helpful and correct, though limited in range. The work is clearly paragraphed, though there might be better ways of arranging some of the ideas, e.g. the warning about addiction in the second paragraph is weakened by the renewed information about non-addictive drugs in the third. This serves to distract the reader. The writer wavers between a detached approach ('People that take drugs ...') and a direct form of address ('Once you take drugs you can get addicted to them'). The latter is by far the more effective style in this persuasive piece, as the writer realises. The final paragraph is written exclusively in this 'button-holing' style and works well. She finishes particularly strongly: 'Drugs cost you your health and looks. Remember in the end the drug is the one that gains by killing YOU!' Expression is not perfect, but one is left with a memorable warning, forcefully emphasized by the use of capitals for 'YOU', and the final exclamation mark.

QUESTION 2

Plan the curriculum of your ideal school.

This might be partly based on what you already know – your own school curriculum, partly on research done from finding out about other schools' curricula, and probably quite a lot on what you imagine would be ideal. There has been much discussion about the new National Curriculum. One starting point could be to sketch out a time-table. Think about getting a balanced curriculum, firstly, in terms of how you as a pupil would experience it; secondly, of meeting the basic educational requirements of every pupil; and, thirdly, in terms of offering variety and interesting options. Your true 'ideal' curriculum may well have to be restricted because of a realistic appraisal of necessary and obtainable resources: staffing; finance for books, laboratories, cookery, craft or sports facilities; art equipment, etc. After sketching out your ideas, discuss the differences between what you would really like and what seems possible.

Here is a pupil's effort at a similar topic:

ANSWER 2

The school I'd want to go to would probably be freaky and not boring. I'd want it to be big with about three halls and three activities blocks. As I like doing athletics a lot, I'd like there to be teams and competitions every month. And mainly sports like swimming, football, American (not rugby), baseball – mostly boys' games and far less of netball as I'm quite boyish. Red, black and yellow is the colour of the uniform I'd like, because it would mix well, better than the dull colours, green, brown, etc. There would be six lessons a day because school will start 9 o'clock and finish 5.30 p.m.

My timetable would look like this:

Monday	Maths	Music	3 lessons of P.E.		
Tuesday	Maths	English	Fashion Design		Typing
Wednesday	Computers		W.Processing	Maths	English
Thursday	3 lessons of P.E.			Swimming	Computers
Friday	Music	Computers	Maths	English	Fashion Design

That would be my ideal picture of a time-table. The teachers would be average age, around 25 to 35. Mostly men because they're more strict. Punishment mustn't be from jumping off Waterloo Bridge to standing on the rails in Waterloo Station.

Tutor's comments

This piece of work shows the pupil's clear sense of priorities; she likes sports, so there would be plenty of time devoted to them on the time-table. She is also realistic about the need for a balanced curriculum: the basics, Mathematics and English, are there, as well as practical skills, such as Typing and Computing. Another aspect of balance is the provision of time for the Arts: Music and Fashion Design are represented. The sample time-table is clearly drawn up. Given that the pupil has thought out her ideal school curriculum quite well, it is a pity that she didn't enter more fully into a discussion of its advantages and disadvantages. The day seems to be very long, for example, but we are given no reasons for this. Would there be no homework in the evenings to compensate, perhaps?

Organization of the piece could have been better: details of the time-table are mixed in with more personal references – the colour of the uniform, for example. The paragraphs are short, but then this is a small-scale piece of writing.

There are some attractive examples of individuality, e.g. the humour 'Punishment mustn't be from jumping off Waterloo Bridge to standing on the rails in Waterloo Station'! The confession that the writer is 'quite boyish' and would prefer a 'freaky' school, is individual and appealing. These touches enhance the writing considerably.

On the whole, the tone and style are appropriate – fairly formal, but also with a strong individual point of view. There are some errors e.g. starting a sentence with a conjunction "And mainly ...", instead of joining it to the last sentence; finishing a sentence lazily with 'etc.' However these errors do not seriously impede communication. The piece, though lively, is rather short and underdeveloped.

QUESTION 3

Trace your family tree and tell something of the history of your ancestors.

The obvious starting point is what you know: a sketch of your family tree, as far as you can fill in the details. Next, what you need to know and could try to find out would be apparent from the gaps in what you had drawn. The first source of information would be older relatives, then family records. If you were very lucky there might be a Family Bible, with names written inside the covers. There could well be old documents – birth, marriage and death certificates, old letters, and so on. At the very least there should be photographs. As your investigations grew you could ask at your parish church if your family had lived in the same area for many, many years, or at the Public Records Office, where records going back to the nineteenth century are kept. Once you had gathered your material, you could follow some of the sorting, planning and writing up methods suggested in this chapter.

QUESTION 4

Compare transport in your area as it must have been in the late nineteenth century to how it is today.

A starting point here is what information you can gather about modern-day transport. You could make two lists – Public Transport and Private Transport – then gather facts about local trains and buses, also the availability of cabs, and estimate the number of private cars per head in your road. A similar parallel list for the nineteenth century would look very different. In the first would be horse-drawn buses, main line trains and, if you lived in London, the beginnings of the Underground (the Metropolitan line was begun in the nineteenth century, for instance). There may be a Museum of Transport in your area and the local newspaper, if it were founded early enough, may have information and pictures of older forms of transport.

Organizing your piece of writing would provide opportunities to bring out the great changes within less than a hundred years by contrasting sections or paragraphs.

QUESTION 5

Discuss the difference between job prospects now and in your parents' youth.

Adults at home could provide you with what you need to know about earlier job prospects for school-leavers, and the current scene is one you probably know well. With this topic there would be a need for careful evaluation: it would be easy to overstate your case or become personally involved in a way that might distort the facts.

QUESTION 6

What is good and what is not-so-good about commercial television?

This question clearly asks for your opinions, so that you would be free to air your own likes and dislikes about commercial television, or even to support one side of the proposition heavily. You should allow some time, though, for considering the other side, since both are represented in the question. Two lists would be a likely starting point: the 'Good' and the 'Not-so-good' aspects. You would need to consider how wide your discussion should range: should it concentrate on programmes or the commercials themselves? What about other forms of commercial television, e.g. cable TV? These choices would need to be made early on in your planning.

Quite a lot of what you would need could come from your own viewing and past experience, as well as from the opinions of friends and family. There are also books and articles available about audience figures, and so on, that could be researched for a larger scale project.

QUESTION 7

Find out what kind of Youth Club teenagers in your area would prefer, and plan a suitable scheme to provide one.

This topic would need some consumer research from the start. You would have to draw up a questionnaire, or interview as many teenagers as you could to canvas opinion and preferences. If your scheme is to be realistic you would also need to consider your area very carefully, e.g. what about location – is there a place that could be acquired for premises? What about the authorities? Could the local church or the local council help? There are some important large issues to sort out before you begin with any detailed consideration of the clubhouse furnishings! Altogether, though, this could be a worthwhile and quite extensive piece of work.

QUESTION 8

Investigate the history of some well-known building or landmark in your locality.

The advantage of this topic is that you could begin with some definite source material. Any landmark or well-known building is likely to have been recorded either in local history books or a town guide. It may have its own visitors' information sheet. There will be old photographs and you can take your own. There may be a guide or local person who could tell you a great deal about the monument or landmark. One danger here could be that there was so much information, so well written down that, in making notes, without meaning to do so, you could lose your own style and copy someone else's – even copy part of the texts themselves. Guard against this. Always make notes in your own words: you may miss some details, but they have the advantage of providing a fresh and individual view.

QUESTION 9

Plan a field trip to investigate the environment in a part of the country that you know well.

A field trip involving even one person requires a good deal of careful planning, and much of it would depend on the location chosen. An advantage of writing on a place that you know – perhaps that you have visited with the school – is that you would have accurate details to rely on. This topic lends itself to being planned in sections: *Before the Trip* – deciding the route, means of transport, what to take, and so on; then *During the Trip* – observations to make, unexpected happenings, timing the visit, arrangements on site, and so on; and finally *After the Trip* – return journey, records to make, etc.

QUESTION 10

Investigate a conservation project in your area.

If you choose this topic it is likely that you will be interested in conservation and possibly involved in a project already. The range of possible projects is vast as each has its own concerns and problems. There are many organizations, including enthusiastic local groups, to supply information. One strength of this topic is the opportunity it gives both for detailed recording of what is to be preserved as well as for showing an individual or group enthusiasm for the importance of saving what we have from the past.

A TUTOR'S ANSWER

Here is a tutor's answer for the first topic-based question in the previous section.

DRUGS – THE DANGERS!!

'I want to tell you about drugs – the facts and the dangers.

'First, here are some facts you should know. There is a wide variety of substances grouped under the term 'drugs'. Some are prescribed by doctors; when you react well to these they are relatively harmless. They are medicines to make you better. Some you take every day yourself for enjoyment or refreshment, like tea or coffee. Did you know that even these drinks are stimulants and, in excess, can lead to addiction? Some drugs, though are definitely harmful.

'Here are the names of some of the harmful drugs: crack, speed, ecstasy, cannabis, cocaine and heroin. These are all addictive, though heroin is the most destructive. Once you take these drugs you will quickly become dependent on them. You will do anything to get them, even things which you would not have thought possible a year ago. Some addicts, for example, leave their families, steal or go so far as to kill to get drugs.

'Of course it should not be easy to get these destructive drugs. They are illegal. People smuggle them into Western countries for greed, because they know that for a very small quantity of cocaine or heroin, they can get a high price. They do not think about the higher price paid by their victims: indignity, pain, suffering, perhaps a life of crime, even death.

'If you take these drugs you are likely to belong to a particular age-group; from as young as thirteen to about forty-five. You will turn to drugs if you are depressed, or under some kind of pressure. This could be because you are unemployed, or have no family, no security.

'At first, you may think you will just have a taste, to be like some of your friends. That taste can lead you to drug addiction. You may think it won't happen to you. You may believe you can control yourself, but gradually drugs will take over your life. Drugs can cost you your looks, your health, your job and your family. Remember, in the end, you can be the loser. Drug addiction can win by killing you.'

COURSEWORK – A STEP FURTHER

Get into the habit of reading critically other people's attempts to convey information. Collect a selection of pamphlets on a topic in which you are interested, or cuttings from newspapers. You will notice that they tend to obey certain rules. For example:

(a) **Material is set out clearly,** with headings, side-headings, wide spacing, paragraphs of varied lengths, and so on. Compare articles from two newspapers on a topic of current interest and see how the lay-out differs and what this tells you about the readers the papers expect to be addressing.

(b) **Information is carefully staged and sequenced.** Try rearranging your own ideas when draft writing, to see which is the best order.

(c) **Clarity of expression is important.** Try to say exactly what you mean.

(d) **Conciseness can be important.** Many forms of communication to inform are very much to the point – they don't waste words.

You should be able to learn from how others go about instructing and informing. Remember, though, that your own way of presenting ideas is distinctive, and can add interest and quality to your communication as long as you do not distort the facts.

R E V I E W   S H E E T

 Reduce this passage to **note form** with suitable headings and subheadings. Give the finished notes a title.

A teaching machine seeks to emulate the ideal teaching situation which is that of one teacher to one pupil and it does so in this manner.

A specialist in a subject takes the area of information to be imparted to the pupil and breaks it down into very short, logical and progressive steps. Each of these small steps requires some sort of answer or response from the pupil to signify that he has understood the step being made. The steps may be so small and so easily understood that it is impossible for a pupil to give a wrong answer to any question. This breaking down of information into short items or steps is known as programming, and each step with its question to the pupil is known as a frame.

The making of a programme is a slow process which involves testing, checking and rewriting over and over again until it is certain that there is no mistake in communication with the pupil.

Programmes may vary in their approach from the staircase or step-by-step type to the kind which offers the pupil a choice of answer. The former is known as a linear programme and the latter a branched programme. Linear programmes have a single question to be answered for each frame but branched programmes have a multiple-choice answer.

Much of the research on programming was carried out at Havard University and two American psychologists, B. F. Skinner (linear programmes) and N. A. Crowther (multiple-choice answer) may be regarded as the fathers of the teaching machine movement.

The finished programme, on rolls of paper or film may then be fed into any number of teaching machines in any number of schools, thus bringing thousands of pupils into individual contact with the mind of the subject-matter specialist.

The machine into which the programme is fed may be a complex mechanical device or a simple wooden box. Basically each has a window in which one frame appears at a time and some means by which the pupil can answer the related question without cheating. This may be done by writing the answer on paper which appears at another window and which disappears behind a transparent screen when the next question and the correct answer appear. In the more complex machines a frame of a branched programme may be answered by pushing one of a number of buttons. The correct button brings forward the next frame but an incorrect button will automatically display an additional frame with supplementary information which will enable the pupil to make the correct answer.

Programmes may also be supplied in book from, but the difficulty here, even with scrambled answers, is to prevent cheating by the pupil.

_____

_____

_____

_____

_____

_____

_____

_____

 Paraphrasing means putting what you read into your own words. It is a useful skill for developing clarity of expression and conciseness.

Paraphase the story below. Retain, as far as possible, the meaning and the mood of the original.

Found asleep in the bedding department of All Things Worldwide Hypermarket, Chicago, Mrs Mandy Palm, a widow of 73, explained that she had been in the giant store for over a month because she could not find her way to the exit.

"After the first day I asked a detective the way out" she said. "But he told me that I looked like a tramp and if I didn't get out he would arrest me on suspicion."

"After that, I opened an account and lived off the things I bought, eating in the restaurants and taking a bath at night. There was no-one to worry about me and I soon got used to the new routine."

_____

_____

_____

_____

_____

_____

✎ Paraphrasing and other types of writing are easier if you have a good command of vocabulary. Being able to find *synonyms* (words of the same meaning) or *antonyms* (words of opposite meaning) can be most helpful here. Find a word to fit in each column below, replacing the word underlined.

	Synonym (same meaning)	Antonym (opposite meaning)
1 a <u>stubborn</u> person _____	_____	_____
2 an <u>industrious</u> child _____	_____	_____
3 to <u>dedicate</u> your life to _____	_____	_____
4 to <u>predict</u> something _____	_____	_____
5 to <u>propose</u> a plan _____	_____	_____
6 to <u>comprehend</u> something _____	_____	_____
7 to <u>select</u> something _____	_____	_____
8 an <u>illicit</u> activity _____	_____	_____
9 <u>obligatory</u> work _____	_____	_____
10 to do something with <u>resolution</u>	_____	_____
11 deep in <u>meditation</u> _____	_____	_____
12 a <u>notorious</u> person _____	_____	_____

✎ Some words are commonly confused. Decide which of the words at the end of each sentence fits the blanks in the sentence. Note that you may need to change the form of the word sometimes.

1 She _____ him not to listen to Helen's _____ .
    (advise/advise)

2 Fiona was badly _____ by the rise in oil prices and it had a very serious

    _____ on the Italian economy too. (affect/effect)

3 The reviewer _____ the cast on their performance, saying that he felt the

    different styles of the three main stars _____ each other very well.
    (compliment/complement)

4 I would strongly _____ the new city _____ against
    complacency. (council/counsel)

5 He has just completed the first _____ of his report on the declining use of

    _____ animals in modern farms. (draft/draught)

6 More people _____ from the UK to other countries each year than

    _____ into the UK. (emigrate/immigrate).

7 _____ of people crowded into the Museum each day to see the exhibition of

    the newly discovered _____ of ancient gold jewellery. (hoard/horde)

8 Being fully _____ should _____ a certain peace of mind.
    (ensure/insure)

CASE STUDY-PREPARING AN ASSIGNMENT

GETTING STARTED

It has been pointed out in this book that the great advantage you have when submitting coursework, instead of doing written papers, is *time*. No piece of work in your folder needs to have been written against the clock, except perhaps occasionally when you are working in supervised conditions. In GCSE oral work, too, you will normally be allowed plenty of time to prepare work which will be assessed.

Having more time has a number of advantages.

In WRITTEN WORK, you can:
- note down first thoughts
- think about and order first thoughts
- obtain any information and supporting material needed
- write a draft
- develop the draft
- edit and correct the draft
- decide on the type of presentation required
- make a final fair copy.

In ORAL WORK, you can:
- decide on a subject to talk about
- obtain background information to help sustain a discussion subsequently
- prepare any necessary aids
- practise talking (but there are dangers here)
- take part in the final talk
- perhaps record it.

One difference between preparing written and oral work is that it is difficult to spend too much time improving the first, whereas over-preparation may damage the second – but this will be considered more fully below. It is assumed throughout the chapter that you will have researched anything you are working on, if that is necessary, *before* reaching the stage of presenting it finally to an audience, whether readers or listeners. How to go about this *research* has been discussed fully in Chapter 7.

NOTING DOWN FIRST THOUGHTS

THINKING ABOUT AND ORDERING FIRST THOUGHTS

WRITING A DRAFT

IMPROVING THE DRAFT

EDITING AND CORRECTING THE DRAFT

DECIDING ON THE TYPE OF PRESENTATION REQUIRED

MAKING THE FINAL FAIR COPY

ESSENTIAL PRINCIPLES

Whatever kind of writing you are attempting, whether it is setting out arguments of your own, summarising other people's ideas, communicating to others your response to something you have read, or inventing a story or poem, the way you approach it will depend very much on your own personality. Your individuality will show particularly strongly in your *first thoughts* about what you are attempting; however different the finished piece may be from where you started, you should try not to lose the freshness and vitality of the beginning. But liveliness of mind and good ideas are no excuse for careless or half-thought-through pieces of work, so the various *stages of preparation* are necessary, and well worth the effort, because you will want your work to be the best you are able to create and communicate.

1 ▶ NOTING DOWN FIRST THOUGHTS

Of course, it is very convenient if your good ideas for coursework come to you when sitting, pen in hand, in front of a clean sheet of paper, but usually this does not happen. It is more likely that your ideas will come to you from the stimulus of talking among friends, or with a teacher or tutor; they may even come on top of a bus. But whatever the circumstances, try not to lose these ideas. Hold them in your mind and think around them, so that they develop greater cohesion, until you can discuss them with someone or start staight away on a draft.

You may, though, prefer to keep a notebook and to jot down ideas. Many famous authors have done this: John Milton, the poet, wrote out a long inventory of the titles of poems he intended to compose, and I myself once, in a rare bout of creativity, took up a pen and wrote down 56 titles of novels I hoped to write – when I had some spare time; but I haven't actually started on any of them yet!

Let us take a particular example of the way a piece of writing might evolve. Turning over the pages of a daily newspaper, you read the following:

SEARCH FOR LONG-LOST LOVE

Mr Wilfred Reynolds, a seventy-two-year-old retired manufacturer, is hot on the trail of his war-time sweetheart, a former nurse called Angela Carter. Angela, he says, was beautiful, with a pale oval face, blue eyes, and a mass of golden hair, and she was as good as she was lovely. Mr Reynolds has placed advertisements in all the national newspapers in order to find her, and intends to leave her a fortune in his will.

It stays in your mind. Intriguing, isn't it? It poses so many questions. Why has Mr Reynolds waited for over forty years before looking for Angela? Will she still be beautiful and good? What has her life been like since they parted? If he finds her, how will she react to his reappearance? You revolve these ideas in your head for a while, and then forget Mr Reynolds and his problem.

Shortly afterwards, in school or college, you are asked to write a short story. Then you have a good idea: why not a story about Mr Reynolds and Angela, his long-lost love? You pick up a pen and write Lost Love. Then you underline it: <u>Lost Love</u>. You have your title. And it's a good one: it gives some clue to the story that will follow, but it doesn't give much away. Will it be a happy or a sad story? Will the love lost be found or not? You begin to get enthusiastic, and search through your memory for what you can recall of the article, still with pen in hand. You jot down:

Mr. William (?) Reynolds
Angela – fair, with blue eyes
The War
Newspapers
Wants to leave her all his money.

It was only half a minute's work, but your short story has begun.

<table>
<tr><td>

2 ▷

</td><td>

THINKING ABOUT AND ORDERING FIRST THOUGHTS

</td></tr>
</table>

For many people this is often the most important stage in the process of composition, because it is here that the communication takes its essential shape. However much you develop the piece of work later, the first way of seeing it rarely becomes entirely lost. In our example above you were *given the form*, a *short story*, but if that had not been so you might now be thinking of a poem, a play – or even a piece of investigative journalism, where you pose as a reporter researching the case. The original stimulus, the newspaper article, offered several possibilities. But you have no problem in this case, as you have been asked to develop your first thoughts, as you jotted them down, into a *short story*.

You find your piece of paper and look again at what you wrote, then you make one or two changes:

Lost Love
Mr. Wilfred Wright
Angela - fair, with blue eyes.
War-time romance.
Wants to leave all his money to her.
Newspapers - advertises in

You can't remember whether the man's name was William or Wilfred; you decide it was Wilfred. Oh, but if he is a real person you probably should change the name. What about Mr Wilfred Right, as Angela's 'Mr Right'? You decide this is too obvious, so change it to Mr Wilfred Wright. You like this, because it is a punning reference to your hero's idea of himself and it patterns nicely. You leave the details about the girl – they fit many people and seem appropriate. Of course, it was a war-time romance, and he advertised in the newspapers. You put your pen down and pause. This seems good, so far. But it is not a story outline. You need time to think about what shape this story will take. You take up your pen again and strike through the first thoughts, writing what follows instead:

Lost Love
Para. 1. Mr Wright remembers the past, as he composes his advertisement.

Para. 2. A few days later, Angela reads the advertisement - her reactions.

Para. 3. Mr. Wright collects his mail from the Post Office.

Para. 4. The meeting.

Para. 5. Mr. Wright visits the estate agents alone OR
Mr Wright visits the estate agents with Angela.

You add several questions to answer:

Did Mr. Wright never marry?
Why did he wait for forty-years before
looking for Angela?
What does he put in the advertisement?
What has her life been like since the war?
Will she still look beautiful?
What does she think of him?
Does she answer the advertisement?
How does he recognise her?
Does he find her?
What happens in the end.

A/W

You have asked yourself a series of questions – those you feel would need to be answered in your story – and then have a rough outline plan of the plot, developing two separate strands, Mr Wright and Angela, and then bringing them together in paragraph 4, the meeting. You haven't yet decided which of the two endings to choose – maybe you will give both, leaving it to the reader to decide.

3 > WRITING A DRAFT

You now feel ready to write a draft of the story, not necessarily worrying too much about correct paragraphing, punctuation or spelling at this stage, though it is best to be as correct as you can, otherwise you will have more work to do later. This is how the story might take shape as a first draft.

Lost Love.

Mr. Wright slowly put his pen back in its case and adjusted his reading glasses on his nose with a sign. He read over the advertisement he had just written. 'CARTER, Angela. Will Angela Carter, last heard of when working at the Royal Naval Hospital, Dover, get in touch with Mr. Wilfred Wright, with a view to meeting and exchanging old memories. Reply to Box 14.' Before him, on the oak dining-table, was a photograph of a pretty golden-haired girl with an oval face and sparkling eyes. He signed. 'Ah, Angela. What good times we had in 1940. I wonder where you are now?' Life had been lonely since Mrs. Wright had died.

He shuffled towards the front door, put on his overcoat and scarf, picked up his stick – he had trouble walking far nowadays – and slowly went down the broad gravel drive of Laburnums, and round the corner to the Post Office ......

'Will you leave off pulling that plant to pieces! If I've told you once I've told you a hundred times!' Mrs Brown sank down into a battered armchair, wiping her forehead with the back of a grimy hand. 'Grandchildren are all right,' she though, 'but not not when you have them all day and all the housework to do, too.' She slowly stirred the blackish tea in her cup and lit a cigarette, then glanced at The Daily News. She turned at once to the horoscope 'The Secret of Your Stars'. 'Acquarius' she read 'Today you will learn something to your advantage. Don't let it slip through your fingers!' Scanning down the page her eye caught what had once been her own name – CARTER, Angela... Will Angela Carter, last heard...' She read on eagerly. This was it – 'Something to your advantage'. It must be one of those young men she had met during the war. Was it the one who had red hair, who was always getting up to practical jokes? Or what about that pale quiet one...? Angela's face broke into an unaccustomed smile as her mind travelled back over the years. Little Jason continued to pull the leaves off the rubber plant one by one.

A week later, on Monday morning Mr. Wright fumed impatiently. It was always busy in the Post Office on Mondays – pensioners came for their money, and shop assistants for cash for the tills. He had come for something else.

'Box 14? Are there any letters for Box 14?' he asked tremulously, when at last he reached the counter. The clerk called across the room.

'Bring those letters for Box 14, will you'. A minute later Mr. Wright was handed a large grey Post-Office bag, brimming with letters, mostly in pink or mauve envelopes. A strong smell of rose water, eau de cologne and 'Spring Violet' met his nose.

'Oh, good gracious!' he said 'You'll have to deliver them'.

It took a long while to work through the sack, but it was worth the effort. Among the hundreds of letters from Anita, Agnes, Angel-face, 'your own Petal' and the like, he found what he was looking for: a short letter, written on sky-blue note-paper. It read:

Dear Fred,

How are you? I've often thought of you during all these years. I've still got the red rose you gave me when you left hospital I pressed it in a book. I'll meet you on Friday, 12th, by the lions in Trafalgar Square.

Yours ever,
Angela.

Friday the 12th, was one of those days when you know it is going to be wet, as soon as you wake up. Mr. Wright had had a long journey to Trafalgar Square, but it would be worth it to see 'Angela again'. He stood damply under a dripping umbrella, by one of the lions among hurrying passers-by, eagerly looking out for a lady with fair hair, blue eyes and an oval face – but there was no-one like that. Maybe he'd picked the wrong lion? There were three more to choose from. He began slowly to walk around the Square. Suddenly there was a yell from near him.

'Freddie! Hallo! I'd have known you anywhere!' It was the right voice, but where was Angela? Before he could think further he was clasped by a large, strong stout woman in an old fur coat, dragging a grizzling little boy behind her.

'Oh! Freddie' she cried 'I've found you at last – after all these years

It was raining hard again when the door of Gale and Pearson Ltd. the estate agents, swung open and crashed shut. The dripping figure of Mr. Wright entered.

'Yes, sir. Can we help you?' a charming young woman with golden hair and an oval face greeted him.

'Well, yes. I'm looking for a retirement cottage — something small, very small — on a remote island. Something in the Hebrides, perhaps?'

Yes, she had something like that. Mr. Wright had found what he was looking for — at last.

OR

It was still raining hard when the door of Gale and Pearson Ltd., the estate agents, swung open and crashed shut. A strange couple entered with dripping umbrellas and damp coats, but they looked happy unaware of all that.

'Yes. Can we help you?' a young woman greeted them.

Mrs Brown spoke up:

'Yes you can, young lady. We're looking for a retirement house — something up-market with a lot of space. Better be near the shops and the schools — I like shopping a lot, and there's the grandchildren to think of. Oh, and with a double garage...' Yes, she had something like that. Angela Carter smiled. She had found what she was looking for — at last.

4 > IMPROVING THE DRAFT

You may feel that this story has quite a good shape already. However, wouldn't the opening be more effective if the advertisement came first? You decide that it would and re-arrange the first paragraph. You consider following through some of the untied knots left in the plot. For example, it hasn't been established clearly what Angela Carter is looking for. Something can well be added, then, in paragraph two, e.g.:

'Grandchildren are all right', she thought, but not when you have them all day and all the housework to do, too. Since Mr. Brown had died a year or so ago times had been hard. The house that had been big enough for two was bursting at the seams when her five children and all the grandchildren came around to visit. If only she could manage to come into some money...

Then there's the ending. You don't want to choose between the two, so decide to keep both, leaving the story open-ended. You may consider moving the paragraphs around, but the pattern already works quite well and follows your original plan. You decide against changing the sequence of events, but re-arrange the first paragraph, so that the story begins with the advertisement, 'CARTER, Angela. Will Angela Carter ..., etc.

5 EDITING AND CORRECTING THE DRAFT

You now go through the draft very carefully, checking for any changes of phrasing you may want to make and correcting any inconsistencies, as well as making sure that spelling and punctuation are correct. You wonder about one of your statements: are there really four lions in Trafalgar Square? You aren't certain, and will have to find out. Even if you are writing fiction, your readers will not accept the situation as realistic if they know that part of your description of a familiar scene is wrong. Also, have you spelled 'Trafalgar' correctly? Yes. 'Acquarius' looks wrong; of course, there isn't a 'c'. Read your story quickly to yourself to see if punctuation seems all right. Do full stops correspond to the main pauses, and the commas to lesser pauses? You give characters' thoughts in the story, as well as direct speech. Have you shown the difference by using single inverted commas for their thoughts and double for speech? You have quoted a letter. How should you set that out? You decide to indent it a few spaces, on either side.

You could work with a friend or in a small group discussing the piece of work, or your teacher or tutor may have made some helpful remarks and corrections. Remember, if that happened, to include the draft work, with any corrections made during the process and information about the help given, with your final version for assessment in the coursework folder.

If your piece of work has been done under supervised (controlled) conditions – and each folder of work has at least one piece of this kind included in it – you would, of course, have had to see to the final correction and presentation by yourself.

6 DECIDING ON THE TYPE OF PRESENTATION REQUIRED

You wonder whether to have a try at printing the story on the word-processor, but decide it would be simpler just to write it out by hand. Your handwriting is quite good when you try, and that is fortunate, since it would certainly detract from the effect of the story if the assessor had to struggle with an illegible scrawl.

The layout presents other problems. How should the advertisement at the beginning be done? You decide to display it – that is, separate it from the rest of the text. And what about the two endings? You could write them side by side in two columns, but decide to make one follow the other.

These matters being settled, you are ready to produce the final copy.

7 > MAKING THE FINAL FAIR COPY

A fair copy is one where all previous alterations and corrections are incorporated. You supply yourself with some clean sheets of paper, and write or type out the story as neatly as you can. The short story would look something like this:

LOST LOVE

'CARTER, Angela. Will Angela Carter, last heard of when working at the Royal Naval Hospital, Dover, get in touch with Mr Wilfred Wright, with a view to meeting and exchanging old memories. Reply to Box 14.'

Mr Wright slowly put his pen back in his case, and adjusted his reading glasses on his nose with a sigh. He read over the advertisement he had just written. Before him on the oak dining-table was a photograph of a pretty golden-haired girl, with an oval face, and sparkling eyes. He sighed. 'Ah, Angela. What good times we had in 1940. I wonder where you are now?' Life had been lonely since Mrs Wright had died.

He shuffled towards the front door, put on his overcoat and scarf, picked up his stick – he had trouble walking far nowadays – and slowly went down the broad gravel drive at 'Laburnums' and round the corner to the post office …

'Will you leave off pulling that plant to pieces! If I've told you once I've told you a hundred times!' Mrs Brown sank down into a battered armchair, wiping her forehead with the back of a grimy hand. 'Grandchildren are all right,' she thought, 'but not when you have them all day and with all the housework to do, too.' Since Mr Brown had died, a year or so ago, times had been hard. The house that had been big enough for two was bursting at the seams when her five children and all the grandchildren came round to visit. If only she could come into some money … She slowly stirred the blackish tea in her cup and lit a cigarette, then glanced at *The Daily News*. She turned at once to the horoscope: 'The Secret of Your Stars'. 'Aquarius' she read. 'Today you will learn something to your advantage. Don't let it slip through your fingers.' Scanning down the page her eye caught what had once been her own name: CARTER, Angela. Will Angela Carter, last heard …' She read on, eagerly. This was it – 'Something to your advantage'. It must be one of those young men she had met during the war. Was it the one who had red hair, who was always getting up to practical jokes? Or, what about the pale quiet one? Angela's face broke into an unaccustomed smile as her mind travelled back over the years. Little Jason continued to pull the leaves off the rubber plant, one by one …

A week later, on Monday morning Mr Wright fumed impatiently. It was always busy in the post office on Mondays – pensioners came for their money, and shop assistants for cash for the tills. He had come for something else.

'Box 14. Are there any letters for Box 14?' he asked tremulously, when at last he reached the counter. The clerk called across the room, 'Bring those letters for Box 14, will you.' A minute later Mr Wright was handed a large grey post office bag, brimming with letters, mostly in pink or mauve envelopes. A strong smell of rose water, eau de cologne, and 'Spring Violet' met his nose.

'Oh, good gracious!' he said 'You'll have to deliver them.'

It took a long while to work through the sack, but it was worth the effort. Among the hundreds of letters from Anita, Agnes, Angel face, 'Your own Petal' and the like, he found what he was looking for: a short letter, written on sky-blue note-paper. It read:

Dear Fred,
How are you? I've often thought of you during all these years. I've still got the red rose you gave me when you left hospital. I pressed it in a book. I'll meet you on Friday 12th, by the lions in Trafalgar Square.
                              Yours ever,
                              Angela

Friday 12th was one of those days when you know it is going to be wet, as soon as you wake up. Mr Wright had had a long journey to Trafalgar Square, but it would be worth it – to see Angela again. He stood damply under a dripping umbrella, by one of the lions among hurrying passers-by, eagerly looking for a lady with fair hair, blue eyes, and an oval face – but there was no one like that. Maybe he'd picked the wrong lion? There were three more to choose from. He began slowly to walk around the Square. Suddenly there was a yell below him. 'Freddie, hallo! I'd have known you anywhere!' It was the right voice, but where was Angela? Before he could think further he was clasped by a large, strong, stout woman in an old fur coat, dragging a grizzling little boy behind her. 'Oh Freddie!' she cried. 'I've found you at last – after all these years …'
    It was raining hard, again, when the door of Gale and Pearson Ltd, the estate agents, swung open and crashed shut. The dripping figure of Mr Wright entered.
    'Yes, Sir. Can we help you?' a charming young woman with golden hair and an oval face greeted him. Mr Wright sat down and smiled.
    'Well, yes, I'm looking for a retirement cottage – something small, very small – on a remote island. Something in the Hebrides, perhaps?' Yes, she had something like that. Mr Wright had found what he was looking for at last.
    It was still raining hard when the door of Gale and Pearson, the estate agents, swung open and crashed shut. A strange couple entered, with dripping umbrellas and damp coats, but they looked happily unaware of all that.
    'Yes, can we help you?' A young woman greeted them. Mrs Brown spoke up: 'Yes, you can, young lady. We're looking for a retirement house; something up-market, on the large side, so that the grandchildren can come and stay and with plenty of space. Better be near the school and the shops – I like shopping a lot, and there's the grandchildren to think of. Oh, and with a double garage …' Yes, she had something like that. Angela Carter smiled: she had found what she was looking for – at last.

You feel rather satisfied with the story, now it is finished. Soon it will be read by your teacher or tutor for assessment, and later it will go into one of your coursework folders. The preliminary notes, plan and draft could be included with it, so that the moderator can look at the whole evolution of the work.

R E V I E W   S H E E T

 In any piece of writing it is important to have a good opening paragraph. Here are six positive points and six negative points about opening paragraphs. It may help if you start by:

   i) stating which particular aspects of the topic you are planning to discuss in your writing.
  ii) defining or clarifying any important terms in the title.

You must try to arouse the reader's interest perhaps by using one of the following methods:
  iii) making a short sharp strong statement about the topic;
  iv) posing a question to the reader;
   v) giving an example from one's own experience;
  vi) making an appropriate analogy (comparison).

You must try not to:
  vii) suggest that you do not have the knowledge to give an adequate answer to the question;
 viii) imply that you are not particularly interested in the subject;
  ix) make language errors;
   x) wander off the point;
  xi) misinterpret one or more words of the question;
  xii) evade answering the question asked.

Each of the following opening paragraphs illustrates *one* of these twelve points. Can you say which one?

A) In this essay I shall limit myself to a discussion of what makes a feature film produced for the cinema great. I shall not, therefore, consider the use of film in television as this would broaden the subject to include such varied genres as news reporting, nature and social documentaries and other types of filming, which would make the discussion too complex for an essay of this length.

B) It is not particularly interesting to write about history as a school subject but the other topics are even worse. Most of the pupils at my school found history the most boring of all our subjects. Had it been used to foster more of a pride in our country, we might perhaps have been more interested in it.

C) A worldwide afforestation programme is not a project that could reasonably be considered. There are a number of reasons why this is the case and, in my essay, I shall discuss each of these in turn.

D) One of the most shocking experiences of my childhood was visiting Leningrad Zoo and seeing elephants and giraffes in evil-smelling cages where there was scarcely room for them to turn round let alone move about. My picture books had shown them as magnificent creatures in the splendid open spaces of Africa. From that moment on I have been against zoos.

E) The term, culture, can be used in a number of ways. In this essay I shall use it in its broadest sense to refer to all the arts, social customs and habits characteristic of a particular society.

F) Music can be like a gentle hand caressing us until we lose all our tension and relax. However, the same hand can also take on other functions. It can whip us into a state of busy activity; it can pummel us until we feel full of renewed energy; it can support us as we do something that we find difficult.

G) Electrical power can be generated, or used, in many different ways and they all have their own particular merits or advantages. Electrical power, for example, is widely used in industry for a whole range of purposes; it is used to provide us with basic services like lighting, heating and hot water; it is used for a variety of processes connected with preparing food.

H) To answer this question fully one would need to know much more about demography and the factors affecting man's ability to survive than I yet do. However, it is an interesting question and I shall do my best to answer it on the basis of my rather meagre knowledge.

I) Tobacco-smoking should be held to be as serious a crime as the use of heroin. We must stop tolerating smoking as a mildly anti-social habit and begin to recognise it for what it really is: a major killer in the modern world not only for those who indulge themselves but also for those who are obliged to live and work with smokers.

J) It is certainly true that a successful politician needs to be able to persuade his or her audience. Would you vote for someone if you felt there were obvious flaws in the arguments they presented? Would you change your views on reading a badly presented political pamphlet?

K) A large number of different newspapers and magazines is produced in my country. In this essay I am going to examine critically the most important of those.

L) There is a great deal of scope for industrial development in my country as the rich resources which we possess have not yet been exploited to any significant degree. Indeed there is much scope for development of all kinds in my country as our social services are negligible and the arts would also benefit from much more funding. I particularly should like to see much more government attention devoted to education and health. To return to the main focus of the essay, however, industrial development is undoubtedly of vital importance to the future of my country.

In order to be able to make your sentences and paragraphs connect effectively together you need to have a range of connecting words and phrases at your fingertips. These words and phrases serve a variety of purposes. These purposes are summarised in the table below and one example of a word or phrase to match each of the purposes is also included in the table. Can you find *two* more words or phrases for each purpose?

Adding and amplifying information	moreover; _____ ; _____
Comparing	similarly; _____ ; _____
Talking about consequences	therefore; _____ ; _____
Sequencing (ordering) information	firstly; _____ ; _____
Expressing contrast	however; _____ ; _____
Concession	admittedly; _____ ; _____
Emphasising	indeed; _____ ; _____
Giving examples	for instance; _____ ; _____
Restating and defining	in other words; _____ ; _____
Summarising and generalising	in conclusion; _____ ; _____

CHAPTER 9

READING COMPRENHENSION

READING THE MATERIAL

ANSWERING THE QUESTIONS

TYPES OF COMPREHENSION TEST

MULTIPLE-CHOICE QUESTIONS

GETTING STARTED

Skill in comprehension is an essential part of all examinations in English. First you have to read instructions about how to fill in your answer book, then read and understand the questions asked in a written examination. This level of reading is for literal meaning, or 'the words on the line', as it has been described. Much of our reading, though, is done 'between the lines', looking for more than one level of meaning, changes of tone, and so on. It can even be important to read 'beyond the lines', by, for example, working out what happened before or after an incident you have just read about, or by considering the moods and motives of some of the people involved. But your search for meaning should always be based on the words on the page; unless they are read with care and thought, problems of understanding will be sure to arise.

The best way to prepare to do well in reading comprehension is to make a habit of reading for information and pleasure as wide a range of texts as you can – novels, newspapers, manuals, reports, autobiographies, and so on. Wide reading should be something to enjoy, especially if you use it to follow and extend your own interests and enthusiasms. It will do far more than help you to build up a vocabulary beyond the average: it will increase your ability to use and understand language in everyday situations, as well as when you are concerned with literature. It is reassuring to remember that you almost certainly have an excellent grasp of ordinary spoken English already. What you need to keep extending is 'book language', in all its varieties.

In the examination you may be reading for a variety of purposes. In the oral examination you may read aloud an unseen or prepared passage. To do this well you obviously have to understand it. You may be asked questions about a passage read silently, or be invited to discuss it with fellow students or an assessor. Coursework will, for most candidates, involve reading a very wide range of material, including at least one literary text. Preparation for reading comprehension in these areas is dealt with elsewhere (Chs 5–7 and 10) in this book. The present chapter is about tests of comprehension of the kind found in *written* examination papers.

E S S E N T I A L   P R I N C I P L E S

1 > READING THE MATERIAL

" Read once quickly; read once steadily; answer relevantly: "

The **most important thing** to do when tackling any comprehension test in a written paper is, first, to **read the material through quickly** to get an overall idea of what it is about. Some Groups give extra reading time. Candidates are told in general terms what to concentrate on when they read and may make brief notes. When you have read the passage, **read it through again steadily** before looking at the questions. On your second reading, or even third if time allows, try to get involved and interested in some aspects of the material and to become aware of its overall structure and the main idea or topic. When you are satisfied that you have a fair grasp of what the passage is about, look at the questions.

2 > ANSWERING THE QUESTIONS

The second principle, whatever type of response you are asked for, is to **answer relevantly**. One way of ensuring this is to try to answer in your own words, thinking the question through in your mind first, then checking your ideas carefully against the wording of the text, using the line references, if they are given. Even in questions where you are invited to give some sort of imaginative or personal response, be sure to link it to the text. If you feel that you have no idea of an answer, do not despair and do not guess wildly. Go back to the text and look for clues which will help you to work out something that seems likely. Work progressively through the questions, as they will follow the development of the passage: it is more difficult to go back to a question later, because you will have to remind yourself in detail of what has gone before.

Whatever the form of the text, questions will cover both its literal meaning and that between and beyond the lines. In passages by most of the Groups, the questions get harder as you go on, and move from the literal, by gradual stages, to more indirect levels of meaning, and often to 'open-ended' personal response questions. As well as showing your understanding of setting and immediate situation you will be asked about some of the following aspects of the passage:

- organisation
- pace of the narrative
- details of an argument
- author's or narrator's points of view
- characters' point of view
- style.

Some or all of these affect how you respond as a reader and examples of all of them will be considered in the following sections of the chapter.

3 > TYPES OF COMPREHENSION TEST

There are *two* kinds of comprehension test:

- those which have questions requiring a written answer from the candidate, in his or her own words

and

- those which give a set of options from which the candidate chooses one (Multiple Choice or Objective Tests).

Your answer to the **first** type should be as compact and correct as possible, unless it is a personal response 'open-ended' question, where there is more scope for your own thoughts and feelings.

With the **second** type, try to answer the question from the text without looking at the alternative answers given, then see which one is closest to your own answer and mark it out. There are collections of passages, with questions, which you can use for practice but, again, regular wide reading is probably the best preparation you can make.

In the papers produced so far for GCSE by the Groups little use has been made of the second kind of test. It will receive a comparatively small amount of space for comment here.

Reading comprehension is tested by compulsory written papers in all Groups.

You will be asked to:

- show that you can understand information and opinion
- select material relevant to whatever you are asked to do
- show that you can understand straightforward (and some subtle) meanings
- recognize different uses of language for different occasions
- comment on a writer's aims and intentions.

Coursework, showing response to your reading – literary and non-literary – is offered by all Groups, and will be discussed in Chapter 10.

EXAMINATION QUESTIONS

In this section it is suggested that you

- read each passage with its questions
- try to tackle it yourself
- look at the general notes on each passage in the Outline Answers below.

The **simplest comprehension test** is a single prose passage, with a list of questions for you to answer in your own words. In the GCSE examinations some questions will require an answer based directly on the language of the passage, and others will require a more personal or imaginative response. The following question is of this type.

QUESTION 1

You should spend about ¾ hour on this section which carries 15% of the total marks for the examination.

Answer ONE question only from this section. (*One of these questions is now presented*)

Look carefully at the advertisement (*on page 108*). You should look particularly at the picture, the headline and the other words. Write about the advertisement making clear how you think it makes its appeal to the public. Give reasons why you think it might or might not be effective.

QUESTION 2

ULEAC Specimen Question: Reading and Response Higher Tier: Levels 6 to 10 Two hours

Read the short story below and answer Questions 1a, 1b and Question 2. You should divide your time equally between Question 1 and Question 2.

You are reminded of the importance of clear English and orderly presentation in your answers.

INSTRUCTIONS TO CANDIDATES: Read the short story below.

The Trout by Sean O'Faolain

One of the first places Julia always ran to when they arrived in G—— was The Dark Walk. It is a laurel walk, very old; almost gone wild; a lofty midnight tunnel of smooth, sinewy branches. Underfoot the tough brown leaves are never dry enough to crackle: there is always a suggestion of damp and cool trickle.

5   She raced right into it. For the first few yards she always had the memory of the sun behind her, then she felt the dusk closing swiftly down on her so that she screamed with pleasure and raced on to reach the light at the far end; and it was always just a little too long in coming so that she emerged gasping, clasping her hands, laughing, drinking in the sun. When she was filled with the heat and
10   glare she would turn and consider the ordeal again.

This year she had the extra joy of showing it to her small brother, and of terrifying him as well as herself. And for him the fear lasted longer because his legs were so short and she had gone out at the far end and while he was still screaming and racing.

15 When they had done this many times they came back to the house to tell everybody that they had done it. He boasted. She mocked. They squabbled.

"Cry babby!"
"You were afraid yourself, so there!"
"I won't take you any more."
20 "You're a big pig."
"I hate you."

Tears were threatening, so somebody said, "Did you see the well?" She opened her eyes at that and held up her long lovely neck suspiciously and decided to be incredulous. She was twelve and at that age little girls are
25 beginning to suspect most stories: they already found out too many, from Santa Claus to the stork. How could there be a well! In The Dark Walk? That she had visited year after year? Haughtily she said, "Nonsense."

But she went back, pretending to be going somewhere else, and she found a

30 hole scooped in the rock at the side of the walk, choked with damp leaves, so shrouded by ferns that she uncovered it only after much searching. At the back of this little cavern there was about a quart of water. In the water she suddenly perceived a panting trout. She rushed for Stephen and dragged him to see, and they were both so excited that they were no longer afraid of the darkness as they hunched down and peered in at the fish panting in his tiny prison, his silver

35 stomach going up and down like an engine.

Nobody knew how the trout got there.

Her mother suggested that a bird had carried the spawn. Her father thought that in the winter a small streamlet might have carried it down there as a baby, and it had been safe until the summer came and the water began to dry up. She

40 said, "I see," and went back to look again and consider the matter in private. Her brother remained behind, wanting to hear the whole story of the trout, not really interested in the actual trout but much interested in the story which his mummy began to make up for him on the lines of, "So one day Daddy Trout and Mummy Trout ..." When he retailed it to her she said "Pooh".

45 It troubled her that the trout was always in the same position: he had no room to turn. All the time the silver belly went up and down; otherwise he was motionless. Hunched over him she thought how all the winter, while she was at school, he had been in there. All the winter, in The Dark Walk, all night, floating around alone. She drew the leaf of her hat down around her ears and chin and

50 stared. She was still thinking of it as she lay in bed.

It was late June, the longest days of the year. The sun had sat still for a week, burning up the world. Although it was after ten o'clock it was still bright and still hot. She lay on her back under a single sheet, with her long legs spread, trying to keep cool. She could see the D of the moon through the fir tree – they slept

55 on the ground floor. Before they went to bed her mummy had told Stephen the story of the trout again, and she, in her bed, had resolutely presented her back to them and read her book. But she had kept one ear cocked.

"And so, in the end, this naughty fish who would not stay at home got bigger and bigger and bigger, and the water got smaller and smaller ..."

60 Passionately she had whirled and cried, "Mummy, don't make it a horrible old moral story!" Her mummy had brought in a fairy godmother then, who sent lots of rain, and filled the well, and a stream poured out and the trout floated away down to the river below. Staring at the moon she knew that there are not such things as fairy godmothers and that the trout, down in The Dark Walk, was

65 panting like an engine. She heard somebody unwind a fishing-reel. Would the beasts fish him out!

She sat up. Stephen was a hot lump of sleep, lazy thing. The Dark Walk would be full of little scraps of moon. She leaped up and looked out of the window. Quietly she lifted the ewer of water and climbed out of the window and scuttled

70 along the cool but cruel gravel down to the maw of the tunnel. Her pyjamas were very short so that when she splashed water it wet her ankles. She peered into the tunnel. Something alive rustled inside there. She raced in, and up and down she raced, and flurried, and cried aloud, "Oh, gosh, I can't find it," and then at last she did. Kneeling down in the damp, she put her hand into the slimy

75 hole. When the body lashed they were both mad with fright. But she gripped him and shoved him into the ewer and raced, with her teeth ground, out to the other end of the tunnel and down the steep paths to the river's edge.

All the time she could feel him lashing his tail against the side of the ewer. She was afraid he would jump right out. The gravel cut into her soles until

80 she came to the cool ooze of the river's bank. She poured out, watching until he plopped. For a second he was visible in the water. She hoped he was not dizzy. Then all she saw was the glimmer of the moon in the silent-flowing river, the dark firs, the dim mountains, and the radiant pointed face laughing down at her out of the empty sky.

85 She scuttled up the hill, in the window, plonked down the ewer, and flew

through the air like a bird into bed. She hugged herself and giggled. Like a river of joy her holiday spread before her.

In the morning Stephen rushed to her, shouting that 'he' was gone, and asking 'where' and 'how'. Lifting her nose in the air she said superciliously,

90 "Fairy godmother, I suppose?" and strolled away patting the palms of her hands.

QUESTIONS

Answer Question 1a, 1b **and** Question 2. You should divide your time equally between Question 1 and Question 2.

1a What do you find in the story to suggest that Julia is growing out of childhood and away from childish things?

and

1b The writer of the story gives clear descriptions of the place where Julia and her family are staying on their holiday. Choose two of these descriptions and explain why you think they are important to the story.

and

2 Freeing the trout is a small incident but it is important in Julia's life. Write about an incident in your own life which has marked a stage in your growing up.

END

QUESTION 3

NEAB Specimen Question – Levels 5–9

Read the following passage and answer the question below. You should spend about 30 minutes on this question.

Read the following passage from a short story by the Cuban writer Enriqué Serpa, translated into modern English then answer the question which follows it.

Suddenly a shark had started to swim round his boat. It was a hammer-head, about fifteen feet long, with long broad fins. Instinctively Felipe reached for his harpoon, but he was stopped by the idea that he was not supposed to catch sharks. So he watched the shark, which looked like a dark, flexible tree-trunk. Yes, it was like a tree-trunk, he thought. How much would it be worth? Felipe calculated that any Chinese in Zanja Street would pay at least two dollars for the fins and tail. He felt he should take those two dollars which the sea was offering so generously, to relieve his extreme poverty. Two dollars meant three good meals for his starving children. But then there were the Police and the agents for the Shark Fishing Company to think about.

On the water-front they were always on the lookout for any fisherman bringing in shark fins or tails. And if sometimes they merely confiscated the catch, at others they arrested the fishermen. And after that five dollars fine and they were not even allowed a defence. But two dollars were two dollars, and however hard he worked, it was possible that that day his wife would have nothing to cook. Fishing was always a game of chance and often one's luck did not depend on one's efforts. If only it were possible to make the fish bite! And those fins there, within the reach of his hands. Two dollars.

He made up his mind. Two dollars, for him. What the hell! Quickly, while he was preparing his harpoon, he threw out all the bait he had to keep the fish around. The shark surfaced, showing its stiff dorsal fins, its white under-belly flashing in the sunlight. When it had eaten the bait, it dived slowly, to emerge a few moments later behind the boat.

The harpoon, skilfully cast by Felipe, caught it in the neck and it struggled convulsively, churning up a whirlpool of water with its tail. A few blows with a mallet on the head were enough to quieten it down. Half an hour later its body, without fins or tail, sank, turning on itself to be eaten by its fellows in the depths of the sea.

Behind the mutilated body, like a silent protest, remained a wake of blood.

After tying the fins and the tail with a piece of cord, Felipe rowed towards the coast. He wanted to get ashore as soon as possible, to go early to China Town in search of a buyer. Perhaps with Chan, the owner of the *Canton*, he might strike a bargain. At worst he ought to exchange the fins for food.

And then suddenly fate, dressed in a blue uniform, arrived. Felipe had scarcely tied up his boat when he was startled by a harsh, sarcastic voice: "This time you can't deny it, I've caught you red-handed." And as he turned, his heart in a vice, he saw a policeman smiling maliciously and pointing with his fore-finger at the fins and tail. After a moment's silence he added:

"I'll take those."

He bent down to pick them up. But he did not get to touch them because Felipe, jumping forward, grabbed them in his right hand.

"They are mine!" he muttered violently.

For a moment the policeman seemed astonished at meeting such behaviour. But he reacted quickly in an attempt to recover his authority:

"Come on, hand them over or I'll take you and the fins along with me."

Felipe looked at him carefully. He was a small man, skinny and ungainly. His precarious physique was in sharp contrast with his hectoring voice and the stance of a fighting-cock he had assumed. Felipe scowled and felt his arm-muscles contract. And aware of his own strength and of the elasticity of his body, he said to himself:

"This fellow isn't even half a man."

In the meantime, a group of onlookers had collected around him and the policeman.

"Hand them over or you'll be sorry."

"Give them to him," advised a voice, that of an old copper-faced fisherman. And changing his tone:

"Perhaps he can see a doctor with what he gets for them."

Felipe felt the weight of innumerable eyes fixed on him and he imagined the scornful smiles and ironical comments with which the witnesses of the scene would taunt him afterwards. And apart from this, the feeling that he was being made the object of an intolerable injustice goaded him on to disobedience, whatever the consequences may be.

"I'm waiting. Are you going to hand them over or not?"

The bullying voice of the policeman was angry and threatening.

"Neither of us gets them," Felipe said suddenly. And whirling them round his head, he threw the fins into the sea.

QUESTION

Write about what you learn of the different aspects of Felipe in the passage. Give evidence from the extract to show how you came to your conclusion about:
a) his situation;
b) his anxieties;
c) his skills;
d) and his attitude to authority.

QUESTIONS 4 AND 5

Another form of question consists of two or more passages, connected in theme but varied in style or approach. They may be from any kind of writing (narrative, descriptive, personal, factual, informative) and in a variety of forms (diary or novel extracts, letters, reports, articles, etc.). In your answers you will need to draw on both passages and, to some extent, compare and contrast them. Questions 4 and 5 are of this type.

QUESTION 4

SECTION A

Read the following two passages and then answer the questions.

From If Only They Could Talk by James Herriot

'If Only They Could Talk' is one of a long series of books describing James Herriot's work as a veterinary surgeon in North Yorkshire in the 1930s.

I stroked the old dog's head as I tried to collect my thoughts. This wasn't going to be easy.

'Is he going to be ill for long?' the old man asked, and again came the thump, thump of the tail at the sound of the loved voice. 'It's miserable when Bob isn't following me around the house when I'm doing my little jobs.'

'I'm sorry, Mr Dean, but I'm afraid this is something very serious. You see this large swelling. It is caused by an internal growth.'

'You mean … cancer?' the little man said faintly.

'I'm afraid so, and it has progressed too far for anything to be done. I wish there was something I could do to help him, but there isn't.'

The old man looked bewildered and his lips trembled. 'Then he's going to die?'

I swallowed hard. 'We can't really just leave him to die, can we? He's in some distress now, but it will soon be an awful lot worse. Don't you think it would be kindest to put him to sleep? After all, he's had a good, long innings.' I always aimed at a brisk matter-of-fact approach, but the old clichés had an empty ring.

The old man was silent, then he said, 'Just a minute,' and slowly and painfully knelt down by the side of the dog. He did not speak, but ran his hand again and again over the grey old muzzle and the ears, while the tail thump, thump, thumped on the floor.

He knelt there a long time while I stood in the cheerless room, my eyes taking in the faded pictures on the walls, the frayed, grimy curtains, the broken-springed arm chair.

At length the old man struggled to his feet and gulped once or twice. Without looking at me, he said huskily, 'All right, will you do it now?'

I filled the syringe and said the things I always said. 'You needn't worry, this is absolutely painless. Just an overdose of an anaesthetic. It is really an easy way out for the old fellow.'

The dog did not move as the needle was inserted, and, as the barbiturate began to flow into the vein, the anxious expression left his face and the muscles began to relax. By the time the injection was finished, the breathing had stopped.

'Is that it?' the old man whispered.

'Yes, that's it,' I said. 'He is out of his pain now.'

The old man stood motionless except for the clasping and unclasping of his hands. When he turned to face me his eyes were bright. 'That's right, we couldn't have let him suffer, and I'm grateful for what you've done. And now, what do I owe you for your services, sir?'

'Oh, that's all right, Mr Dean,' I said quickly. 'It's nothing – nothing at all. I was passing right here – it was no trouble.'

The old man was astonished. 'But you can't do that for nothing.'

From Intimate Relations by Jacqui Durrell

Jacqui Durrell shares with her husband, Gerald Durrell, a love of animals. In the following episode she gives an account of an Emperor Tamarin monkey. This pet is particularly troublesome and has a bad influence on others in their care!

It is lovely having animals living with you, but we feel that, in fairness to them, it is essential that they should have a definite routine. It is also unwise to inflict one's own routine on animals; the best thing is that they should evolve their own. One creature that we did have in the flat who utterly refused to be influenced by us in any way at all, was Whiskers, the Emperor Tamarin. Whiskers is a magnificent creature, being very attractive to look at and getting his name from his enormous white moustache. Gerry had always had a passion for these little monkeys from South America, since the days before the war when he had had a black-headed Marmoset as a pet. They are bird-like in character and fearless, a rule to which Whiskers was no exception.

He arrived in pathetically bad condition (from a dealer, of course) and was obviously suffering from the cage paralysis that often afflicts these South American primates. With the help of our veterinary friend in Bournemouth, we had evolved a perfect answer, but unfortunately, it involved a massive injection of vitamins D and B12. No one liked administering these injections, but unfortunately, if the animals were to be saved, there was no alternative. Poor old Whiskers was given the shot. Unlike others of his species who accepted it philosophically and did not connect the pain with the person who was giving the injection, he immediately turned round, looked at Gerry, and bit him severely on the hand; a warning as to what would happen if he was to try to repeat the operation. Gerry was so amused and taken aback that all he could do was laugh. This pugnacity was characteristic of Whiskers; later he became, for his size (a mere six inches), one of the most ferocious specimens in the zoo. If he adored you, you were fine, but if he did not, he would leap upon your head and try to bite you viciously.

As he was in such a weakened condition when he arrived, it was decided to keep him in the flat for a little while, in order to build up his strength. At this time our Common Marmosets had a youngster who was approximately the same size as Whiskers and so they were brought up as companions. They spent most of their day in a large cage in Gerry's mother's bedroom. She, of course, doted on them. Nothing was too much trouble. She would spend two hours every morning cooking delicacies for them, stewing apples with honey or brown sugar, boiling rice and lentils, making other little tit-bits that she was sure they would like. Of course, this was entirely the wrong treatment for Whiskers and, from being naturally arrogant, he became unbearable. He refused to go into his cage until he wanted to, and he and his friend Popadum tore round poor Mrs. Durrell's bedroom, rioted over the bed, played havoc with her possessions and really completely took her over. They did have their moments of rest when they would sit calmly in her lap, but most of the time they were tearing her knitting out of her hand, hiding her wool, getting in and out of her knitting bag, strewing bits of wool and patterns all over the place – in fact, becoming totally unmanageable.

The questions which follow are based on the two passages you have just read. Answer **ALL** the questions using the information you have gained from reading the passages.

1 What do you learn from these two passages about the feelings and attitudes of the various humans to the animals concerned? (10 marks)

2 The first passage is mainly sad, the second mainly humorous. Show how these effects are gained in each case. (10 marks)

3 Jacqui Durell says: 'It is lovely having animals living with you.' How far do these passages prove that it is true and how far do you think they show that it is a matter of opinion? (10 marks)

4 How does your own experience in dealing with *either* animals *or* people compare with the events in the passages? You may refer to *either* one *or* both of the passages. (10 marks)

(SEG)

QUESTION 5

NEAB Specimen Paper ½ hour – Levels 5–9

RESPONSE TO UNSEEN TEXTS

Read the following two passages and then answer the questions which follow.

You should spend about 30 minutes on this question.

Passage A is part of Psalm 107 in the Bible, in the translation made for King James in 1611. Read the passage carefully in order to be able to answer the question which follows it.

PASSAGE A

23   *They that go down to the sea in ships, that do business in great waters;*
24   *These see the works of the Lord, and his wonders in the deep.*
25   *For he commandeth, and raiseth the stormy wind, which lifteth up the waves thereof.*
26   *They mount up to the heaven, they go down again to the depths: their soul is melted because of trouble.*
27   *They reel to and fro, and stagger like a drunken man, and are at their wits end.*
28   *Then they cry unto the Lord in their trouble, and he bringeth them out of their distresses.*
29   *He maketh the storm a calm, so that the waves thereof are still.*
30   *Then are they glad because they be quiet; so he bringeth them unto their desired haven.*
31   *Oh that men would praise the Lord for his goodness, and for his wonderful works to the children of men!*
32   *Let them exalt him also in the congregation of the people, and praise him in the assembly of the elders.*

Passage B is an Anglo-Saxon riddle dating probably from the eighth century and translated at the beginning of the twentieth century into Modern English which tries to give some of the flavour of the original. Read the passage carefully in order to be able to answer the question which follows it.

PASSAGE B

SHIP

[The generally accepted solution is ship which moves on its keel ship (the "one foot"), which is braced by beams ("many ribs"), and which has a hole in the deck ("mouth").]

This world is beautiful in various ways, decked with adornments. I saw an artful work go forth, excellent in journeys, grind against the sand, move with a cry; the strange creature had not sight nor hands, shoulders nor arms; the curious thing must move on one foot, go quickly, pass over the plains; it had many ribs; its mouth was in the midst, useful to men; it brings to the people provision in plenty, bears food within it, and each year yields to men a gift of which men, rich and poor, make use. Tell, if thou canst, O sage, wise in words, what the creature is.

QUESTIONS

a) What are the "wonderful works" in Passage A?
b) What are the different ways in which the ship in Passage B is described as if it were a person?
c) Using examples from both passages explain how language has changed over time. You might comment on such matters as vocabulary, grammar, meanings, structures and usage.

Some groups combine Reading and Writing assessment on one paper. Treatment of the combined skills needed for these papers will be considered more fully in Chapters 10–11, 15, and 17.

QUESTION 6

WJEC Specimen Paper (1½ hours) Tier 1, Level 4–6

Answer all the questions in Section A (Reading) and B (Writing). You will be assessed on the quality of presentation in your answers as a whole.

QUESTIONS

SECTION A: 20 marks
To answer this section you will need to look at the leaflet: Big Pit (pages 116–117)
  You should spend about 30 minutes on this section.

Look at the leaflet under the heading 'How To Get There'.

A.1. a) What telephone number would you ring to find out more information about a
    trip to Big Pit?
  b) At what time of the day does the first underground tour start?
  c) Who are not allowed to go down Big Pit? Why do you think this is ?   [5]

Now look at the section headed 'The Underground Tour'.

A2. What would you see and hear underground on a visit to Big Pit?   [5]

Now look at the leaflet as a whole.

A.3. Choose **two** pictures in the leaflet. Say what is in them. Why might these
  pictures have been chosen to appear in the leaflet?   [5]

A.4. How does the leaflet try to attract visitors to Big Pit?   [5]

Think about the information it gives, the pictures shown, the overall layout.

SECTION B: 20 marks
*Answer Question B5 **and** Question B6.*
  You should spend about 30 minutes on each question.

B5. Your class has been on a visit to Big Pit. You have been asked by your teacher to
  write an account of this trip for the school magazine.

Write your article.   [10]

Remember to think about:how the day was planned;
                the things you saw and heard;
                whether the trip was a success

B6. Think of a place not too far from your home which people might like to visit. It
  could be a castle, a farm, a factory, a theme or wildlife park or a zoo. **Now
  design a leaflet, like the one on Big Pit, which sets out the attractions of
  this place.**   [10]

*You may use pictures and diagrams if you wish but remember to include the
important information.*

There is another type of comprehension test – **Multiple Choice** – which has
questions called 'items'. Each question has an introductory statement, called the stem,
then four or five suggested 'answers', called options. Only one option is the key or best
answer to the question put in the stem. The other options are the distractors. Notice
that the options are normally similar in form and length, so that none stands out more
than the rest.

  Try the following items, which illustrate the three most common types, and are
based on the passage in Question 2 (pages 107–109). They are designed to test the
same range of skills as traditional comprehension questions.

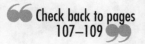
Check back to pages
107–109

a) SINGLE-RESPONSE ITEM

Which of the following words is closest in meaning to 'incredulous' as used in line 24?

A Unhelpful; B Unconvinced; C Unaware; D Unconcerned; E Unheeding

BIG PIT

UNIQUE UNDERGROUND TOUR OF A COALMINE

BLAENAFON, SOUTH WALES

SOME OF THE FEATURES AT BIG PIT, BLAENAFON

A unique underground tour, with an ex-miner as your guide.

The original colliery buildings, including the winding engine-house, the blacksmiths' shop and the pithead baths.

Exhibitions illustrating the history of the South Wales coal industry and the way of life of the mining communities.

The miners' canteen, now offering a range of hot and cold snacks and meals, confectionery and ice cream.

A gift shop well stocked with souvenirs and publications.

A professional photographer to record your visit.

Ample free parking space; and a picnic area.

HOW TO GET THERE

Big Pit is within easy reach for a day trip for anyone in South or Mid Wales, the West of England, the Midlands, or even London. From the M4, turn off at junction 26 and take the A4042 to Pontypool, then the A4043 to Blaenafon. From the A465 Heads of the Valleys Road turn off at Brynmawr and take the B4248 for Blaenafon. From the M50 take the A449 to Raglan, then the A40 to Abergavenny, and the B4246 to Blaenafon. Big Pit is about a mile out of Blaenafon on the B4248, and is well signposted.

Big Pit is Open Daily from March to November

At other times ring for details. The first underground tour starts at 10.00a.m.; the last underground tour starts at 3.30p.m. Parties please book in advance.

Disabled visitors please 'phone in advance to discuss arrangements. We regret that children under 5 years of age cannot be taken underground.

For further details, discounts and bookings, ring

BIG PIT

Blaenafon (0495) 790311

A UNIQUE UNDERGROUND TOUR THROUGH 19TH. CENTURY COAL AND IRONSTONE WORKINGS

Big Pit closed as a working colliery in 1980, exactly 100 years after it first produced coal. In Blaenafon the mining of coal and ironstone on a large scale began in the 1780s and some of these older workings are connected with Big Pit. The pit is now a museum where visitors can go underground and discover how miners have worked and lived over the last 200 years.

The photographs show you something of what you will see – underground roadways, coal-faces, haulage engines, and on the surface the blacksmiths' shop, the baths, and exhibitions.

THE UNDERGROUND TOUR

First you will be kitted out with a safety helmet, cap lamp and 'self-rescuer' just like a working miner. Then you will ride down in the cage to the bottom of the shaft – 294 feet deep. Ex-miners will be your guides and their explanations and anecdotes will bring your trip to life.

The underground tour lasts nearly an hour. During this time you will walk through workings some of which are over a hundred years old. There are many fascinating relics of mining history preserved here, including stables and haulage engines. At the coalface your guides will explain the different methods of extracting coal and the working conditions of the miners.

Although Big Pit no longer produces coal it is still a real mine, so please remember to wear practical shoes and warm clothing.

Layout of Underground Workings

b) A DOUBLE COMPLETION ITEM

Which two of the following are reasons why Julia cried "Mummy, don't make it a horrible old moral story!"   (lines 60–61)

1   She is angry with her mother for telling a story.
2   She is bored by stories with moral endings.
3   She is pretending that stories do not interest her.
4   She is afraid to hear the unhappy ending.
5   She is aware there are no fairy godmothers.
    A 1 and 3 only   B 1 and 5 only   C 2 and 3 only
    D 3 and 4 only   E 4 and 5 only.

c) AN EXCEPT ITEM

In the passage Julia experiences all the following EXCEPT
    A fear; B anger; C hatred; D pride; E pity

OUTLINE ANSWERS

ANSWER 1

This question looks deceptively easy, because there is no set of specific questions to answer. You are asked to look at the picture and headline and explain how the advertisement makes its appeal.

The chief aim in this kind of writing is to persuade the reader, in this case, to buy a number of books. Your answer should bring out, as fully as possible, any means the writer uses to persuade. The first form of persuasion to comment on in the piece is what it looks like. The illustrations, size of type in the headline, arrangement of the text on the page – all contribute to the total effect. The second form of persuasion is the choice of words. Here space is very important. There is no room for long sentences or paragraphs, as short ones are easier to read quickly, and they pack in more information. Repetition, though, especially of the name of the product, is space well used, as it tends to make the reader remember the product. Jingles and rhythmic phrases have a similar effect. The words chosen to describe the product must praise or recommend it: 'special', 'unique', 'invaluable', etc. A vital factor is the kind of person the writer thinks he is addressing. Here the writer is addressing parents of primary school-age children, and perhaps the children themselves. He gives information but also tries to amuse, and to build up the readers' feelings of self-importance, playing on their wish to do their best for their children, with such phrases as 'you can afford', 'build their vocabulary', 'encourage them to learn'. You are asked, finally, to evaluate the advertisement, saying why it might or might not be effective. Consider here, as well as the claims made – i.e. that the product is attractive and good value – what is *not* made clear, e.g. the total cost. Has the writer got the tone right? Is he perhaps talking down to readers or mystifying them? Repetition may persuade us but too much can irritate us as well. Pick out as many detailed points of this kind as you can. Your answer will be different from mine, but remember that to be done well, very open-ended questions like this need thinking through carefully, *before* you start writing.

ANSWER 2

If the passage is a story it is easy to grasp quite a lot about it when you first read it. Look at the questions: you will see that they move from questions about ideas and characters in the story (1(a) and 1(b)) to a more personal response, related to an incident in the story. Questions 1(a) and 1(b) need a concise statement of detail, and it would be worth making a list of relevant points first, then attempting a quick draft, before writing your final answer. The repetition of the adverb "always" in the first two paragraphs show that Julia had been visiting the Dark Walk for some years. This year would be different because now she could share it with her young brother i.e. he now has the experience she had, but presided over by an older sister who can call him "babby" – all an indication that she is growing out of childhood. Her attitude to childish things is shown when we are told that "She was twelve and at that age little girls are beginning to suspect most stories". She dismisses them with disdain: "Nonsense" and "Pooh". Another sign of her growing maturity is a concern for the safety of the trout and her understanding that it is at risk – a fairy godmother won't rescue the fish; it needs a human being to act. She overcomes her fear of the night and the Dark Walk to go herself and carry out the planned rescue. She also is able to keep the secret and joke about the possibility of the rescue being the work of a fairy godmother. For 1(b) you have to deal with inference by thinking for yourself why these places are important to the story – a step forward in critical reading. You could, perhaps, choose the Dark Walk, and explain that it is a splendid example of a journey through what seems to be a dangerous and frightening place; that Julia feels she has to keep going through it and by doing so learns to control her imaginings. It is of vital importance to the story because that is the place of opportunity for her, later. The best answers would make the point that this is a small example of what we all have to face in life at some time.

In Q.2. you are asked to use your understanding of the story, applying it to an experience in your own life when you felt you had taken a step towards maturity.

ANSWER 3

The questions all explore aspects of Felipe's character. 1(a) is literal comprehension. You simply have to pick out what is his situation. This seems to involve where he is, what he is doing and why he is doing it. Felipe is a fisherman, tempted to kill a shark for its fins and tail for the two dollars price he will get for them, even though he knows it is against the law. (b) This answer is a continuation of the first, isn't it? He has two sources of anxiety: the need to feed his children and the fear that he might be found out by the police or the agents for the Shark Fishing Company. (c) His skills are those of his calling – he is very fit and "aware of his own strength and of the elasticity of his body", and is able to harpoon the shark after it takes his bait. Quote occasionally in your answers, to show that you are drawing ideas from careful reading of the text. (d) We learn about his attitude to authority towards the end of the passage, after he encounters "fate, dressed in a blue uniform". Notice that this is a two-sided affair: the policeman's attitude and behaviour evokes a response in Felipe, doesn't it? Pick out the words and phrases that tell you firstly about the policeman's attitude: he is "harsh" "sarcastic" "smiling maliciously"; he gives orders: "Come on, hand them over" and threatens: "I'll take you and the fins along with me". He has a "hectoring" (bullying) voice", and continues being angry and threatening. Now, let's look at Felipe's side of the encounter. He is taken by surprise and reacts instinctively "They are mine!" He feels he is more of a man in strength and physique than the policeman. Then a crowd gathers, and they also affect Felipe's attitude. He is taunted by what he thinks is their scorn, and by the supposed injustice of the situation. He finally acts in defiance, regardless of "whatever the consequences may be".

ANSWER 4

See Tutor's Answer on page 121.

ANSWER 5

Here you are asked to consider each passage in turn. In your answer, do not be content with one or two points: a careful search will find several. This question requires close reading of the passage.

a) The "wonderful works" in Passage A are the wonders of the sea, part of God's power in calling up storm winds and great waves, which terrify and threaten the lives of sailors.. It also praises his power to calm the storm and bring men safely to shore.

b) You may have noticed how vividly the riddle is expressed. Part of this effect is personification, that is, giving the inanimate thing described human characteristics. Look again closely, and then make a note of these human features. I have listed: "journeys", "grind against the sand", "cry", "strange creature had not sight nor hands, shoulders nor arms", the thing "must move on one foot"; "it had many ribs"; "its mouth was in the midst". That's quite a lot, isn't it.

Question (c) is more difficult. Here you need to look at the different aspects of the writing and compare them with modern English. You could take each feature in turn e.g. vocabulary. In Passage A (the seventeenth century English text) there are unfamiliar words: "the deep" (for "the depths of the sea"); "reel" (for "walk unsteadily"); "haven" (for "place of safety"); "assembly" (*gathering – rather like a school assembly!). Though written in Modern English, Passage B has phrases with an archaic tone e.g. "artful work" (we would say now "well-made by a craftsman"); "go forth" (for set out) and so on. You probably noticed the endings to the verbs in Passage A "lifteth" and "bringeth" – English used to be conjugated. By close examination you can pick out many changes, and perhaps add that, as English is not a dead language, it is changing constantly, even today.

ANSWER 6

A1. a) *What telephone number would you ring to find out more information about a trip to Big Pit?* [5]

b) *At what time of the day does the first underground tour start?* [5]

These questions are simply tests of location.

Give one mark for each correct answer.

c) *Who are not allowed to go down Big Pit? Why do you think this is?* [5]

This question allows for location but also encourages some inference.

Give one mark for the correct answer.
Give an additional 1–2 marks for sensible inferences.

A2. What would you see and hear underground on a visit to Big Pit? [5]

This tests location, reorganisation and some inference.

Give 1–2 marks, according to quality for those who merely locate relevant material in the text.

Give 3–5 marks according to quality for those who reorganise the material with some success.

A3. *Choose two pictures in the leaflet. Say what is in them. Why might these pictures have been chosen to appear in the leaflet?* [5]

This tests location and inference.

Give 1–2 marks for simple description of picture content.

Give a further 1–3 marks for sensible suggestions/comments on content.

A4. *How does this leaflet try to attract visitors to Big Pit?* [5]

This tests appreciation of style at a fairly simple level.
Give 1–2 marks for recognition of features.
Give 3–5 marks for comments.

SECTION B and PRESENTATION

B5 Account of trip to Big Pit [10]

Levels 4–5

(Marks 4–7) These answers are likely to rely very heavily on the Resource Material to produce simple content but with some understanding of the nature of the task.

Level 6

(Marks 8–10) These answers will show understanding of the nature of the task and some sense of audience. Content will begin to have shape and coherence.

B6 Leaflet on attraction near home [10]

Levels 4–5

(Marks 4–7)   These answers will show some understanding of the demands of the task and show some awareness of appropriate form and content.

Level 6

(Marks 8–10)   These answers will show understanding of the demands of the task and awareness of appropriate form and content for a particular audience.

MULTIPLE-CHOICE ANSWERS

a) B; b) E; c) C.

TUTOR'S ANSWER TO Q.4

This answer, to Question 4 above, is by no means the only one possible, but it indicates a way of tackling it that will cover the chief requirements of a typical mark scheme. It is likely that marks would be awarded for picking out information from the passage and, to some extent, responding to implied meanings.

1. The people whose feelings and attitudes to animals are shown in the two passages are James Herriot, a veterinary surgeon; Mrs Jacqui Durrell, an animal lover; her husband, Gerry; his elderly mother; and Mr Dean, an old man who owns a dog. In general terms, the feelings and attitudes of the people concerned depend on the way that they come into contact with animals. James Herriot takes a professional attitude and has expert knowledge. We know this by what he says, e.g. his diagnosis: 'You see this large swelling. It is caused by an internal growth'; 'it [the cancer] has progressed too far for anything to be done …' His attitude to treatment is realistic. Bob is to him a patient, not a pet. It is his job to advise action, however painful his advice may be, and he recommends that 'it would be kindest to put him to sleep'. His behaviour throughout is also considerate: He strokes the dog's head and allows time for a final leave-taking of master and dog. He speaks reassuringly as he injects the fatal dose and his refusal to take payment shows that he has a deeper compassion than mere professional kindness.

In contrast, Mr Dean sees Bob as a pet and much loved companion. He responds with strong feeling. He speaks 'faintly' and looks 'bewildered'; his lips tremble and he falls silent and avoids the vet's glance. He is near to tears. Most readers of this passage will identify with him and share some of his grief.

Jacqui Durrell is more like James Herriot – animals come and go in her life: Whiskers is one of a number of animals to share her home. She, too, knows how to treat them professionally. She has an affectionate, amused view of Whiskers and his antics: 'Poor old Whiskers was given the shot.' (Compare how differently the expression 'the old fellow' in the first passage affects the reader.) Gerry's mother, however, like Mr Dean, has such a passion for animals that she treats them too tolerantly, allowing them to become totally "unmanageable'. There is a contrast between her and Mr Dean: his attitude is shown with approval, but the reader is made to feel that she is misguided: 'of course, this was entirely the wrong treatment.'

2. The passages are contrasted in mood. The first is mainly sad. The writer achieves this effect by the use of affectionate terms – 'the old dog's head', 'Bob', 'the old fellow', 'the loved voice', and in the way the bond between master and dog is shown to be threatened. The dog is helpless and at the mercy of the humans and, ironically, they must, as an act of kindness, kill it. The pathos of the old man is established in the description of his behaviour throughout, especially the strong feeling he shows. This pathos is increased by the stark and cheerless account of his environment. We see things through the eyes of the narrator, James Herriot, and share his compassionate mood as it grows; for example, he finds it difficult to open the discussion, and he speaks briskly but feels 'the old clichés had an empty ring'. The details of the final caress by the old man are sensitively observed and the contrast of the room, 'faded', 'cheerless', 'frayed', 'grimy', anticipate the bleakness the old man will feel when Bob has gone.

A great deal of the humour of the second passage results from the lively behaviour of the animals, and of Whiskers in particular. His name is comic as it reminds us of 'his enormous white moustache'. The reader is invited to share Gerry's amusement when he is bitten for his act of kindness, which is not appreciated. (Compare here the passive, and therefore pathetic, behaviour of Bob in a similar situation.) His size, 'a mere six inches', makes his ferocity and aggression seem funny. The list of his antics with Popadum, resembling those of very naughty children running riot, amuses, and the doting response of Gerry's mother, because it is so inappropriate, is humorous too. Looking closely at this part of the passage we are struck by the vitality of the language, full of exuberant action in such verbs as 'tore', 'rioted', and in the participles 'tearing', 'strewing'.

3. Evidence from the passages to support this statement can be found. Mr Dean definitely expresses his appreciation of Bob's companionship when he remarks: 'It's miserable when Bob isn't following me around the house when I'm doing my little jobs.' Man and dog have been together for a long time and Bob returns his master's regard by thumping his tail 'at the sound of the loved voice'. The reader is in no doubt at all, as the many references already given in this answer illustrate, that Mr Dean finds the thought of separation from his dog very painful. The positive side of this emotion is the love he feels, but it is clear, too, that having animals living with you is not always a 'lovely' thing. In the second passage we are told that 'Gerry had a passion' for animals and the couple usually had several living with them in their home, and that Gerry's mother indulged them like children, even allowing them to rest in her lap. This shows the pleasure of living with them. On the other hand, it is possible to form a very different opinion from the passage. The creatures are demanding and probably costly (the need for a vet's advice, for instance); they impose a routine upon the household, and readily create havoc and do quite a lot of damage. Finally, they are not always grateful for the attention of humans, and may reward them with a bite!

4. (Here you are asked for your personal opinion, so your answer will inevitably be different from mine, and everyone else's, to some extent.)

In the first passage a pet owner has noticed that his dog is ill. When the vet is called in he confirms that the dog has a terminal complaint and should be 'put to sleep'. The owner agrees, but is heart-broken. This made me remember an occasion when I was given a puppy as a Christmas present, fulfilling a wish that I had had for a very long time. It was tiny, beautiful and helpless. The house was full of people and activity because it was Christmas and the puppy scrambled about, amusing everyone with its antics. Suddenly it crawled, whimpering under a sofa: it was clearly hurt. When the vet came (after a long delay in which we helplessly watched the puppy suffering) he said that its back was seriously damaged and it would die in agony if he did not painlessly end its life. It was a terrible moment: the contrast between the special happiness of the gift on Christmas Day and the unexpected tragedy was almost too much to bear. I have never forgotten it.

On the other hand, being dominated by your pet is humiliating and annoying. In the second passage, Gerry's mother goes to endless trouble to prepare delicacies for the marmosets, and allows them to share her bedroom and even sit on her lap, but they begin to presume on her good nature and become 'unmanageable', 'rioting' and behaving mischievously, to the disapproval of the other adults in the household. I was similarly repaid for my care and doting affection for a stray cat. He quickly changed from a skinny, timid creature, hiding in the corner of the kitchen, to a huge over-fed monster, imposing his will on everyone. He demanded entry to all parts of the house, behaving in a very unpredictable fashion, and if he was thwarted, retaliated by tearing paper off the walls, among other things. Like the Durrells, I learned that it may not be wise to let the animal establish its own routine.

REVIEW SHEET

Here is some further practice in reading comprehension.

Read the following passage carefully and then answer the questions which follow.

"Obuechina Maduabuchi..."

Obu could not contain his joy as the headmaster read out his name. He jumped off the creaking bench on which he sat and dashed out of the school building. After displacing unrehearsed acrobatics on the uneven bahama lawn outside, he ran back to his seat sweating all over as he vibrated with excitement. He came top of Standard I in the end of year examinations,
5   thereby qualifying for the privileges generously conferred by the headmaster on all end-of-year 'firsts'; exemption from fetching firewood for teachers all through the first term of the ensuing school year. He was itching to gallop home to announce his distinguished achievement to his parents, and wished the headmaster could skip the remaining names and let him go.

Obuechina was the only boy out of seven children born to Mazi Lazarus Maduabuchi and his
10   wife. Little wonder they literally worshipped him and showered on him all the names they had been saving up for boys who never came. After the birth of their fifth daughter, the husband's family had intensified their pressure on him to marry another wife who could give him male issues. With Obu's arrival, his mother's place had been firmly secured; she could sleep in spite of thunder, no matter how many other wives her husband decided to take. The memorable
15   event - Obu's arrival - had fallen nearly nine years back - in January 1934. Hopes of having a second boy disappeared when, a little over two years later, Mama Obu gave birth to another daughter, Amuche (no one knows God's mind).

Obu's distinguishing features were a large head, which his parents believed carried a giant-sized brain for outstanding scholarship, and a diminutive nose which seemed to have been
20   stuck to his face as an afterthought. The nose had earned him the nickname 'when the war is over', implying that a larger nose would be ordered for him at the end of World War II when all rationing would have ended. His head swung from side to side on a torso that was so thin proportionately that he sometimes reminded you of a tadpole. His legs gradually straightened as he grew older, but a rugby football or a fluted pumpkin could still pass between them when
25   he stood to attention. His father had started off with such legs, which straightened with time and contributed to his impressive height.

Obu's mother, popularly called Mama Obu as if she had no other children, was about to leave for the market when the children came home. Giving birth to seven children had not taken much out of her; at the age of forty she could clip ten years off her age and no one would disbelieve
30   her. There was nothing superfluous about her - average height, an athletic body that was slender without being thin. Two rows of tattoo marks ran parallel to each other from her chest to her navel, and sideways from each corner of the mouth, terminating just short of a crater-sized dimple.

"Mama! Mama!" Obu shouted from the gate leading into the compound.
35   "I'm here, Obiano," his mother replied. She could tell from the boy's excitement that he had passed his examination. She carefully arranged the pumpkins she was taking to the market for sale inside her long basket, smacked the sand off the palms of her hands and moved towards Obu's voice. Obu ran to her, shouting: "Mama! I've passed! I came first in the whole class!"

"What did you say?" Mama Obu spoke as if she did not believe him.
40   "I came first in the whole class, Ma!"

She lifted him up with amazing ease, considering the weight of his head, pressed him to her chest and then lowered him: "Obiano, my son, well done. Well done. Thanks be to God."

She went to the kitchen and pulled down the large basket hanging over the fireplace. From it she tore off a large piece of smoked fish and stuffed it into Obu's mouth. She also tore off a larger piece from the dried meat and handed it to him, advising him to eat that with palm oil and
50   pepper.

Ogechukwa, one of his sisters, sneaked in, weeping as if she had broken a precious pitcher at the stream. Mama Obu asked her superfluously whether she had failed. She replied with a crescendo of weeping. The weeping only stopped when Ogechukwa saw that her mother was too engrossed with Obu to take notice of her penitent sobs.

55   "I'd always maintained that this big head contained nothing but brain for book work," Mama Obu teased Obu. "That was why your father and I did not take you seriously when at the age of five you said you did not want to go to school..."

As she packed her basket for the market, she recounted Obu's earlier refusal to go to school. That was nearly four years ago. It was a story she had told many times over. She repeated it
60   every time Obu excelled in an examination or his teacher extolled his academic ability. Yet on each occasion she told the story as if she had never told it before. Now it did not matter to her that she did not have an audience.

In the following questions, when you are asked to use your own words, you should not copy substantial phrases from the text.

1 In your own words state what visible evidence there was that Obu 'could not contain his joy' (line 1).

_____

_____

2 Why was Obu impatient for school to be dismissed?

_____

_____

3 What evidence is there of this impatience?

_____

_____

4 Explain the meaning of the statement 'With Obu's arrival his mother's place had been firmly secured' (lines 13)

_____

_____

5 What evidence is there that Obu's physique was weak?

_____

_____

6 Quote one word to show that the change in Obu's appearance had taken place over a period of time.

_____

7 From the passage quote one word which shows that Obu's mother did not appear as excited as he was when he first called to her.

_____

8 In the context of the passage, explain what is meant by 'had not taken much out of her' (line 28–29).

_____

_____

9 Why is Mama Obu's question to Ogechukwa described as 'superfluous' (line 52)?

_____

_____

10 Explain the meaning of the following words as used in the passage:

showered (line 10) _____

fallen (line 15) _____

extolled (line 60) _____

11 Why should Obu's mother repeat the story of his not wanting to go to school 'every time he excelled in an examination or his teacher extolled his academic ability' (lines 60–61)

_____

_____

_____

12 Imagine you are Ogechukwa. Write down your thoughts at the end of the day, describing what happened and how you felt. Write about 150 words.

FROM READING TO WRITING

WRITING DOWN YOUR FIRST RESPONSE

USING A FLOW-CHART

ASKING YOURSELF QUESTIONS

GOING FROM FIRST TO FINAL DRAFT

GETTING STARTED

There are many ways in which you can use your reading by writing a response which shows creativity in your coursework. This chapter is about exploring and developing what you read: ideas, themes, aspects, can be taken further, giving you the opportunity to be imaginative or creative, rather than to study in detail the exact meaning of what is read.

The following is a list of some of the types of writing you might do, stimulated by reading of different kinds:

- Suppose you have read two short stories on the same theme, but different in style. Discuss what makes them different and how they compare to any experiences you have had of this kind.
- Read a play and imagine you are one of the characters. Write about what you think of events with hindsight, looking back some years later. Take a story you know and like and consider producing it on television. Which episodes would you want to choose to make the greatest impression on an audience? What would you need to leave out? Would you want to add extra characters or incidents? What difficulties do you think you might meet as a producer?
- After reading a novel, write a review of it, to encourage someone else to read and enjoy it.

You can write on some of these topics immediately, using your own thoughts and feelings. For others, you might need to get more information – do some research. There are ideas for writing in most of what you read, if you are looking out for them.

ESSENTIAL PRINCIPLES

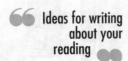

The kinds of writing already discussed in this chapter vary a good deal. For all of them, though, you need to bear certain things in mind. First, you should find something in what you read that will really make you want to write and sustain a response. Then, your first enthusiasm and interest should carry over into the writing you do. Next, take time to think about what you have read: let ideas develop in your mind. When you are ready to start writing, work out some possible approaches on paper. Your writing will probably be more successful if you work through one or more drafts before coming to the final version. Some practical ways of going about writing from your reading are dealt with below.

> **Ideas for writing about your reading**

1 WRITING DOWN YOUR FIRST RESPONSE

To help you prepare to write there are a number of useful skills you can acquire. Capturing your *first* response on paper can be very useful when you come to write. If you make a few notes, you can read them to refresh your memory, but they must be notes that will bring the first experience of reading back to life for your.

Remember to

> **First thoughts are worth noting**

- keep notes short – you don't want to paraphrase the book
- use your own words
- keep your notes well spaced, so that you can make additions later.

2 USING A FLOW-CHART

Some people prefer to make a *flow-chart*. By doing this they can keep their options open, and let their ideas flow for a longer period before they become set into a fixed form. Figure 10.1 is a flow-chart made by a boy preparing to write after reading Harper Lee's *To Kill a Mocking Bird*. He wanted to write about prejudice in the story and began by putting his ideas down quickly as they came to him.

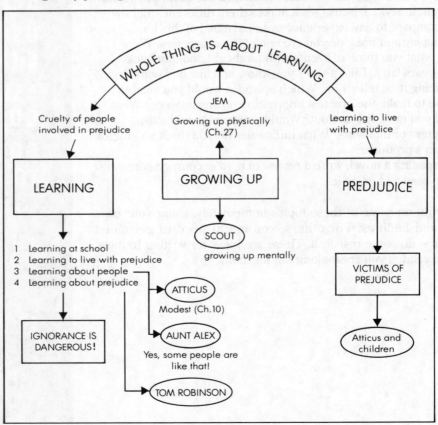

If you make a chart, it is a good idea to discuss it with a friend, or make one as a group.

You may sometimes be given a definite writing assignment based on a book or extracts, but at other times be in an 'open' situation where you decide what you write. To get started, then, it may be helpful *to ask yourself a question* which interests you, e.g. in the example above, the boy may well have asked himself: 'Which characters show prejudice in this novel?' He may have gone on from there to his flow-chart and a plan, and so reached the point of writing a first draft.

Drafting a piece of coursework is another important skill to acquire. You write a first version, or 'draft' as it is called, following your notes, flow-chart or plan, and then you read it through and make alterations, improving the arrangement and wording, the spelling and punctuation. Here are two examples of how the piece of work on Prejudice grew from first to final draft.

This was the first draft the boy wrote:

GROWING UP

1   This book is basically about a childhood which vanishes. It involves learning and prejudice both subjects having strong links with each other. It involves Jem and Scout Finch, who are brought up into a world of prejudice, racial and otherwise. They have a lot to learn, for ignorance is dangerous.

2   They are growing up amongst blacks. They feel slightly uncomfortable, I think, but Scout at least shows no real sign of prejudice. There is a lot of difference between the two races, which can be seen when the children visit Calpurnia's Church in Chapter twelve, when the author says 'Negroes worshipped in it on Sundays and white men gambled in it on weekdays', and before the trial of Tom Robinson when Jem said 'around here once you have a drop of Negro blood, that makes you all black'.

3   They also have to learn about prejudice and people. Scout is prejudiced against the Ewells, because of the way in which they made them lose the court case. They are prejudiced against Mrs Duboise, because they do not know her well enough to form any real conclusive view of her, until she is dead. They have to learn about people like Aunt Alexandria, who plays quite an important part in her growing up, although they do not realise it. They have to learn to control their prejudices, like the one against Boo Radley, where it is not until the end of the book that they form any reasonable conclusion on Boo Radley.

4   There are a very wide range of characters in the book, several of which Scout is unreasonably prejudiced against at first, like Boo Radley, Mrs Duboise and Tom Robinson. However, she does not know her father very well. She thinks of him as rather senile, and a bit cracked, taking on the court case, which she is not very enthusiastic. She is not experienced enough with people to know her father very well. She does not perceive his modesty, and will not let anyone know too much about him. She is immensely pleased in chapter ten when Atticus shoots the mad dog with incredible accuracy. Her view of a father is 'someone to boast about in school' because, as Scout herself says after the incident: 'Ain't everybody's daddy the deadest shot in Maycomb County!'

5   The children are victims of prejudice, which is imposed by Atticus defending Tom Robinson. He is branded a traitor in his elder circles, which penetrates even Scout's social life and she is called names; for example, when her cousin Francis says that Atticus is 'ruinin' the family' by being 'nothin' but a nigger-lover'. This is another 'fact of life', and he intentionally did this in Maycomb County, and an example of the cruelty of the people in those days of the depression, when men have to hate someone, so they hate those of another race. Prejudice is essentially a preconceived idea of someone without any solid evidence. It can be between sexes, classes (esp. England) religion, race, appearance and politics. As I have already said, the main victims of prejudice in this book are: Mrs Duboise, Atticus, Scout and Jem Finch, the Ewells, who bring back their own prejudice, and Tom

Robinson.

6   The two children are not growing up in exactly the same way; Scout is growing mentally more than anything, and Jem, who is thirteen, is growing more physically. Dill, Scout's 'future fiancé', is a very important topic in Scout's maturity, because he impresses on her a more ladylike manner, which shows that she has grown up from her tomboy days in first grade, when she was always fighting and doing the wrong thing. Dill is becoming more masculine towards the end of the book, when he runs away from his 'new' father to join Scout, which is a very fanciful but interesting story. He had matured into a young gentleman since they had first met him, and had helped Scout mature in the same way. However she is still pleasantly, maybe even helpfully, innocent, which is shown when she and Jem walk into the circle of men surrounding her father, and asks Mr Cunningham about his entailment, and tells him how his son does at school. If she was four years older, she would never have done that thing, but in her innocent questions she was uncovering something very important about her character. She, one eight-year-old child, could bring a whole crowd of grown men to their senses. 'Hmp, maybe we need a police force of children ...' said Atticus.

7   One of the major parts in the story was played by Tom Robinson. When the truth is discovered about him (even though it is to no avail in a court of law), Scout realises the error in having preconceived ideas about black people. As she has lived all her life among blacks, she knows them, and should not feel prejudiced towards them. However, there is still a childish misconception in her mind, and a secret dislike for Negroes after what she had been through. But Tom Robinson was different. He seems nice, innocent of the disgusting crime which he is accused of having done, and he tries to make the people like him, although knows that he cannot succeed because he is black. He is honest, and when asked whether he could have raped Mayella, says yes. He is also a very strong man, and he wanted to escape very much. This gives Scout a very different view of him, and of the whole subject of prejudice.

This was the final version:

GROWING UP in *To Kill a Mockingbird*

This book is basically about a childhood which vanishes. It involves learning and prejudice, both of which are strongly connected. It is about Jem and Scout Finch, and Atticus, their father. The children are brought up in a strongly prejudiced world, both racially and otherwise, on which subject they have a lot to learn, because ignorance is dangerous.

They are growing up amongst Negroes, who they have lived with all their lives. They seem unintentionally prejudiced towards them, but it is not a strong feeling of dislike, as towards other characters in the book. There is a great deal of difference between the two races, which is evident when the children visit First Purchase Church with Calpurnia, 'where Negroes worshipped on Sundays, and white men gambled on weekdays'. It is also obvious before Tom Robinson's trial when Jem says 'around here, once you have a drop of Negro blood, that makes you all black'.

They also have to learn about prejudice and people. Scout is prejudiced against the Ewell family, partly because of the way in which they inhabit the Maycomb rubbish tip, and partly because of the way that their lies affected the court case, and helped to convict Tom Robinson. She is also prejudiced against Mrs Duboise, and the way in which she speaks and acts towards the children, but she does not know her well enough and does not have enough experience with people to form any conclusive view of her, until she is dead. She teaches them a lesson not to retaliate without thinking. They have to learn about people like Aunt Alexandra, and to control their prejudices, like those against Boo Radley, because it is not until the end of the book that they form any reasonable judgement on him.

The children are victims of prejudice, imposed by Atticus defending Tom Robinson. He is branded a traitor by his friends and family, and this means that the children are called names, e.g. when their cousin Francis says to Scout that her father is 'ruinin' the family' by being 'nothin' but a nigger-lover'. This aspect is important because it means that the children can learn what it is like to be victimised, and it is a fact of life which Atticus is very eager for them to learn. In fact, it is reasonable to suggest that he took up the court case for one reason that the children could learn this very important fact. The story is set during the depression; times were hard and men had to hate someone, so they picked people of another race. Prejudice is essentially a preconceived idea of someone without any solid evidence. It can be between sexes, classes (especially in England) religions, races, appearances and politics. As I have already stated, the main victims of prejudice in this book are: Mrs Duboise, Atticus, Scout and Jem Finch, the Ewells (who seem to bring back their own prejudice), and Tom Robinson.

The two children are not growing up in exactly the same way; Scout is growing mentally more than anything, and Jem is reaching puberty, and growing more physically. Dill, Scout's 'future fiancé', is a very important aspect of Scout's maturation and helps to change her from a tomboy in first grade, when she was forever fighting and doing the wrong thing, to a more ladylike girl aged ten. Dill himself is becoming more masculine towards the end of the book, when he runs away from his 'new' father to join Scout (a very fanciful but interesting story). He has matured into a young gentleman since they had first met him. Scout, however, is still innocent of the reasoning of men, which is exemplified when she walks straight into the circle of men outside the county jail to be next to her father, and asks Mr Cunningham, who meant business, and not to be played up by eight-year-old girls, about his entailment, and tells him how his son Walter is getting on in school. If she was four years older, she would never have done this, but in her questions she was uncovering something very important about her character, and the character of any child at that age; the innocent, purposeful attitude of the girl, and the don't-take-no-for-an-answer personality. If she, one eight-year-old child, could bring a crowd of grown men to their senses, then as Atticus says, 'Maybe we need a police force of children!'

There is a very wide range of characters in this book, some of which Scout is prejudiced against at first. There is her father, whom she does not seem to know very well. She thinks of him as being rather senile at times, and maybe even a bit crazy, taking on the court case in the way that he does.

She does not have enough experience to perceive his modesty, his strange methods, like making Jem go and apologise to Mrs Duboise, knowing full well that he might have had his head blown off, his experience in life, and his being a good father. His modesty, not letting anyone know about his talents, is important. She is very pleased in chapter ten when Atticus shoots the mad dog with incredible accuracy, because, as Scout herself says, 'Ain't everybody's daddy the deadest shot in Maycomb Country!'

One of the most important parts of the story is played by Tom Robinson when the truth is discovered about him (even though it was to no avail in a court of law), Scout realises the error in having preconceived ideas about anybody. As she has lived all her life among blacks, she knows them, and should not feel prejudiced in any way towards them. However, there is still a childish misconception in her mind, and a secret dislike for negroes. But Tom is different. He seems nice, innocent, incapable of the disgusting crime which he is alleged to have committed, and he tries to make the white people like him, but knows that he cannot succeed because he is black. He is honest in Scout's mind, and strong, and all these factors combine to give Scout a very different view of prejudice.

A similar example is that of Boo Radley, Scout simply bases her evidence that he is mad on tales told to her by the neighbours. But it really seems that he is a bit mad and childish, but he needs someone to exhort him. Scout knows so little about him, that it is not until the very end of 'To Kill a Mockingbird' that she realises that she had given Boo nothing in return for his kindness, and she deeply regrets it. Boo Radley played another very important part, even more than Tom Robinson, in giving Scout a final opinion on the folly of prejudice.

 A final version

Notice how several changes have been made – e.g.. the original fourth paragraph moved to later in the piece – until the boy was satisfied with his version.

EXAMINATION QUESTIONS

All Groups will require candidates to show examples of their written response to a variety of reading materials. **NEAB** (Syllabus B), **MEG** and **SEG** require coursework of the kind considered in this chapter, and **NEAB** (Syllabus A) has similar questions in its written paper (see an example below). You may find you have several pieces of coursework of the right sort to choose from for your examination folder; try to choose a piece or pieces which show that you can:

- fully understand what you read
- clearly convey your thoughts and feelings about it
- select what is relevant
- organise your writing effectively.

Here is a question typical of the kind you might choose to write on.

QUESTION 1

Choose a story you like and write a review of it, so that someone of your own age would know whether he or she would be likely to enjoy it.

Try to think how you would attempt this assignment before going on to the Outline Answers below. Choose a story and make some notes, or a flow-chart, ready for a first attempt at a draft.

The next question represents the type of reading-into-writing opportunities to be found in written papers.

QUESTION 2

In this question a passage and a comprehension exercise, using more closed questions, will already have been attempted by candidates. Read the two extracts carefully, then consider how you would answer Section B here.

SECTION A
*Read the following extracts and then answer **ALL** the questions which follow.*

Passage 1

Going to the shore on the first morning of the holiday, the young English boy stopped at a turning of the path and looked down at a wild and rocky bay, and then over to the crowded beach he knew so well from other years. His mother walked on in front of him carrying a bright-striped bag in one hand. Her other arm, swinging loose, was very white in the sun. The boy watched that white, naked arm, and turned his eyes, which had a frown behind them, towards the bay and back again to his mother. When she felt he was not with her, she swung round. 'Oh, there you are, Jerry!' she said. She looked impatient, then smiled. 'Why, darling, would you rather not
10   come with me? Would you rather ...' She frowned, worrying over what amusements he might secretly be longing for which she had been too busy or too careless to imagine. He was very familiar with that anxious, apologetic smile. His concern sent him running after her. And yet, as he ran, he looked back over his shoulder at the wild bay; and all morning as he played on the safe beach, he was thinking of it.

Next morning, when it was time for the routine of swimming and sunbathing, his mother said: 'Are you tired of the usual beach, Jerry? Would you like to go somewhere else?'

'Oh, no!' he said quickly, smiling at her, feeling guilty that he was neglecting
20   her. Yet, walking down the path with her, he blurted out, 'I'd like to go and have a look at those rocks down there.'

She gave the idea her attention. It was a wild-looking place, and there was no-one there, but she said: 'Of course, Jerry. When you've had enough, come to the big beach. Or just go straight back to the villa, if you like.' She walked away, that bare arm, now slightly reddened from yesterday's sun, swinging. And he almost ran after her again, feeling it unbearable that she should go by herself, but he did not.

She was thinking: 'Of course he's old enough to be safe without me. Have I been keeping him too close? He mustn't feel he ought to be with me. I must be careful.'

30

He was an only child, eleven years old. She was a widow. She was determined to be neither possessive nor lacking in devotion. She went worrying off to her beach.

As for Jerry, once he saw that his mother had gained her beach, he began the steep decent to the bay. From where he was, high up among red-brown rocks, it was a scoop of moving bluish green fringed with white. As he went lower, he saw that it spread among small promontories and inlets of rough, sharp rock, and the crisping, lapping surface showed stains of purple of darker blue. Finally, as he ran sliding and scraping down the last few yards,

40

he saw an edge of white surf, and the shallow, luminous movement of water over white sand, and, beyond that, a solid heavy blue.

He ran straight into the water and began swimming. He was a good swimmer.He went out fast over the gleaming sand, over a middle region where rocks lay like discoloured monsters under the surface, and then he was in the real sea – a warm sea where irregular cold currents from the deep water shocked his limbs.

When he was so far out that he could look back not only on the little bay but past the promontory that was between it and the big beach, he floated on the surface and looked for his mother. There she was, a speck of yellow under

50

an umbrella that looked like a slice of orange peel. He swam back to shore, relieved at being sure she was there, but all at once very lonely.

(Adapted from *Through the Tunnel* by Doris Lessing)

In the following extract the narrator tells us how he prepared to move from his junior school to the secondary grammar school which was some distance from his home. He also tells us how he felt about the change.

Passage 2

All this was during a time which seemed carefree and radiant when I looked back afterwards in such longing, from the middle of my misery. I was still at my first school when I had the bicycle. Then I sat for a scholarship to go to a secondary school. We were given clean squares of pink blotting-paper and pens of unpainted wood with bright nibs which had never dipped in the ink. I sat with a big space around me, tense with fear and importance, trying to breathe properly.

My father had to fill in a long questionnaire asking if he would be prepared to pay for my uniform and books, and I think it was more than he could manage.

10

Everything for that place had extra shillings on it. There were anxious discussions which I was not supposed to hear.

In the summer holidays my mother took me to buy a new cap and tie, and the badge of Memorial Road School for my jacket. The colours were purple and grey, and the badge was just a large 'M' in a purple frame. After that we went to the bus station and set out to find the school itself.

I remember us getting off the bus and twisting through several streets in a quiet district where everything was strange, going over some black dirt near a small park where there was a sand-pit for playing in, climbing slowly most of the time.

20 Suddenly at the top of the road all I could see was a line of railings made from metal tubes, like scaffolding. There was only sky behind it, and I cried out: 'It's like the seaside!' I knew it was impossible for a promenade and the sea to be up there, but I started pulling my mother along, making her walk faster, till we reached the top.

It was a large piece of flat common, dropping gently, with no buildings until a low factory began, behind a line of poplars that seemed a long way off. To the right and left there were houses and streets, but I looked straight out, as I would have done at the edge of the sea. 'That's where Uncle Jim works,' my mother said. She pointed at the unreal factory, glinting innocently behind the far-off trees.

30 We had come a little out of our way. An old man directed us back downhill to our right, and soon we stood in front of a grim, high building that reminded me of the city hospital. It was so large, so forbidding, that I could not imagine myself going there. Because it conveyed nothing I was quite brave, standing beside my mother staring across the queer blankness of the tarmac playground at the dead school with its rows of blind windows. There were three more weeks of holiday before I had to face the first day. My mother murmured: 'You'll be all right,' and the words, or perhaps the anxiety that had crept into her voice, gave me a twinge of uneasiness. I was not really worried until then. I tried to pretend she had spoken without thinking, for something to say, and was not comforting me.

40 We found our bus stop and went home. It was Friday, which meant fish-cakes and home-made chips for tea, with moist new bread. I always looked forward to Fridays.

When the first Monday was still a week away a little fear came into me. Instead of dying it grew stronger, until by the Sunday it was a dread. The next day I would have to go, there was no escape, no way out, and in my despair I felt I should never trust my parents again. They had betrayed me, trapped me in some terrible sly way. I did not stop to think that I would have had to leave my old school in any case, because I was too old to stay there. I only knew I was being wrenched out of a place where I was rooted and happy, though I had never realised it before.

50 Somehow I managed to get up next day, eat some breakfast and then put on the blazer and cap with their hateful badges. But as my mother held open the back gate and I wheeled my bicycle through dumbly, I saw by her face that she understood.

'Never mind, you'll soon be home,' she said hopelessly. 'The first day's always the worst.'

(Adapted from *Native Ground* by Philip Callo)

Answer ALL the questions.

Questions on the first passage

1 Look at lines 1–15. How do you think Jerry regarded his mother and his relationship with her?

2 In your own words, write down the thoughts and feelings of Jerry's mother, which are suggested by lines 16–33.

3 a) Describe in your own words the main features of the 'wild bay'.
   b) Using quotation and/or reference, explain what you think Jerry's reaction was to swimming in the 'wild bay' separated from his mother.

Questions on the second passage

4 Look at lines 1–7. What were the boy's feelings at the thought of leaving his junior school?

5 Look at lines 29–38. How does the writer suggest that the boy disliked the appearance of his new school?

6 In your own words, explain what you understand by the following:
  a) 'There were anxious discussions which I was not supposed to hear' (lines 10–11).
  b) 'The next day I would have to go, there was no escape, no way out, and in my despair I felt I should never trust my parents again' (lines 43–45).
  c) 'I only knew I was being wrenched out of a place where I was rooted and happy' (lines 47–48).
7 By referring to the passage, describe the impression you get of the home life of the boy and his relations with his parents.

SECTION B

Choose **ONE** *of the following, and write 350–600 words.*
Credit will be given for your ability to describe scenes, people, thoughts and feelings and for your choice of words.

1 Write about the return of Jerry and his mother to their villa that evening. You may, if you wish, write as if you are **either** Jerry **or** his mother or you may write a play script.

2 With reference to the second passage, describe the boy's first day at his new school in such a way as to bring out his feeling about what happens to him.

3 Write an account of a visit to the seaside you made with your parents. You may write in any way you like but you might like to try writing about a time when you were younger and particularly enjoyed new challenges such as swimming, climbing on the rocks, or going out in a boat; **or** you might like to write around the idea of being lost, or cut off by the tide. The account can be real or imaginary.

4 The second extract is all about the fears and worries that build up in people when they have to face something new and unknown, like going to a new school, or having an operation; even going to the dentist, or to a party if you do not know many people.
  Write about something **you** worried about a lot. If you like, you can include both what you felt **before** the event, and what it was really like when it happened.

[MEG]

OUTLINE ANSWERS

ANSWER 1

There are as many answers as there are books to review and readers to respond. Even so a good book review has to keep a balance between saying something true about the book's contents – enough to interest but not so much that the reader feels there is no need to go on to the book itself – and offering a fresh and individual response. The main problem with the first requirement is the temptation that some reviewers have to summarise the plot at great length, losing the mood and vitality of the original work and boring the reader. One way round this is to choose one or two key incidents that will attract or intrigue, and offer them as tasters. You might begin with a striking quotation, highlighting one of these incidents. Again, avoid listing characters with just a sentence of description. Think of ways of saying something about them that will arouse interest, leaving the reader wishing to find out more. Your own response is an equally important part of a review. It can be negative, but there is a chance that you will write a less successful review of a book you dislike (if you are trying to be fair) than of one you really enjoy. Additional details worth including are comments on other books of a similar type that you would recommend, or other books by the same author. Finally, a bright review cover, with a picture or design that sums up for you something important about the book as well as showing clearly the author and title, is a good idea.

A pupil's answer to Question 1 is given on page 135.

ANSWER 2

Here are outline answers to the questions set on the two passages in Section A.

Passage One

1 There is clearly some anxiety about his mother, indicated by his frown, and the concern which sent him running to her. He was familiar with her gestures and ways, and felt more secure when he was with her.

2 Using your own words, you can touch on her concern to give Jerry some independence from herself, yet her worry that he be safe and well. She wanted him to know he was loved, yet not to overdo it so that he felt her too possessive.

3 a) The bay was surrounded by high, red-brown rocks. There were bits of sharp rock here and there, some peeping above the water line, with white surf at the waters edge. Beneath the water was white sand and further out, as the water became deeper, the colour became a deeper blue.
   For three marks only some of these points need be mentioned, using your own way of expression.

   b) Clearly there is an element of excitement and pleasure, indicated by how he ran straight into the water and the speed with which he swam out from the shore. There was still a concern for his mother's welfare, indicated by his looking for her even as he was floating on the surface of the water. This concern is re-inforced by the words 'relieved at being sure she was there'. He also felt lonely at being separated from her.

Passage Two

4 His feelings included a sense of importance at having the opportunity to take a scholarship to go to the grammar school. There was also fear, perhaps of the exam itself and of the thought of going to a new and unfamiliar environment, should he pass. He was very happy at his original school, as indicated by the first sentence.

5 The use of the words 'grim', and the likening of the school to a 'city hospital', indicate that the boy disliked the appearance of the new school. This is followed by other words and expressions which suggest dislike, 'forbidding', 'blankness of the tarmac playground', 'dead school', 'blind windows', etc.

6 a) The parents were discussing the cost of sending their son to the expensive new school, and were clearly worried as to whether they could afford it. However they did not wish their son to be aware of these financial problems, but somehow he had overheard them.

   b) The next day was the Monday, the first day at his new school. It was certain that Monday would come, no matter how much he wished it would not, so there was no escape from his dread of going to the new school. He was extremely cross with his parents; he saw it as their fault that he had to leave the happy, familiar primary school and go to the unknown school that had looked so forbidding on his first visit to it.

   c) He couldn't understand the educational system and why children had to change schools at certain ages. What he *did* know was that he was being forced to leave a school in which he had been happy and contented, and at which he had become familiar with all its ways.

7 There are many possibilities here. Remember to *use* the passage as evidence for the points you make about the home life of the boy and his relations with his parents.

In Section B you are invited to write on one topic only. You will see that the four topics are of two kinds: those (1 and 2) which are directly related to the passage read, and those (3 and 4) where you are quite free to respond imaginatively in an individual way.

If you find personal writing difficult, probably one of the first two questions would be the better choice, as you have the material in the passage to give you a start. Even if you enjoy personal writing, the passages will help, if you choose 3 or 4, because your mind will be filled with thoughts of taking up a challenge, struggling to achieve something new or facing a worrying, new experience. Notice that suggestions are made here to help you think along relevant lines from the start.

A PUPIL'S ANSWER TO QUESTION 1

ANSWER 1

Here is an answer to Question 1 above, written by a pupil. The book reviewed is *It's My Life* by Robert Leeson.

A Book Review
Book It's My Life

author Robert Leeson

It's My Life is about a fifteen-year-old girl called Janice who has a lot of trouble to take care of when her mother leaves her father, her brother and her. The reason for this, no one knew. Janice had a lot of trouble also because she had been asked out and wasn't sure of what to say. She told the boy that she would go out with him and they made a date. When Janice came home she couldn't go because her father said that Friday was his night out and that she would have to stay home and look after her brother. Janice got annoyed and didn't turn up which annoyed her very much.

Janice went to try and get a job but the interviewer recognised Janice as Janice's mother used to work there, and told her that he would contact her. Janice had to go to another interview to see if she could get a job. The interviewer told Janice that he told her that her mother left on a train (he didn't know where) because she couldn't take the strain any longer.

You could tell that Janice's mother was up to something when Janice came home and found the kitchen stored up with food. (Valerie stored up the kitchen with food to last her husband, son and daughter for a while.)

I didn't really have a favourite character as I didn't enjoy the book much. I found the book boring and hard to concentrate on because I don't really read books like this. The type of book I like reading is The Pedestrian by Ray Bradbury. They are interesting. I also like adventures, horror and romantic books. The best I like are short stories as I can finish them in one go.

Examiner Comments

The writer has chosen a book that she has read right through and to which she has a definite response, even though it is not one of approval. She has given the title and author clearly at the start. Then she has written three paragraphs giving an account of the story, but the best of these is the third, where an incident is retold, conveying the actual feel of the book. She has given her opinion of the quality of the book in the fourth paragraph. It is rather a pity that she did not really enjoy it: she would almost certainly have had more to say if she had liked it. She concentrates instead on other, similar books she knows about. Overall the result is a little unbalanced; ideally, more space should have been given to evaluation. However, despite the errors, this is a readable review, with sufficient detail to make a reader want to go on to the book itself.

R E V I E W   S H E E T

 You can practice some of the skills involved in analysing a passage before writing about it by first reading the following passage and then answering the questions which follow.

1   For every type of animal there is a most successful size, and a large change of size inevitably carries with it a change of form. Let us take an obvious case, and imagine a giant man, sixty feet tall. This monster would be not only ten times normal height but ten times as wide and ten times as thick, so that his total weight would be a thousand times greater, or about eighty to ninety tons. Unfortunately, the cross-sections of his bones would be only a hundred times larger so that every square inch of giant bone would have to support ten times the weight borne by a square inch of human bone. As the human thigh-bone breaks under about ten times the human weight, giants would have broken their thighs at the first step.

2   Suppose that a gazelle, a graceful little creature with long thin legs were to become large. It would break its bones unless one of two things happened. Its legs must become short and thick like those of the rhinoceros, so that every pound of weight has still about the same area of bone to support it; or its body must be compressed with legs stretching out obliquely to gain stability like the giraffe's. I mention these two beasts because they happen to belong to the same order as the gazelle, and are both quite successful mechanically being remarkably fast runners.

3   To the mouse and any smaller animal, gravity presents practically no dangers. You can drop a mouse down a thousand yard mine shaft and, on arriving at the bottom, it gets a slight shock and walks away. A rat would be killed, a man broken, a horse smashed to pieces. For the resistance presented to movement by the air is proportional to the surface of the moving object. Divide an animal's length, breadth and height by ten; its weight is reduced to a thousandth but its surface only to a hundredth. So the resistance to falling in the case of the smaller animal is ten times the driving force.

4   An insect, therefore, is not afraid of gravity: it can fall without danger, and can cling to the ceiling with remarkably little trouble. It can have elegant slender forms of support. But there is a force which is as formidable to an insect as gravity is to a mammal. This is surface tension. A man coming out of a bath carries with him a film of surface water of about one-fiftieth of an inch in thickness. This weighs about a pound. A wet mouse has to carry about its own weight of water. A wet fly has to lift many times its own weight and, as everyone knows, a fly once wetted by water or any other liquid is in a very serious position indeed. An insect going for a drink is in as great danger as a man leaning out over a precipice in search of food. If it once falls into the grip of the surface tension of the water - that is to say, gets wet - it is likely to remain so until it drowns. A few insects, such as water-beetles, contrive to be unwettable; the majority drink at a safe distance by means of a long proboscis.

5   But it is time that we passed to some of the advantages of size. One of the most obvious is that it enables one to keep warm. All warm-blooded animals at rest lose the same amount of heat from a unit area of skin, therefore they need a food supply proportional to their surface area and not to their weight. Five thousand mice weigh as much as a man, but their total surface area and their food consumption are about seventeen times a man's. In fact, a mouse eats about a quarter of its own weight in food every day, which is mainly used in keeping it warm. In the arctic regions, no small mammals occur naturally. The smallest mammal in Spitzbergen is the fox. The small birds fly away in the winter while the insects die, though their eggs can survive six months or more of frost. The most successful mammals in the arctic regions are the bears, seals and walruses.

(From *Possible Worlds and other Essays* (adapted) by J.B.S. Haldane)

1   Sum up in one sentence what the writer is arguing in this text.

_____

2   What is the topic sentence of each paragraph? (the topic sentence is the sentence which sums up the main idea of that paragraph).

1   _____

2   _____

3   _____

4   _____

5   _____

3   Mark the following ideas as primary '1', secondary '2' or not in the text 'X' according to the points which the writer is making (a primary idea is more important that a secondary idea).

_____ *a* Every kind of animal has its own ideal size.
_____ *b* Most very large people often break their thigh-bones.
_____ *c* A rhino can run as fast as a gazelle.
_____ *d* Gravity is not a problem for creatures the same size or smaller than mice.
_____ *e* When a person gets out of a bath he or she is carrying about a pound of water on their body.
_____ *f* Most insects drown very easily
_____ *g* Small mammals need to eat more proportional to their size than large ones.

4 Find *one* example of as many as possible of the following techniques in the text:

a illustrations or examples to support a general idea
_____

b analogy to clarify an abstract idea or compare a situation
_____

c quotation to lend force to a point made
_____

d metaphor or figurative language to lend force to an argument
_____

e questions to state the problem that the reader should consider
_____

f repetition to reinforce statement of view
_____

g contrast to emphasise or highlight a point
_____

h modification or refutation following statement of a point of view
_____

i definition to define a concept
_____

j listing to enumerate details
_____

k justification of a view through presentation of arguments
_____

l implied or inferred meaning to convey a point indirectly
_____

5 Underline all the words and phrases in the last two paragraphs which serve specifically to make links and connections between points the writer is making.

6 What do we learn about the attitude of the writer in this text?
_____
_____

7 a) Explain why a giant man, sixty feet tall would weight about a thousand times more than a normal man.

_____

   b) Explain why the legs of a rhinoceros are short and thick.

_____

   c) Why does gravity present little danger to a mouse but such great danger to a horse?

_____

8 In what ways are bears, seals and walruses successfully adapted to life in the Arctic?

_____

_____

9 In the Arctic summer, small birds and insects are common, yet there are no small mammals. Explain why this is so.

_____

SUMMARY

WRITING IN AN APPROPRIATE STYLE

SELECTING THE KEY IDEAS

ORGANISING THE KEY IDEAS

LENGTH

PRESENTATION

G E T T I N G   S T A R T E D

Writing a summary typically involves the following steps: reading through the material or listening to gather information, selecting important points that you want to bring out, writing those down in a suitable order, making a draft and writing a final, corrected version. In their written papers GCSE Groups will not usually ask candidates simply to write a summary, but nearly all will set questions and coursework exercises that require some form of task based on printed material for a particular purpose being put in order and then summarised, e.g. an extract from a guide book, a diary, two contrasting eye-witness accounts of the same situation, or extracts from a newspaper article. You may be given information in statistical form, too, occasionally.

The **National Criteria** state that in English candidates must be given opportunities to show that they can.

- understand and convey information
- understand, order and present facts, ideas and opinions
- evaluate information in reading material and in other media, and select what is relevant to specific purposes
- show a sense of audience and an awareness of style in both formal and informal situations.

ESSENTIAL PRINCIPLES

There are several very important things to get right in order to produce a good summary – that is, one that reflects correctly the facts and opinions in the material you are given, and which can be easily followed by the readers for whom it is intended.

66 Bear your readers in mind. 99

There are a number of *questions* to ask yourself at the outset:

- Who do I have in mind as the readers (sometimes called the 'audience') of this piece of writing?
- What sort of style will they respond to most readily?
- Which are the key ideas/opinions that I *have* to include?
- Which are the minor ideas/opinions that I *could* include?
- How long should I make it?
- How should I set the work out: in short paragraphs, columns, as a letter, etc.?

If you are given any instructions, read them carefully and think about the way you need to shape and present your summary, from the start.

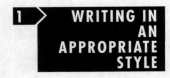
1 > WRITING IN AN APPROPRIATE STYLE

You may have to choose between a fairly formal style in Standard English, if you are writing a report or article, or a more relaxed style to suit, say, members of a youth club or readers of a local paper. In the second case, remember that this could include a wide range of readers, so keep your style generally 'reader friendly', without using slang or writing inaccurately. Good communication is directed *to* someone, so if you want your work to be readable by a particular group you need to find a style to suit them. It may help to try to imagine a typical member of the group you are addressing, and write for him or her.

2 > SELECTING THE KEY IDEAS

At first sight this may seem to be a matter of individual choice but, if you think about it, there are always certain key points which need to be brought out when considering any issue. These points may have details or minor arguments associated with them, of course, and opinions may differ as to how important the points might be. Sometimes you will have to think hard about what to leave out, but the effort should be made, since too many details produce a cluttered effect and make it hard for the readers to take in what you really want them to notice.

66 Go for key ideas 99

3 > ORGANIZING THE KEY IDEAS

How you do this depends on the material you are working with and the directions given. If you are asked to write from one point of view only, keep to that. If you are asked to write a balanced account, give each side about the same amount of space. Sometimes it is good to begin with the key ideas, to think them through so that you can state them clearly, then to write a series of short paragraphs expanding them. Alternatively, you might be able to put your details and minor points into linked sentences, then finish strongly with the key ideas. Another possibility is to contrast key ideas as you go, taking in the details. There are many ways of arranging material and none is necessarily the right one. Whatever you choose, remember to explore all relevant aspects of the topic as clearly as possible. In the following section you will find some techniques to help you to do this.

4 > LENGTH

66 How long *is* a summary? 99

How long is a summary? This is rather like saying 'How long is a piece of string?' The answer is 'As long as it needs to be'. But remember that if you are actually told what the work is to be – e.g. that it is to be a fact sheet, a letter, a pamphlet – you should be realistic and not write something which is obviously much too short or too long. If you are given a word limit, write **that** number of words or **fewer than the number of words asked. Exceeding word-limits usually results in a penalty.**

5 ▷ PRESENTATION Finally, and very important, you need to consider presentation. Most pieces of summary and directed writing need a heading of some kind. It may be a banner headline:

GOOD OLD DAYS RECALLED BY RISLEY SENIOR CITIZENS

or a catchy title

Guide Through the Jobs Jungle

– whatever it is, it should sum up the main topic in a few words.

Probably a piece of continuous writing in three or four paragraphs is the most usual form of presentation, but you may need to consider arrangement and lay-out features if, for instance, you are writing an article for a newspaper, a brochure or a pamphlet. Letters, of course, also have a special lay-out and varieties of style, depending on the degree of formality involved.

USEFUL PRACTICAL APPROACHES

There are a number of useful techniques to help you with summarising and directed writing. Suppose for a piece of coursework you decide to write a short guide book to your town to attract visitors of your own age. You could first look up the official guide book and gather some facts from it, selecting those that seem likely to be worth including. Next, these could be arranged in a form that would allow you to see at a glance the possible arrangements for your own guide. There are several ways of doing this:

a) Key ideas
You list key words or phrases in the most suitable order, e.g.

YOUNG RISLEY

Places to stay; Food; Sights; Sports; Fashion; After dark.

b) A flow-chart
You put down key headings and associated details in a series of circles, then link the circles by arrows. You can experiment with various links and cross-connections, as shown in Fig. 11.1.

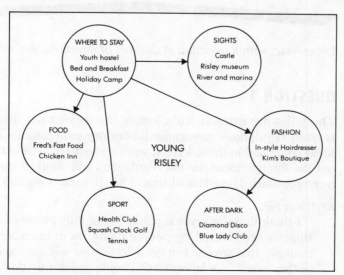

Fig. 11.1

c) A topic tree

You draw a tree-like structure, where each branch is a main idea and each twig a minor point, as shown in Fig. 11.2.

Why not try a topic tree?

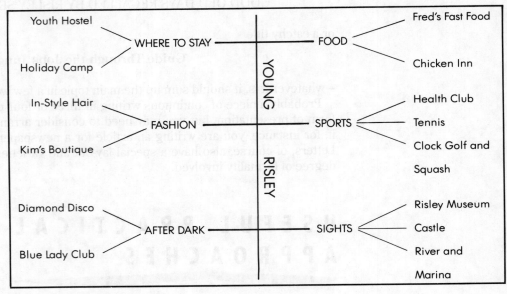

Fig. 11.2

d) Key questions

You list a series of questions you hope to find answers to, e.g.

YOUNG RISLEY

1 Where can visitors stay?
2 Where can visitors eat out?
3 Which sights of the town will appeal?
4 What sports are there?
5 What is on at night?

EXAMINATION QUESTIONS AND COURSEWORK TOPICS

Let us start with a selection of the sort of questions you might find in a written paper.

QUESTION 1

The following extracts from letters to a newspaper discuss the recently proposed revised regulations governing laboratory experiments on animals. Using only the ideas contained in these letters, write a short editorial in *two* paragraphs, one pointing out the limitations of the old regulations and another showing the advantages of the new proposals. The editorial should be approximately 200 words in length.

a) 'Dear Sir,

I think that the general public is not fully aware of the shocking way that many animals are treated by people using them in experiments. Do they know, for example, that anyone can get a licence for so-called 'scientific experiments', as long as they work in a laboratory? People apparently don't even have to say what the experiment is for. True, they are supposed to operate in suitable premises but who is checking up? There are only fifteen inspectors to cover the whole country. That may have been all right when there were only a few hundred experiments a year, but last year there were more than three million.

Animals can be obtained from more or less anywhere. No questions are asked. Some say it's a highly organised business collecting unwanted animals, strays, even the pet from your front lawn, for use in laboratories. There may well be a need for science to make use of animals to some extent to further knowledge, but it is high time that people thought of the rights of animals as well as their uses ...'

b) 'Dear Sir,

I have never written to you before but the letter I read last week about animal experiments made me sad. To think how these animals suffer. I've been told that over eighty per cent of experiments on live animals are done without anaesthetics. Then, when the scientists have found out what they want, the animals are killed.

Surely there must be other ways of getting this information. Why must animals always be used? Some one should put a stop to all this cruel treatment. I thought we were supposed to be a nation of animal lovers!'

c) 'Sir,

As a local councillor closely connected with the working party on the use and abuse of animals in laboratory experiments I should like to draw the attention of your readers to some of the ideas put forward for revising the regulations.

It is proposed that only properly qualified people should be granted a licence and only after details of the purpose and design of the experiments have been considered, and it has been made clear that no alternative to animals could do as well. These licences would be issued to individuals rather than to institutions. The use of strays would be stopped altogether. All animals used for research should come from properly registered agencies.

At the moment there are penalties for performing experiments without a licence – six months in prison, or a fine of up to £2000. We should like to see this increased to up two years in prison or an unlimited fine. We also want more inspectors, so that they could oversee what is going on – not just put their heads around the door of a laboratory.

Scientific enquiry depends on a continuing supply of animals, but as a humane society we must do our best to control conditions and limit animal suffering.

Over one point the committee seems in some doubt: they recommended that the "degree of pain an animal suffers should be balanced against the value of the experiment". Is that really an improvement over the old practice of uncontrolled pain while the experiment lasts?'

Here are some questions for summary and directed writing. Questions 2 and 3 should each take ¾ hour, and would carry 15% of the overall mark.

QUESTION 2

The following letter appeared in the *Belfast Telegraph*. Read it and using the correct letter format write a letter to the Editor, Belfast Telegraph, Belfast BT1 1EB, giving your response to the points raised.

Thugs run the streets

I am writing to inform you of events which occurred in Belfast City Centre on Saturday last. I hope that by bringing these matters to public attention something will be done to ensure that they do not occur again.

I brought my four-year-old daughter with me into town to do some shopping. As soon as we got off the bus we became aware of crowds of young people, both girls and boys of about 16 years old standing around corners and in the doorways of some shops. It was clear that some were in gangs of one kind or another by their dress, hairstyles and general behaviour. I was shocked when suddenly they began to run at each other; my daughter was knocked to the ground and, naturally, became very frightened by this stampede. She became quite hysterical and I had to call a policeman to assist us in getting back on to the bus.

This situation cannot be allowed to continue. Decent people cannot come into town while these thugs run the streets. The authorities will have to do something to keep young people off the streets. It is clear that young people of today lack common sense, maturity and consideration for others. Young people of my generation did not behave like this, possibly because their parents had control over them. If parents cannot control their children then it is up to the Government, the City Council and the Police. As a rate payer I demand that something should be done.

(Mrs) Joan White

QUESTION 3

The following are statements made by witnesses to a road accident, which occurred near a bus stop, in which a schoolgirl was knocked down by a car. Put yourself in the place of a policeman who has to write a factual report on what happened and who was responsible. Base the report on your interpretation of the information given by the witnesses.

A Mr John Black, aged 27 – Passer-by:
'The kid had no chance. The car came speeding up the inside lane, he was just trying to avoid the queue in the other lane. Next thing I knew was that the girl was lying across the bonnet of the Escort. You should have heard the screech of brakes.'

B Mr Peter White, aged 41 – Motorist:
'I was in the outside lane in the line of traffic. The lights were red for traffic travelling straight on along Main Street but the green filter light was on for traffic turning left up Station Road. The red Ford Escort was coming up the inside lane signalling to turn left when I saw the brake lights on and heard the screech.'

C Mr Jim Brown, aged 38 – Bus Driver:
'Those kids are the same every day. I'm surprised this has not happened before now. They are always running around, chasing each other. I was coming behind the car and I had to brake too. I was doing about 15 m.p.h. so I suppose the Escort was doing the same. He was signalling to go up Station Road. I didn't see the wee girl but there was a crowd of kids at the shop.'

D Susan Gray, aged 15 – Schoolgirl:
'It was about 4.15 pm and I was waiting for the bus as usual. Sharon wanted to buy sweets at the shop on the other side of the road. She looked around before stepping out. The red Escort AZB 392 just came from nowhere. The driver was sneaking up the inside lane because there was a line of cars waiting at the lights. I think it was shock more than anything but she went in the ambulance which I called. I wonder who is going to tell Mrs Green?'

QUESTION 4

Read the following newspaper article and then answer both (a) **and** (b).

SCHOOL BUS STOPPED AS PUPILS GO ON RAMPAGE

Police were called last night to Park Road, Midtown, when a school bus travelling from Midtown High School was halted by the driver after a fight among the pupils.

According to the driver, Mr Len Jones, the trouble began with children squirting cans of lemonade at each other, and throwing paper and chewing gum from the bus windows. A fight then broke out between two groups of pupils. Mr Jones claimed that he was unable to concentrate on driving the bus because of the disturbance and distraction behind him. He said that pupils had been warned previously about bad behaviour on school buses.

A police spokesman stated that as a result of a 999 call a Panda car went to Park Road and ten children were taken off the bus and left to walk home. In view of the potential danger to other traffic, the driver had been right to refuse to continue.

The Headmaster of Midtown High School, Mr C. Wall, has promised an immediate investigation and has said that the pupils will be severely punished.

Now answer (a) AND (b), basing your answers on the information given in the newspaper article.

a) Write Mr Jones's report to the Bus Company Traffic Superintendent explaining what happened on the bus.

b) Write a letter from Mr Wall to be sent to the parents of all pupils who travel on the school buses explaining what happened and making it clear that misbehaviour on the buses will be severely dealt with.

QUESTION 5

SEG Specimen Question 30 minutes – Foundation Tier 4–8

Read the following extract, and then answer the question below it.

MRS WEBB

Mrs Webb is elderly. Here she describes her life.

I was brought up in the country, in a cottage on a farm. My father was the cowman, and next door lived the horseman. I always loved the countryside. I remember the woods near us, a carpet of bluebells in the spring; and in the autumn there was blackberrying and mushrooming.

I left school when I was twelve and I had to go into service. I went to a young couple who were farmers, and I had to live in. It was about fifteen miles from home and it seemed to me the back of beyond. It was a big, rambling place, and I was the only help they had. I got one and threepence a week. They weren't bad to me, but they used to go out a lot and I'd be in the place on my own. I was literally terrified.

I helped the mistress make butter, and sometimes I used to milk the cows as well. Anyway, I didn't last long. I got so lonely. I went to a butcher's wife near Wellingborough. She was a terror. There was another maid there, and fortunately we got on well together. We could laugh and cover up for each other if we did anything wrong. We slept in an attic, and we had to be up at six o'clock in the morning.

I had fifteen places in twelve years, and only at one of them was I treated like a human being. They didn't think of us as people like themselves. We were different. Occasionally my father and brother used to come and see me, and I felt really unhappy when they left. I wanted to say 'Take me away with you,' but of course they couldn't. You had to work; your parents couldn't afford to keep you.

I've been married twice. I met my first husband when he was home on leave from the Great War. We were married in Lowick church. It's a beautiful place, a lantern tower and some glass hundreds of years old. Anyway, he was gassed and he had dysentery, and he was never really well after that. A lot of the time he couldn't work at all. In the end, I got a cottage in the country, near where I was brought up. I thought, 'Get him into the fresh air. He'll be better there.' I thought he might be able to do a bit of agricultural work, but he couldn't. We moved in the February, and he died in the August.

Ten years ago I went on a holiday for the elderly, and that's where I met my second husband. We had seven years of real happiness. I don't know, do you think you have to pay for the happiness you have? Do you think you have to give it back in sorrow? But beneath it all there's always been this feeling of being different. I've no children for one thing, and that makes a difference.

Your local librarian is compiling a booklet of short articles by young people who have interviewed elderly citizens in the community. You have interviewed Mrs Webb.

Write your article. Make clear what you found interesting in the things she said.

QUESTION 6

Study these seven extracts from a newspaper article and decide what you think is a reasonable order. (A space has been given at the end of the question for you to write down the numbers of the extracts in your new order.)

Then write a brief summary in your own words of the points which the article puts forward and in the order you have chosen. You should aim to write about 150 words.

1   In 1974 tunnelling work actually began at sites near Dover and Calais, only to be abandoned on environmental grounds after a fierce campaign by Kent villagers. Now, several false starts and mountains of research effort later, a Channel link looks certain to be constructed.

2   Ironically, the one question which has yet to be answered is whether the link will make it cheaper to cross the Channel. Journeys will certainly be quicker – 30 minutes by rail shuttle or driving, against 50 minutes by ferry – with speedier customs facilities. But the rival groups have merely indicated that they will be competitive with ferry fares when a link opens in 1992–3.

3   The stakes are high. Mr Sherwood, whose Sea Containers group owns the Sealink ferry business, says that the ferry business will be forced to close down if a fixed link is built. 'I've got to win,' he said. 'Otherwise I will be out of business.'

4   The sudden enthusiasm for a project which has been on the shelf for so long is easily explained. Britain and France are wracked by unemployment which will be a key issue in forthcoming elections in both countries. President Mitterrand has his eye on the French parliamentary elections next March. Mrs Thatcher is already planning for 1987, when she has to go to the polls again.

5   The idea that a tunnel should link England and France was first suggested by Napoleon nearly two hundred years ago. The proposal was turned down by Britain for security reasons. It was feared that Napoleon would send French troops through the tunnel to invade Britain.

6   Big business is also champing at the bit to win a slice of the Channel action. The three main contenders to build a link – Channel Expressway, Channel Tunnel Group, and Euroroute – have already invested tens of millions of pounds in the battle to build the link.

7   The threat of terrorist attack on a link, the risk of rabies spreading from the Continent, and a welter of other considerations have figured prominently in the debate. But not once has the risk of invasion by French troops been mentioned as a serious option. That, perhaps, is what they call progress.

(Extracts reproduced by courtesy of *The Guardian*.)

QUESTION 7

Some people are opposed to the building of a fixed Channel link. Here are some notes made by an opponent of the scheme who is worried about the effects which it will have on the environment. Study them carefully and then write ONE of the following.

Bridges – would destroy view of cliffs
('last remaining stretch of unprotected coast exhibiting natural erosion'
— Nature Conservancy Council 1985)

Rare species on chalk land
  – spider orchid
  – 4 rare moths as well
could be wiped out?

Waste from tunnel would be
dumped on shore. Visual aspects?
Danger to fish?

'Euroroute' starts in
Farthingloe Valley
– completely unspoilt and
beautiful

Where would construction
sites go? Rail lines, new
roads. Kent crowded anyway!

Villages as well

Newington and Peene

Noise dirt and traffic (ugh!)

KENT (encyclopaedia entry)

Large county in S E England. Often called 'Gateway to England' because nearest county to France. Dover and Folkestone are main ports for ferry services. Tourist resorts like Whitstable and Margate still very popular. Industries – cement and paper making (newsprint for London papers is still produced here). Still called 'Garden of England' as well for apple and cherry growing in rural areas. Also famous for hops, used in beer-making, and oysters near Whitstable.

Write **ONE** of the following:

EITHER

a) A letter to the Editor of *The Dover Gazette* opposing the scheme on environmental grounds.

OR

b) A leaflet to be issued by 'Friends of the Earth' to households in the area, putting these points to local people.

OR

c) A speech to be made at a public inquiry to discuss the proposals.

OR

d) A reply to these arguments suggesting that there are other points to be considered in favour of a fixed link. You can write this as **either** a speech **or** a letter to the newspaper.

[MEG]

QUESTION 8

Using local gazetteers and guide books prepare a leaflet for teenage visitors, pointing out the things of interest about your village or town.

QUESTION 9

Write 'a guide to an interview' for young people applying for a first job

QUESTION 10

Using a tour brochure for far-away holidays, write (a) an advertisement for holidays in India, based mainly on information in the brochure, (b) a letter to a friend and (c) a short letter of appreciation to the tour operator for a good holiday.

OUTLINE ANSWERS
AND ADVICE

ANSWER 1

Make two lists, one giving the limitations of the old regulations and the other the advantages of the proposed new regulations, and try to place the points on them in a logical order. Then draft the editorial. Compare your version with that in the 'Tutor's Answer' below

ANSWER 2

You are asked to write a response to a letter from the correspondence columns of the *Belfast Telegraph*. The writer has adverse views about some sixteen-year-olds and it is likely that you will react strongly against them. There is no reason why your letter should not offer an equally determined defence but, rather than allow yourself to get carried away, recognise that the writer has been genuinely upset by her experience and make some positive efforts to reassure her. In addition, you must answer the points raised in the letter, and not be tempted to put in a lot of material of your own. The main charges to be answered are as follows: the liking for young people to go around in crowds, to wait about aimlessly; to dress the same and to behave in an excited and unruly way. These are based on direct observation by the writer. She also alleges that young people are 'thugs', who lack common sense, maturity and consideration for others and are not like their parents' generation when young, probably because of a lack of discipline in their homes. The writer urges strong intervention by the authorities – e.g. the Government, the City Council and the Police – to maintain order.

Remember to write in an appropriate style – that of a responsible teenager, addressing the public, and with an appropriate lay-out, i.e. formal, for a letter to an editor of a leading newspaper.

ANSWER 3

Here the point of view is that of a policeman gathering information from eye-witnesses. He has to decide which pieces of information are substantiated, and therefore can be considered to be 'facts', and which are opinion. This may be quite a difficult thing to do. The facts may be no more than the following: the girl's name, the time of the accident, the details of the car involved, the place of the accident, the state of the lights at the junction and anything about the driver's behaviour that observers agree on.

A report presents balanced arguments, backed up by evidence, and should be written in a formal style – Standard English.

ANSWER 4

Here you are asked to write a report and a letter, based on the same piece of material – a newspaper article about the behaviour of school children on a bus. As in Question 3, the report will need to be a careful statement of fact, with sensible arguments which are supported by evidence. Should the Bus Company superintendent want to follow up this report he will need sound evidence to work on. The facts are few: the driver stopped the bus in Park Road, Midtown, and a police car, responding to a 999 call, arrived at the scene and ten children were taken off the bus. The driver also alleges that school children have been warned before about bad behaviour on the bus and that, on this occasion, there was fighting and other unruly behaviour by the children. Those statements are not proven, and would need to be closely investigated. The report should be written in a formal style, in Standard English and be correctly sequenced.

The letter from the headmaster is likely to treat the same information rather differently. He is addressing parents and his purpose is to prevent any future disturbance on the school bus by impressing on them the importance of their children behaving in a disciplined fashion. He may well highlight those aspects of the situation that will suit his purpose, e.g. the alleged fighting, squirting cans of lemonade, paper throwing from the bus windows, etc. His tone will be serious and his style fairly formal, but, as he seeks the parents' co-operation, the letter may be semi-formal in lay-out, e.g.

'Dear Mr and Mrs. ....
....
....
....
....

Yours sincerely,

(Signed)'

ANSWER 5

The extract is monologue – a transcript (probably edited, as it is rather too fluent and non-hesitant for speech). Your task is to turn this into a report in a style suitable for young people who will read your article bringing out points of interest in Mrs Webb's account. You have no word limit, but time is short, so you should aim to write no more than 200 words or so. First, made a list of points that you want to include, maybe covering Mrs Webbs' country childhood, her years as a servant, her marriage, her husband's ill-health and death, finally her second marriage. Draft the points probably in that order, as she is telling her life story, then read through what you have written for suitability of style, paragraphing and correctness of expression. Remember that 5% of the marks will be for these skills. Don't forget to give your work a suitable title – something to distinguish your article from the rest, and make the reader want to know more e.g. *Mrs Webb: the Cost of Happiness*.

ANSWER 6

This question is close to a straightforward summary. You are asked to read the seven extracts, sequence them in a reasonable order, then give a short account (in about 150 words) of the article, following the sequence you have already decided upon. You are helped with part of the preparatory work in the sequencing exercise. You still have to move from that to your own compact account, though. A draft version is highly recommended here so that in rough you can write out your points in order, check the length of the piece and improve the style before writing your final version. Style needs to be formal, as in the original article, but try to use your own words as far as possible, so that it is clear that you really have understood the points you are putting forward.

ANSWER 7

Using a page of notes made by the opponent of the building of a fixed Channel link, you have the choice of kinds of writing: either a letter, or a leaflet, or a speech or a considered statement in favour.

Again, it is best to start by listing the key points to be made, either for or against, depending on the question you choose. How you proceed depends on the topic on which you are working. If it is (a), then you need points opposing, in a formal letter, in Standard English, with appropriate lay-out. If you choose (b) you must consider especially the readers of your piece of writing (local people) and its form (a leaflet). Your style should be lively (though correct) and fluent. You should put points for both sides of the case in a way that draws attention. This demands an eye-catching lay-out, with banner or sub-headings. You could consider numbering points for and against. If you choose (c) you should offer the same balance of material, but remember that oral communication works rather differently from the written word. In your speech think of the audience you would be addressing – the general public. As part of your style find some ways of drawing them in, of persuading them to your point of view. (As more will be said about speech writing in Chapter 13, you may find it helpful to refer to that chapter now.) Question (d) requires the same approaches as either (a) or (c), but notice that it has to be in favour of a fixed link.

ANSWER 8

To begin here find a guide book (better, find two) on your area. Then make a flow-chart or topic tree of the key points, adding minor details next, to be included in your leaflet. Try writing it out in draft, and aim at producing three or four paragraphs.

ANSWER 9

List some key areas and then rewrite your list in what seems the most helpful order.
    You might begin by suggesting a letter confirming attendance: then stress the importance of suitable dress and arriving on time. Your audience will be young people seeking advice, so keep your tone lively and choose a style that is likely to appeal to them. You could consider some presentation aspects, too, suitable for a leaflet.

ANSWER 10

Ask yourself some key questions: 'What would I enjoy on the holiday described in the brochure?'; 'What are the basic amenities on offer?'; 'What about the price?'; and so on. List them, and jot down an answer to each, using details from the brochure. You now have the basis for your advertisement and letters. Think how the tone and style of the letter to your friend will differ from that to the travel company. Write the letter to your friend first. How will you begin and end it? Will there be an address and a date? You have quite a range of choice here. Now turn to the second letter and think about its form. Keep it short, and begin and end it suitably.

A TUTOR'S ANSWER TO QUESTION 1

Here are two lists of points that could serve as the basis of a summary. Check them against your own:

Limitations of the old regulations

1   The old regulations are out of date because the number of experiments has increased vastly.
2   Licences have been issued to unqualified applicants, without enquiring about the purposes of the experiments.
3   There are not enough inspectors to cover premises throughout the country regularly.
4   Licences allow experiments without anaesthetic, which leads to suffering.
5   No enquiries are made about the source of animals used for experiments.
6   It is permissible for animals to suffer until the main point of the experiment has been gained.
7   Penalties for unlicensed experiments are only six months in prison as a maximum, or a fine of up to £2000. This is too little.

Advantages of the proposed new regulations

1 Provision will be made for many more experiments.
2 Only properly qualified persons will be eligible for a licence.
3 The purpose and design of experiments will be carefully considered.
4 Animals must only be obtained from registered agencies.
5 Uncontrolled pain will not in general be permitted.
6 The committee may refuse permission for use of some animals, especially cats, dogs and horses.
7 Penalties for unlicensed experiments will be increased: up to two years in prison or an unlimited fine. This will be a more realistic deterrent.

An appropriate editorial might read as follows:

'ANIMAL RIGHTS IN THE LABORATORY'

'Few issues have brought such a large post-bag from readers as this one. Certainly the old regulations no longer reflect a world where experiments on animals have increased vastly. Inspectors have always had a limited role, and there aren't enough of them to monitor the work done or to ensure that experimenters are properly licensed and controlled. The issue of licenses needs investigating; the maximum penalty of six months in prison or a fine of £2000 just does not deter. No questions are asked about the source of animals used and over eighty per cent are experimented on without anaesthetic. The pain suffered is disregarded, until the main results of the work have been established.

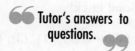

Tutor's answers to questions.

'By the revision now proposed, most of these abuses would stop. Only those qualified would be licensed, and only after the purpose and design of the experiment had been approved, the onus being on the applicants to justify their need to use animals. Penalties for unlicensed experiments would be increased – up to two years in prison, or a large fine. Animals would be supplied only from registered places.

'One problem would remain: the need to balance outcomes of research against the pain inflicted. Many would say that we still haven't got that right.'

PUPILS' ANSWERS AND TUTOR'S COMMENTS

Here are the preparations made by a pupil for a summary – a guide to an interview.

Summary and Directed Writing

ROUGH

Note points   A Guide to an interview   150 words

1 Careful not to be criticised for being slow and unenthusiastic.
2 First impressions very important. Appearance and manner of movement. Personality.
3 Bold with views of your own/news etc. Warm, friendly and outgoing.
4 Like people that take an interest in the real world and can keep up discussion on current affairs.
5 Independence, don't ask too keenly about hours and salary.
6 Seem keen and enthusiastic. Don't be monosyllabic.
7 Be punctual.
8 Keep a clear head, use initiative.

Pupil's answers to questions.

The writer has decided on eight main ideas. They do not seem to be in any particular order, e.g. first impressions' comes second and 'be punctual' seventh. Points (1) and (6) are more or less the same, in reverse. He has chosen a title, which is a good idea.

A better summary might have resulted if he had gone through a second planning stage and reorganised the sequence of his points: (7), (2), (6) and (1), then (8), (3), (5) and (4) would make a more logical order.

Here is his final version

> First impressions are very important in an interview, both of appearance and manner of movement. Be careful not to be criticised for being slow and unenthusiastic. Personality is also very important, so be bold and stick to your views. Young people with views of their own are particularly admired. Also be warm, friendly and outgoing. Most employers like people who take an interest in the real world, so make sure you're able to keep up an intellectual and interesting discussion of current affairs and news.
>
> Do not seem too keen about knowing your possible hours and salary – remember they're interviewing you, and not vice-versa. Independence is also very much admired; seem keen and enthusiastic, answer questions properly and don't be monosyllabic. Make sure you turn up punctually with no feeble excuses. Keep a clear head, use your initiative and Good Luck!

You will see that he has rearranged the points as follows: (2), (1), (3), (4), (5), (6), (7) and (8), which makes quite a good summary, except for the repetition of the ideas mentioned above, in points (1) and (6). That could have been weeded out at the planning stage. Notice that the tone of the guide is appropriate – there are quite a few commands: 'Be careful ...!', 'Don't seem too keen!'; but also a friendly tone: 'Good Luck!'. It ends well.

PUPIL'S ANSWER TO QUESTION 10

Here is a pupil's version of this topic

a)
> *Holiday Brochure*
> *'Intersun'*

> Having problems? Need a break? Then come and see any of our Intersun travel agents. We've any place to suit any one in India. And the unbeatable prices:
>   Bombay £480
>   Delhi £575
>   Madras £520
> These are just some of the cities from which you can choose. You may choose Bombay then we can arrange for you to see some of India's famous film stars.

> The beaches are golden from the everlasting sun which beats down on sun bathers. You can pick the right spot for you to sun bathe.

> The food is just fabulous. There's no time for any particular food. You can eat anytime. Apart from Indian food you can have any other food that pleases you.

> Rush now before it's too late!

★ ★ ★

Five Star Hotel
51 Central St.,
Bombay
Fri 22nd Nov.

b) Dear Sonia,

Hi, how are you? I am sorry I couldn't write sooner. I've been really busy enjoying myself with Saqib. I didn't think that £480 would be so cheap for all this. There's guided tours, good food, air-conditioned bedrooms, bathrooms. The view from our window is just beautiful. We've taken some photos for you to see.

The beach is just five minutes away; the best time to go there is in the evening sunset. We made some friends at the beach yesterday. They also came for a holiday from London.

Tomorrow we're going to the Indian Film Industry; I've heard a lot about that. I am looking forward to going there and so is Saqib. You know how he is with acting, plays, films etc.

We've only been here a week and we've got three more weeks; I wish it was longer. It's so nice to get away for a while. You should do that and I'd advise you to go to Intersun travel agents – they are the best. Hope to see you soon.

Love,
J

P.S. I've written the address. If you wish to write, then please do, and let me know what you want from here.

★   ★   ★

40 Court Gdns.,
London SW1
Tues 26th Nov.

c) Intersun Ltd.,
142 Union Rd.,
London W1

Dear Manager/ess,

Thanks to your wonderful travel agency 'Intersun' my boyfriend and I had the best time of our lives. We both visited Bombay for four weeks. Everything was just perfect the way you described it. It was just like a dream land. We didn't want to come back. I hope to go back there again. Thanks again.

Yours sincerely

(Miss J C)

P.S. Your surprise hotel in Bombay was excellent.

The pupil has included four key ideas, so that her advertisement is clear and uncluttered. She includes those in the letter to her friend. This has a casual tone: 'Hi, how are you?' and 'Love, J', but it is correctly expressed. In contrast, the letter to the tour operator is friendly, but more formal. It has few details, but one main idea: to express thanks for a wonderful holiday. All three pieces are readable and clear – successful communication, in short!

COURSEWORK –
A STEP FURTHER

This chapter is quite closely related to others – Chapters 7, 10 and 15

You probably use summarising skills frequently in your general work, but further practice is always useful. Try out some of the ideas here when you are making your own notes. If you are reading a play, novel or short story, take a scene or incident, and try to write about it from the point of view of one character.

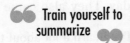

Train yourself to summarize

Compare news items in different newspapers, and try writing your own version. Look at advertisements, prospectuses and brochures, and select points of interest from a particular angle. In these ways you can train yourself to read accurately and write clearly and concisely – the basic requirements for good summarising.

REVIEW SHEET

A skill often involved in summary writing is the ability to get across the same idea while using fewer words than in the original writing.

    Look at the sentences below. Try to reduce the sentence by about one third in each case (the number of words is given in brackets).

Example:

It is possible to say more or less the same thing. = You can convey roughly the same idea.

1 Even if the letter is a formal "Dear Sir or Madam" letter, you know the job of the person you are writing to. (23 words)

2 You can, therefore, in a letter make definite assumptions about what your reader knows or does not know about what you are writing about. (24 words)

3 Even if it is for your workplace newsletter, it may be read by management, by your closest colleagues, by visitors from other companies and by the cleaners. (27 words)

4 All these people will have very different degrees of knowledge about your subject and so, ideally, you must write in a way that is appropriate for them all. (28 words)

5 Even work letters are usually interesting in some degree to the recipient. (12 words)

6 You can be pretty certain that the person who receives your letter will read it to the end. (18 words)

7 The potential readers of an article, however, are probably not particularly interested to see your article. (16 words)

8 They have to be attracted to start reading it, and, once caught, their interest has to be held or else they will not continue reading until the end. (28 words)

9 An article is never going to consist of only two or three short paragraphs. (14 words)

10 It usually has to have much more weight than the typical letter. (12 words)

To summarise effectively you must have a good understanding of what the original text is about. Finding a *title* for a piece of writing is a useful check on your understanding.

Read the short passages below and then suggest a title for each of them.

1   A shark weighing 457 lbs was caught off Antigua. Its stomach contained one pair of two-tone suede beach boots, a human skull and a copy of the Gospel of St John printed on polythene.

Title: _____

2   Returning to his car, a motorist found its bodywork severely dented and the following note tucked behind the windscreen wiper.

"I have just run into your car. People have seen me and are watching me write this. They think I am giving you my name and address. They are wrong!"

Title: _____

Being *concise* is an important skill in summary writing. Find a word or shorter phrase to replace each of the longer sayings in this table.

at the same time as	_____
the reason for this is that	_____
a little at a time	_____
in spite of	_____
due to	_____
as a result of	_____
for what reason	_____
moves into line with	_____
miss out on	_____
on the other hand	_____
in addition to	_____
while we must accept that	_____
in every nook and cranny	_____
there is every likelihood that	_____
with the exception of	_____
give the impression that	_____
reach the conclusion that	_____
draw the deduction that	_____
draw the inference that	_____
make quite certain that	_____
reach the decision that	_____
bound to happen	_____
to all intents and purposes	_____
on many occasions	_____
leaves a lot to be desired	_____
as well as	_____
in order to	_____
many and varied	_____
which would lead to	_____
this has caused	_____
period of time	_____

12

WRITING NARRATIVE

RELEVANCE

SELECTION OF INCIDENTS

POINT OF VIEW

STRUCTURE

STYLE

GETTING STARTED

It has been suggested that narrative is a 'primary act of mind'; that is, we all shape our experiences in life into a narrative form. How do you tell people in the evening what your day has been like? You cannot include everything that has happened, every feeling you experienced, every thought you had. Nor do you spend time thinking out the best way to recount your experiences. No, you simply narrate selectively, highlighting what was most important to you, in roughly chronological order: this is basic narrative. Quite often, when telling about what has happened, you have to present yourself acting against someone, or acted against. When doing this, if you think about it, you are likely to show the qualities in yourself that you want others to admire, and if you came out of the experience badly, use humour to lessen your humiliation. Suppose you had been picked on by a school bully or superior and had been too afraid to stand up for yourself? Aren't you more likely to cast yourself in a heroic role than admit to your cowardice? If so, then you are not only narrating events, but introducing an element of imagination. This is similar to telling a story.

That is not to suggest that composing narrative comes naturally, and is easy. You will have many opportunities to write narrative on various subjects for coursework and will probably be set a question of this sort if you take a written paper. What follows in this chapter is advice on how to go about writing effective narrative.

ESSENTIAL PRINCIPLES

A successful narrative is likely to be satisfactory as regards

- relevance
- selection of incidents
- point of view
- structure
- style

Consider each in turn.

1 ▷ RELEVANCE

Whether you are writing on a theme chosen by yourself entirely or answering a question in a written paper, it is important to focus clearly on the chief area of concern for your narrative, and keep to it. Only move away to a parallel set of happenings or ideas, or flash back or predict forwards if by doing so you will make the central theme clearer or increase its power. When we are narrating our everyday experience, as mentioned above, most of us do so automatically, and those who do not are soon labelled as speakers who offer a 'rigmarole' or 'go all around the houses to get to the point'. These commonly used phrases indicate how impatient listeners can become when forced to listen to the rambling account of others' experiences. Certainly, when many pupils write a story they depart from the directness and pointedness of many of their real life accounts. It is a mistake, for instance, deliberately to decide to be extremely original. What you intend as striking and refreshing may seem to the reader perverse or even obscure. One pupil chose the title 'Day Trippers' and wrote about a disco with this name; another devoted several pages to events about a cruiser named *The Catch* in a story of that title.

A more usual form of irrelevance is when the writer has an opening or closing sentence or two relating to the title, and then continues with something quite different. 'Day Trippers' might begin with a group of friends setting off for a day by the sea and, by the second paragraph, finding that they had become caught up with a gang of criminals in a car chase. 'The Catch' could easily tell the story of a family holiday: sight-seeing, shopping, sun-bathing, visiting museums, cafés, sampling the nightlife – and then, in the final paragraph, going on a fishing trip on which father lands a salmon.

There is one way of departing from the obvious meaning of the title but still writing relevantly. Many titles can be considered in two ways, both literally and figuratively. In the example of 'The Catch' a pupil wrote an excellent short story about a fishing boat called 'The Catch', taken out by two young boys for a first attempt at the sport. Starting with the boys pushing off from the shore, with their hearts full of excitement and their heads of grand dreams of the three-pounder they hope to hook, the story proceeds through the calm of waiting, the slow hours dragging by and the false alarms, and culminates in the dramatic moment when there is a sharp tug at the line. Feverishly, one boy winds in, his rod bending and line taut under the weight. With a jerk which topples him backwards into the boat, he swings his prize catch clear of the water: it is an old bicycle tyre! As the writer pointed out in his final reflections – there was a catch to the day's sport in 'The Catch', and the boys laughed at the deluding name of the boat as they rowed home.

2 ▷ SELECTION OF INCIDENTS

Suppose you are writing a story called 'The Catch' and have decided to combine a literal and figurative treatment, as described above. After a few moments thought many ideas will clamour for attention.

First, you have to choose your main focus, your *theme*. Let the story be, as an example, about a tense moment when a lowly member of the cricket eleven tries to make a catch which would dismiss the opposing team's best batsman – and drops it! Secondly, you need to decide which *events* to discard and which to keep. Obviously, the moment of the catch is essential. Will you work up to it slowly, building suspense, or start dramatically with it, and let the rest of the story go back to the earlier hopes and fears of the would-be catcher? These are just two possible arrangements among many. Certainly, the story has to give some kind of context to the significant moment. But that is all. It is not even necessary to give the feelings of the fielder when he drops the ball: as a strong anti-climax it would make a fitting end to a story – but more of that below. Now you must try to give your story *effective shape*. Will you write about all the events of the morning, from when the fielder got up, had his breakfast, put on his whites, etc.? Probably not. On the other hand, if he did all these things in a daze, dreaming of future glory on the field, anticipating saving his team from defeat, all this could be included, because it would make the moment of dropping the catch such a let-down for the hero. Will you give an account of every ball and run in the match? Of course not: you will choose parts of the match which will help the main focus.

Choice depends very much on the individual writer. No two treatments will be the same. The important thing is to think about how the events you select help your theme to have maximum impact on, and interest for, the reader.

3 ▷ POINT OF VIEW

Who tells the story? Often stories are told from the point of view of the so-called 'omniscient' author; that is, one who knows everything and chooses what to tell and what to withhold. Often, again, the point of view offered is that of a character in the narrative, possibly speaking in the first person. Some students find this hard to maintain. They become so involved in what they are writing that they switch from the name of the character to the personal pronoun, and back again. Beware of this elementary mistake. Henry James, the novelist, liked to have the story told by a wise friend of the main character, who would be likely to know a great deal about the situation but also was close to the hero or heroine. In the story about 'The Catch' outlined above, for instance, it would make a good deal of difference whether the chief point of view was that of the star batsman, or the hopeful fielder. Try experimenting with different angles in the narrative: it can have quite dramatically different effects. Some stories are even deliberately told from two contrasting points of view – a 'two-sides-of-the-truth' approach, where the reader is left to decide which is preferable, or whether both are equally acceptable.

4 ▷ STRUCTURE

" Begin and end well. "

What has already been said implies a number of important things about structure. Learn to make the most of your material by organising it effectively. You may prefer to do a brief outline *plan*, or have a plan in your head. Five minutes' thinking before you write can make a lot of difference. Also, *beginnings* and *endings* are very important: you need to catch the reader's attention at once, and hold it, perhaps through developing events to a climax, to make him or her want to read on. Try to include some unexpected turns in the action, or some variety of narrative approach, so that your story is not a level, even piece of writing, unless that is an effect you really want to achieve. Finally, find some way of resolving the situation in a satisfying or challenging way, perhaps leaving the reader guessing. This sort of story is called 'open ended'. The reader forms his own idea of how matters end, using the clues you have given.

An essential part of your organisation will be *paragraphing*. Paragraph logically, as phases of the narrative evolve, not just every ten lines or so. If you paragraph logically you can control the pace and growth of your narrative. Practice in plotting a narrative is worth the effort. After deciding on a beginning and concluding idea, break the body of your story into say, four or five paragraphs (remember, economy is essential if you are given a work limit), each with a *key idea* for development.

For example, a possible plan for the cricketing story entitled 'The Catch' might look like this:

- **Opening paragraph** – The moment of the catch; hero feels weak at the knees as he sees the ball falling towards him from a great height. The crowd goes quiet, in anticipation.
- **Body of the story** – The morning of the event; excited preparations; good luck wishes of friends and relatives hardly heeded by hero in dreamy state of mind.

■ **In the pavilion before the match** – Hero notices photographs on the wall of old teams going back many years; dreams of personal glory as he walks eagerly out onto the field.

■ **Concluding paragraph** – The ball is nearly on him. He cups his hands. The ball goes into them and then – out again! He has DROPPED IT!

STYLE

Good style has been described as 'mind style', because it reflects individuality. Even so, there are several ways of making narration more interesting by varying your approach. Stretches of dialogue can carry the story forward sometimes, and a descriptive passage may help to set the scene. Characters' reflections on what is happening often give depth to the events of the story, and so on. Try to show plenty of variety and don't be afraid to experiment.

EXAMINATION QUESTIONS

Here is a collection of suggested questions.

QUESTION 1

Write a story about the 'Marathon'.   **(WJEC)**

QUESTION 2

'They don't understand me.' Write a short story about a young person who might have said this.   **(NEAB)**

QUESTION 3

Write about an incident in your own life which has been important to you because it has marked a stage in your growing up.

QUESTION 4

Write a story which ends with the words 'Neither of us won.' (You may use as a starting point for writing, the short story printed earlier in this book, on page 110–111).

QUESTION 5

Write your own story beginning like this: '… It was late at night and quiet. I had been playing my favourite computer games. Then my eyes began to feel heavy and the screen blurred. I seemed to be falling towards it … through the screen …'   **(MEG)**

QUESTIONS 6–11

Write a story about each of the following: (MEG)

    6 A question of loyalty.
    7 The hunt.
    8 Hijack!
   9 Return journey.
  10 An animal you have known well.
  11 A frightening experience.

QUESTION 12

'The fungus was suspiciously innocent-looking but strange. It was milk-white, mottled with purple splashes. Chris had never seen one like it before and knelt down eagerly to look closer to smell, to taste. Suddenly he/she experienced a weird sensation and the world seemed to be revolving, changing …' Continue this story as you wish, perhaps adding new characters. What you write should relate closely to the opening situation.

PUPILS' ANSWER TO QUESTIONS 7 AND 8

ANSWER 7

Here is a pupil's story, written about a hunt (Question 7).

Tiger Hunt

The scent of humans fell upon his nose. He scampered from the shallow pool he lay in. He ran like a paper being pulled in a hurricane. The men kept track of him flashing past at the speed of light. The hunters kept chasing him.

The tiger was terrified now, but there seemed to be no escape. as he ran along the plains the black stripes on his coat kept showing up, like bands of darkness.

The poacher took his aim but – disappointedly – missed.

The tiger trampled through the long grass. He desperately ran on. The hunter raised his gun, tightly pulled the trigger and sadly, and very sadly the tiger stopped running. He stopped panting. He stopped breathing. He was no longer terrified. He rested in peace: a gun shot wound, as big as an apple, lay deep in him.

The poachers retired. Another skin to sell, more money and another innocent tiger slaughtered illegally and viciously.

ANSWER 8

Here is another story, this time on the topic 'Hijack!' (Question 8).

Essay Plan

Para 1: Despite unsuperstitious, Mondays always bad – boring, then various things happening – generally bad.

Para 2: Sunday night contemplating this Monday, thinking it might be a better day/uneasy feeling about it/going away.

Para 3: Monday morning – bitterly cold, etc. Describe the journey to airport, action there.

Para 4: Getting on plane – Describe activities, etc.

Para 5: The hijack – Describe fear and confusion. Describe what happens – Intercom announcing time on Monday.

Para 6: The hijackers are won over, we manage to get off the plane. As we do we hear an announcement at the airport – *Tuesday morning*.

First consider the pupil's outline plan above. Paragraph one anticipates Monday. Paragraph two concerns Sunday evening, but also anticipates Monday. Paragraphs three to five concern events on Monday. Paragraph six has action taking place on Tuesday morning. Overall, some forty-eight hours is the planned time sequence, and it is economically handled in the narrative plan.

The second thing to notice is that there is a theme related to the time-sequencing, i.e. that Mondays are always dull days and at first the Monday of the hijack ran true to form. Ending with the announcement that it was Tuesday morning is a good idea, then, suggesting double relief: both the hijack and Monday are over!

The third thing worth mentioning is that the plan gives a few necessary details of happenings: journey to the airport; the weather (when it is considered important to mention it); the chief character's feelings – early depression, then confusion and fear and relief when the hijack is over; the idea of two announcements, etc. This plan promises a well-organised story. Now read the story itself, noticing how closely the writer kept to the plan, and considering how successful a piece of narrative you think it is.

Hijack

Mondays had always been bad for me and considering I'm a very unsuperstitious person, that probably sounds rather hypocritical yet something always did seem to go wrong on a Monday, rather than any other day. I was born on a Monday. I broke a leg on a Monday and my grandfather died on a Monday and there were many more disasters as well!

I was sitting by the open fire in our living room on a Sunday night, thinking about this and wondering if it really was mere coincidence. It was in the middle of January and we were going skiing tomorrow and I wondered if anything would go wrong. We got up very early the next morning, as our plane was leaving at seven a.m. London was going through a very cold spell and the roads were covered in ice and snow, so the traffic was hideous. When we finally arrived at the airport it was still bitterly cold and we were all feeling very annoyed, and our tempers certainly didn't improve when we discovered that our plane had a two hour delay.

Eventually we were allowed on board and as the 'fasten your seat belt and no smoking' light went on, a surge of relief swept through us … we were finally on our way. A few minutes after take off we were served breakfast.

Suddenly two men stood up at the front of the plane, holding guns. I'm not quite sure how it happened. I don't think anyone was. Many people didn't seem to realise what was happening and the people who did were in a blind panic; several women fainted and the rest were screaming or trying to clamber to the back of the plane. The rest, like me, were obviously still not able to fully take in the awfulness of the situation. The hijackers started to shout and threatened to shoot and gradually the noise subsided. The plane it seemed had been ordered to land as planned in Austria which it did. As we came into the airport we could see guards all around yet they didn't approach us. The plane was completely silent now and everybody sat waiting.

As the hours went by the tension mounted. Some attempts were made by the police to talk to the hijackers but to no avail. By this time one shot had been fired but luckily no-one had been hurt. The electricity suddenly went off too and so we had no lights or heat. As it began to go dark the hijackers were evidently getting more and more nervous. For some reason I didn't feel scared – just numb. I suppose it was shock. In the distance I heard the intercom at the main airport announce that it was 9.30 p.m. on Monday night. It was rather ironic, I thought to myself, how this happened on a Monday. Several hours later a spot-light was put on us. This must have been the last straw for the hijackers who leapt up and started shouting 'Everybody off! Get off! Everybody off!' There was a hysterical plunge for the door and when I got out into the fresh air I heard the airport intercom again, this time announcing that it was one o'clock on *Tuesday* morning. Thank God, Monday was over!

A TUTOR'S COMMENTS

ANSWER TO QUESTION 7

'Tiger Hunt' is a most economically written short story. What it leaves out in detail is made up for in pace and dramatic suspense. Notice the direct opening. Here is a group of verbs which move on the action. See how many more good words and phrases are used: 'scampered', 'kept track', 'flashing past'. Sparsely written though this is, the writer has included some *figurative* expressions: 'flashing past at the speed of light' is rather a well-worn comparison, but the idea of a paper in a hurricane is original and interesting. The short paragraphs have the effect of moving attention quickly from the tiger to the hunter, and back again. The death of the tiger is described almost in slow motion. Notice how the very short sentences produce this result, and also the repetition of 'stopped', and the drawing out of the phrase 'and sadly, and very sadly', which also has a powerful emotional appeal. The final paragraph stresses the cruelty of the attack, the grotesque joy and speed of the poachers and the pathos of the victim. The word 'illegally' stirs our conscience, and widens the issue.

ANSWER TO QUESTION 8

In some respects 'Hijack' works well as a story – the opening offers a definite point of view and strong sense of anticipation: 'Mondays had always been bad for me and considering I'm a very unsuperstitious person, that probably sounds rather hypocritical yet something always did seem to go wrong on a Monday, rather than any other day.' The rest of the paragraph enlarges our awareness of the first person narrator's wry sense of humour, too!

Notice how suspense is gradually built up, from the narrator's thoughts on the Sunday evening as he reflects by the open fire: 'I wondered if anything would go wrong.' Things aren't very comfortable on the Monday morning: 'the traffic was hideous'; 'it was still bitterly cold'; everyone is ill-tempered when they hear about the two hour delay to the flight. All these preliminaries help to confirm our suspicion that this Monday will be as bad as the narrator feared it might be. There is one short paragraph, lulling our fears, but in the next the disastrous climax is reached: 'Suddenly two men stood up at the front of the plane, holding guns.' The final sentence of this action-packed paragraph indicates an uneasy calm, just as frightening as the frantic activity it follows: 'The plane was completely silent by now and everybody sat waiting.'

Next, with excellent economy the writer copes with time passing and anxiety in one sentence: 'As the hours went by the tension mounted.' Then, unfortunately, paragraphing breaks down. The 'I hate Mondays' theme, though, is picked up again, echoing the first paragraph: 'It was rather ironic, I thought to myself, how this had happened on a Monday.' The eruption of action in the finale, when the hijackers 'leap up' and shout 'Everybody off! Get off! Everybody off!' and the passengers all make 'a hysterical plunge' for the door, is dramatic and exciting. The escape into fresh air would make a suitable conclusion, but the writer neatly ends his story by reminding us that 'it was one o'clock on *Tuesday* morning. 'Thank God, Monday was over!'

There are some errors here – weak indication of where new paragraphing begins, sparse use of commas and some slips of expression, but overall this is a good short story.

COURSEWORK –
A STEP FURTHER

A great deal may be learned from being alert to the narrative techniques of others, especially writers you admire. Remember to notice effective openings and conclusions, twists of plot, aspects of character development, and so on. Remember, too, that few writers, even great ones, are wildly original: they have learned a great deal of their craft from reading other writers, and often name authors who have influenced them in their work, so there is no reason why you shouldn't take some tips from other writers, too. Study especially collections of short stories. There are many collections that you will enjoy and from which you can learn a great deal.

REVIEW SHEET

✎ If you are writing narrative it is important to decide at the beginning who is telling the story. Can you name three different 'points of view' for telling a story.

1 _____

2 _____

3 _____

✎ Suggest the point of view used in each of these three extracts from stories.

> 1 I'm easily led and swung, my mind like a weather-vane when somebody wants to change it for me, but there's one sure rule I'll stick to for good, and I don't mind driving a nail head-first into a long rigmarole of a story to tell you what I mean. Jim Scarefdale.

Point of view _____

> 2 Anne bent down and peered into the dark hole of the tunnel. She did not want to enter it. The enveloping blackness was the suffocation of her dream that could not be pushed away. She turned her head. It was day. She turned back and quickly went into the tunnel.

Point of view _____

> 3 Poor Fanny! She sang little, and looked beautiful through that inappropriate hymn. ... Brilliant she looked, and brilliant she felt, for she was hot and angrily miserable and inflamed with a sort of fatal despair. Because there was about him a physical attraction that she really hated, but which she could not escape from. He was the first man who had ever kissed her. And his kisses, even while she rebelled from them, had lived in her blood and sent roots down into her soul.

Point of view _____

✎ What techniques are being used in each of the following extracts to capture the attention of the reader at the beginning of the story?

1 Whizz! Zoom! The rockets sped upwards and illuminated the night sky. The faces of the children glowed with pleasure as the sounds of the fireworks exploded in their ears.

_____

_____

2 'Hey look!' shouted Jane, 'up there! Something's wrong with that plane.' The children stared into the sun. At first their eyes were dazzled by the blinding rays but even so it soon became horrifyingly clear that the aircraft was falling from the sky, spinning helplessly and hurtling towards the city below.

_____

_____

3 Waiting on the platform for his morning train to his office, something familiar about the back of a fellow commuter caught Jack Grigg's attention... There he stands, Basher Bradley, the notorious, belligerent fifth-former who is held in awe by all.
   'Ah!' a chronic spasm electrified Jack's back as a picture of Basher inflicting pain crystallized in his mind, and memories of the past came flooding back to him.

_____

_____

_____

After developing your story, you must decide on your *ending*. Here are some different types of ending

1 *Neat endings*, where all loose ends are sorted out.
2 *Circular endings*, where the events at the end of the story have not really changed anything from the situation at the beginning.
3 *Descriptive endings*, where you leave the reader with a picture of a scene which creates a mood you want your reader to go away with.
4 *Surprise endings*, where you produce a surprise or 'twist' in the story.
5 *Open endings*, where you leave it to the imagination of the reader to work out an appropriate ending.

 Look at the following five endings and write down which type you think it is.

> For one moment I hoped. All the buildings stood as firmly as before. I could see them like a town plan in the Surveyor's office, small, distant but perfect and very clean. Not a speck of dirt. All white ... and not a soul stirring.
>
> R.W. Mackelworth, *Cleaner than Clean*

> I turned into the street where our new flat was, and where I knew Rodney would be waiting for me. We were to have dinner with Sybil and Arnold that evening. It seemed a happy and suitable ending to a good day.
>
> B. Pym, *A Glass of Blessings*

> I lingered round them, under that benign sky; watched the moths fluttering among the heath and the harebells; listened to the soft wind breathing through the grass; and wondered how any one could ever imagine unquiet slumbers for the sleepers in that quiet earth.
>
> E. Bronte, *Wuthering Heights*

> Sitting opposite a middle-aged man who was hiding behind a copy of the Telegraph, reading about guerillas in Latin America, was an urban freedom fighter. And as the train followed its customary and prescribed route - East Finchley, Archway, Camden Town, Warren Street - Sumitra knew that when she stepped for the last time off the Northern Line, she would be stepping into a new life.
>
> R. Smith, *Sumitra's Story*

> ... I put my nose to the undercarriage and sniffed for five seconds, nothing spiritual happened but my nose stuck to the plane! My father took me to Casualty to have it removed, how I endured the laughing and sniggering I don't know.
>
>   The Casualty doctor wrote 'Glue Sniffer' on my outpatient's card.
>
>   I rang Pandora; she is coming round after her viola lesson. Love is the only thing that keeps me sane ...
>
> S. Townsend, *Secret Diary of Adrian Mole Aged 13¾*

WRITING DIALOGUE

DIALOGUE AND SPONTANEOUS TALK

DIALOGUE AND DIRECT AND INDIRECT SPEECH

IDENTIFYING DIALOGUE

WRITING DIALOGUE

GETTING STARTED

Writing dialogue is something that you may be given an opportunity to do in a written paper for some of the GCSE Groups, and it is certainly well worth attempting dialogue if you are submitting coursework. In the imaginative writing section of WJEC papers some questions will require writing of a particular form, but others may leave candidates free to choose their approach; here then may be an opportunity for writing dialogue, or a short play. The coursework guidelines of the same Group say 'one of the two pieces of imaginative writing may be either poetry or a drama script', and ULEAC says similarly that coursework 'may include dialogue and verse'. The NEAB syllabus for GCSE offers candidates opportunities to recount real and imagined experience in any appropriate form such as narrative, description or drama.'

ESSENTIAL PRINCIPLES

1 DIALOGUE AND SPONTANEOUS TALK

The **first** thing to remember is that **dialogue is not simply spoken English that has been written down**. Compare the following list of some of the features of **spontaneous talk** and **written-down speech**:

Talk
a) Loosely structured and often rambling – repeating itself or missing out information that is known or shared;
b) not in complete sentences;
c) often ungrammatical;
d) has a wide vocabulary range which can include slang, technical terms, formal words, etc.;
e) depends on stress, pace, pitch and volume to convey mood;
f) depends on contact with a listener – uses non-verbal features, e.g. gesture and facial expression.

> **"** Dialogue isn't just written down talk **"**

Dialogue
a) Selected to make a dramatic point;
b) often in complete sentences;
c) less often ungrammatical;
d) vocabulary is more controlled by dramatic situation;
e) moods to be conveyed indicated by stage directions or by including adverbs, e.g. 'Goodbye!' (wistfully);
f) lacks non-verbal features.

Some kinds of talk, e.g. a radio cricket commentary, having a telephone conversation or making a formal speech to the school assembly, are perhaps mid-way between spontaneous talk and dialogue. Check each against the lists above and think how each poses special problems for the speaker in terms of the situation he or she is in. Take a radio commentary, for example, where listeners depend on the speaker for full details of the scene. There may well be a considerable range of types of people listening, so any commentary must be widely intelligible in choice of language, as well as lively and accurate. Contrast talking on the telephone: you cannot see how your listener is responding and he or she cannot see you waving your hands or frowning. What do you do to your speech to compensate for this? You may have written out a speech to be given at assembly, but how are you to keep a live audience's attention in the way you deliver it?

2 DIALOGUE AND DIRECT AND INDIRECT SPEECH

A **second** point to remember is **that dialogue in a play is not the same as a stretch of direct speech in a story**. (It is, incidentally, often a good idea to include snatches of talk in your personal writing – it adds liveliness and a touch of realism.) These two kinds of written speech will be rather different, though, and if you use indirect speech in a story, that will differ again.

Compare the following:

■ Jane (*sadly*): It's bad news, I'm afraid. I won't be allowed to come.
  John (*angrily*): Oh, that's not fair!
■ Jane came into the room slowly and sadly. She paused before she said 'It's bad news, I'm afraid. I won't be allowed to come.'
  John shouted out 'Oh, that's not fair!'
■ Jane came into the room slowly and sadly. She paused before she said that she was afraid it was bad news. She wouldn't be allowed to come. John replied angrily that it was not fair.

The three examples differ in effect.

The first – **dialogue** – has most impact: it is vivid and seems to be happening now. On the stage, or in a television play, you would hear the tone of voice and the extra volume of John's angry retort, and see the expressions and gestures of both speakers.

The second – **direct speech** – happened in the past. The only hints that you are given as to the mood of the speakers are the occasional adverbs 'slowly and sadly', or verbs such as 'shouted'.

The third – **indirect speech** – has an even more distanced effect. The speech is in the past and is reported. We lack a sense of either speaker being immediately present and responding personally to the situation.

In order to convey these degrees of immediacy, each type of speech has to be presented differently, in terms of punctuation and lay-out. How to do this will be discussed below.

Can you tell the difference between dialogue, and direct and indirect speech?

USEFUL PRACTICAL APPROACHES

3 ▶ IDENTIFYING DIALOGUE

Compare the following extracts: one is a stretch of dialogue from a play and the other is a transcript of an actual conversation. Can you tell which is which?

A **Gus**: I saw the Villa get beat in a cup tie once. Who was it against now? White shirts. It was one-all at half-time. I'll never forget it. Their opponents won by a penalty. Talk about drama. Yes, it was a disputed penalty. Disputed. They got beat two-one, anyway, because of it. You were there yourself.
Ben: Not me.
Gus: Yes, you were there. Don't you remember that disputed penalty?
Ben: No.
Gus: He went down just inside the area. Then they said he was just acting. I didn't think the other bloke touched him myself. But the referee had the ball on the spot.
Ben: Didn't touch him! What are you talking about? He laid him out flat!
Gus: Not the Villa. The Villa don't play that sort of game.
Ben: Get out of it.

B **Mary**: Hello … hasn't it turned cold!
Sally: Um … it's freezing.
Mary: I'm …
Sally: You're making sausage rolls. Having a party?
Mary: No-o.
Sally (*laughs*).
Mary: No, they're for our tea.
Sally: Um … they look very, very 'more-ish!
Mary: Get off! (*laughter*) Get away! You … you … (*laughter*).
Sally: Lena come home, then?
Mary: Yeah.
Sally: How long'a she staying, 'cos I …
Mary: Don't know. Let's hope it's a bit longer than last time!

It's quite difficult to tell which is which isn't it. Extract A is from a play by Harold Pinter called *The Dumb Waiter*, whereas extract B was written down from a recording of two women talking. Go back to the check list of features of talk and dialogue and you will probably agree that the first is really much more orderly than the second, even though the speakers are conversing casually. The second has 'Ums', and false starts of a kind that could be very confusing in writing, whereas the first has clearly defined utterances – often complete sentences. The vocabulary in the second could range very widely, as the chat continues, but in the first it is very much concentrated on the matter in hand. We cannot gauge the changes of mood in either extract, because we cannot see and hear the speakers. Nevertheless, features and facial expression, as well as stress, changes of pace, pitch and volume would be a very important aspect of the second extract, and would be added by the actors in the first. So dialogue, however informal, is usually more orderly and clearer than normal speech, and each speaker usually responds directly to what the last has said.

4	WRITING DIALOGUE

66 Did you know that punctuating dialogue is easy? 99

66 Why not try a story board? 99

Dialogue is easy to write because it is simple to punctuate, if you follow a system of presentation such as that shown above, i.e. write the names of the speakers on the left, followed by a colon, and end each remark with a full-stop. Put any brief directions, e.g. about the speaker's mood, in brackets, before the colon. Avoid long narrative stretches between dialogue. If you must have stage directions, keep these as short as possible, and preferably put them at the beginning of the scene.

Scripts for television drama require a rather special approach. One device worth knowing about is a 'story board'. Here, you break down the action into a series of shots, maybe some long shots (for scenes at a distance), a few panning shots (where the camera sweeps around the scene) and occasional close-ups. Next, you draw a series of strip pictures, indicating below each which shot it is and the dialogue you want to use to match it.

Middle-distance shot – sets scene.

Close-up of Clare: – looks worried.

Middle-distance shot – close to school gates.

Middle-distance shot – at the disco.

C: Hi, Sam.
S: Watcha! Have you finished with the stuff I borrowed?
C: No, not quite.

S: What's wrong?
C: Oh, nothing. Just thinking about something.
S: What are your thinking about? You look as if you've done something really bad.
C: Not really.
S: Anyway, when are you going to bring 'em?
C: Soon
S: How soon?
C: Say in a week's time?
S: All right.

C: Going to the disco tonight? It's going to be really good.
S: Yeah, I'm going, but guess who's taking me?
C: Who?
S: Clinton.
C: You mean Clinton Jones?

S: Oh, Clinton. This is great!
CJ: I can see that you're enjoying yourself.
S: Yeah. Oh, there's Clare – soon come ...

Fig 13.1

Figure 13.1 shows the start of a story board for the play entitled *Excuses* – see Question 1 below. This helps to keep to the point and achieve an effective dramatic pace and overall tight structure. It is well worth trying – even in the planning stage of any piece of drama.

EXAMINATION QUESTIONS

Here is a selection of the types of question that will give you opportunities for writing dialogue:

QUESTION 1

Write a short play entitled *Excuses*.

QUESTION 2

Write a short dramatic scene about a memorable incident at school or college.

QUESTION 3

Write an episode as a continuation of a television drama series that you enjoy watching.

QUESTION 4

Write an exciting episode from a story you have read, as if it were a scene from a play.

QUESTION 5

The 'phone rings several times before Speaker A picks up the receiver.
A: Hello. Canning Town 45678.
B: Is Frankie there?
A: Well, yes. Speaking.
B: Well, you don't know me, but Ron Fisher suggested I should ask you if you'd like to be included next Saturday …
(Continue the conversation in a suitable way).

QUESTION 6

Continue the following dialogue in a manner which develops the dramatic situation, adding one or two more characters, or a further scene, if you wish.

At eleven o'clock pupils troop into the hall for a special assembly. The staff and head teacher come in, grim-faced. The head teacher rises to speak.
Head teacher: I have asked you to assemble today for a special announcement. Rarely, in my long experience in this school, have I had to face such a stuation.
Chris (*whispering*): Oh, he'll talk for half an hour now. I know him.
Head teacher: It appears that some of you saw fit to spend the lunch-hour yesterday in activities which created a local scandal. I have some idea of who the culprits may be, but I will give them a chance to come forward …

QUESTION 7

Continue the following dialogue in a manner which develops the dramatic situation, adding one or more characters, or a further scene, if you wish.

A car comes to a halt in a snowy lane. The driver leaves his car and crunches his way up a long drive to a big house. There is one small lighted window on the second floor. He knocks and pauses.
Traveller (*calling*): Hello. Is there anyone there? Hello!
(*The door opens slowly and a boy looks out cautiously*).
Traveller: Look, I've broken down. Could you give me a push while I try to get started, or something.
Boy: Well, I don't know about that. Why don't you come in for a moment …?

P U P I L S '   A N S W E R S

ANSWER 1

Excuses

Clare: Hi Sam.
Sam: Watcha! Have you finished with the stuff I borrowed?
Clare: No, not quite. (Pause)
Sam: What's wrong?
Clare: Oh nothing, just thinking about something.
Sam: What're you thinking about? You look as if you've done something really bad.
Clare: Not really.
Sam: Anyway, when're you going to bring 'em?
Clare: Soon.
Sam: How soon?
Clare: Say in a week's time?
Sam: Alright.

(*A week goes by*)

Clare: Going to the disco tonight? It's going to be really good.
Sam: Yeah I'm going, but guess who's taking me?
Clare: Who?
Sam: Clinton.
Clare: You mean Clinton Jones?
Sam: Yeah him.
Clare: Boy, he's gorgeous.
Sam: Yes, Clare.
Clare: What you going to wear then?
Sam: Well, I'm going to wear my short white skirt with my white Wham-style jacket top. I was going to wear my black leather jacket with them but you've got it and two weeks have gone.
Clare: Yeah, I know and I thought I might wear it to the disco tonight.
Sam: *You* thought, you might wear it. What about *me*? It's my jacket, you know. Oh forget it.
Clare: See you tonight then?
Sam: Yeah.

(*The Disco*)

Sam: Oh Clinton, this is great!
Clint: I can see that you're enjoying yourself.
Sam: Yeah. Oh, there's Clare soon come.
Clare: Watcha Sam.
Sam: Hi, Clare. I thought you said you were going to wear the leather jacket.
Clare: I changed my mind.
Sam: You changed your mind. I could have worn that rotten jacket.
Clare: Alright don't get so heated!
Sam: Clare, if you've done something to the jacket let alone the LP's and the bicycle I'll *kill* you …
Clare: Keep your flippin' voice down, the music's not so loud you know.
Sam: Clare, I want to know what you've done with my things.
Clare: Alright let's go in the toilets.
Sam: And don't try to sweet-talk me.
Clare: Sam, just listen, will you. I was going to Julie's house on your bicycle with some of the LP's in the bag I had on my shoulder and, of course, I was wearing your jacket. Anyway, as I got to the gate I parked the bike behind the brick wall but I forget to chain and padlock it. Anyhow, Julie opened the door and we went up to her room but then your jacket got caught on one of the hooks on Julie's door and tore half of the arm off and there was no way I

could do that. After playing the records I was about to go when Julie's brother Michael came in, jumping on the records and smashed them to bits. I came running down to take the bike and that was gone. Sam, I nearly went through Julie's window! I thought I'd keep giving excuses while I thought of a way to buy them back, without you knowing …

Sam: Oh my God, Clare, you're right. You're going to buy them back. What am I going to tell me mum?

Clare: Sam, please don't be angry with me …

Sam: Don't be angry, you must be crazy. Just buy back my things and don't ever ask me for anything again. Never!

ANSWER 2

The next short play is called *The Governors' Meeting*, and concerns the investigation of an incident between a pupil and teacher (Question 2):

The Governors' Meeting

This play is set in the Headmistress's office, Mrs Catherine Williams. Five people are attending this meeting: Margaret Keating (the mother of the pupil being discussed), John Andrews, (best friend of Ken Samuels, the teacher who was attacked), Walter Richmond (friend of Margaret Keating's husband) and Elizabeth Walker (Chairperson of School Governors).

Walker: Would you like to come in, ladies and gentlemen?

(*They all go into the room*)

Williams: Take a seat, please.

(*They all sit around a large table.*)

Walker: First I must say, thank you for attending this meeting. Now, we are all here to discuss the incident involving Jennifer Keating and Mr Ken Samuels, the Humanities teacher. I have made out five copies of the report. Would you all please take one.

(*They all take one and read them.*)

Keating: This isn't fair at all! This is not what happened! He's lying! This report is all lies!

Williams: Calm down Mrs Keating. Perhaps you would like to give your account of the incident.

Keating: Well, Jennifer was talking quietly to a class mate when she was told to shut up in the most rude way. Anyway she refused because of the way he spoke to her. She was then asked to leave the room and she refused still. So he took her by the arm and pulled her out of the chair to lead her out of the classroom and she pulled away and he fell over and hit the floor. That's what happened. No big deal. You see, Mr Samuels should be sacked for dragging my daughter about, not my daughter expelled for just defending herself.

Williams: Well, Mrs Keating, if that's the case, then it makes no difference. You see, she still refused to do as she was asked, so she still would be punished.

Keating: Yes, but why should she do anything anyone tells her to do? I'm her mother, I tell her what to do, no-one else!

Walker: Mrs Keating, you are not being very co-operative at all! While Jennifer is in school she is under our authority and we have every right to tell her when she is in the wrong.

Andrews: Mrs Keating, imagine if you can, that you are looking after a friend's daughter. Now this little girl happened to be helping herself to your dinner for the night. Tell me, Mrs Keating, would you think that you have no right to tell this little girl what is wrong to do and what is right to do or would you tell her that it is wrong to take something not belonging to her, and take it away?

Keating:	I'd kill the little cow if she pinched my dinner!
Andrews:	Well, there you are, so what makes you think that only you can tell people what to do and nobody else is permitted to, especially with your daughter?
Keating:	Yes, all right, I was being a bit stupid, wasn't I? But that's still no reason to expel my daughter.
Williams:	Well Mrs Keating we will decide that at the end of this meeting.
Walker:	Let's get on with the meeting shall we? Now, going by Mr Samuel's report, Jennifer was talking and chewing when the rules clearly say that chewing is strictly forbidden. So that's one rule broken. Another is, one way or another Jennifer Keating did actually assault Mr Ken Samuels.
Richmond:	Yes, but only because he assaulted her!
Williams:	Ah, but Jennifer gave him reason to.
Richmond:	I see. If it was the other way round then Jennifer would probably still get the blame.
Walker:	Mr Richmond. It doesn't matter what you would like to think, the truth is she did assault Mr Samuels so there are no ifs and buts about it.
Richmond:	Yes, O.K. I'm sorry.
Walker:	Now, another broken rule was swearing, and swearing is also strictly forbidden and we will not have our pupils abusing the teachers no matter what!
Williams:	Well I'm sorry but the only possible thing we can do is to suspend Jennifer for a little longer, in order to be fair to both sides. It is not a serious enough case for Jennifer to be expelled. Mr Samuels was hurt but it wasn't intended that way. So I have decided that she should be given a clear warning and told not to do it again. If she can abide by these rules then I am willing to have her carry on at this school. Is everyone agreed?
Keating:	Yes, that sounds fair to me. I'm sure she won't do it again.
Walker:	Well, we shall have Jennifer back in two weeks from today.

(Everyone mumbles, some with relief and some with disagreement. They all get up and leave the room.)

ANSWER 3

The third example concerns two brief incidents from an imagined continuation of the television serial *Eastenders* (Question 3):

East-Enders

(Hannah and Tony are re-wed and living happily in the house, done up nicely.)

Tony:	Hannah, I just want you to know that I'll do my best to make things work out … for us.
Hannah:	Tony it will work out, it must. I don't want it to go wrong again, especially with the children.
Tony:	I know. By the way did I tell you Kelvin took his exams again? He passed some of them, but he had a little problem in …
Hannah:	… Maths?
Tony:	Yes

(They both laugh.)

East-Enders

(In the laundry Caroline drops a box of soap powder just as Kelvin and Ian walk in.)

Kelvin:	Oh let me 'elp you!
Caroline:	Thanks.
Kelvin:	Grm … You new around 'ere or you just poppin' in for a quick wash?
Caroline:	No, I just moved in, in the council flats just around the corner. Near the doctor's place.
Kelvin:	You mean Dr Legg? I see.
Caroline:	I got to go now, my room-mate will be wondering where I got to.

Kelvin: Who's she then?
Caroline: No. HE. He's my boyfriend. You see we got engaged just before we moved
            here.
Kelvin: Boyfriend! Engaged! Oh no!!
Caroline: What's wrong – did I say something wrong or something?
Kelvin: No. Here's your powder. I gotta get out of 'ere. Come on Ian!

(They leave quickly.)

Why not try one or two of the above topics yourself?

A TUTOR'S COMMENTS

ANSWER TO QUESTION 1

This has been quite well laid out: notice the brief setting of the scene and the notes, to
indicate music playing. The characters interact through the dialogue, which is
appropriately casual, and some slang is used as tempers rise. Clare's long speech at
the end is getting dangerously like a stretch of narrative, though, isn't it.

ANSWER TO QUESTION 2

Notice how economically the scene has been set and the characters introduced.
Further directions are given in brackets between speakers, and the scene ends with a
final brief direction. The dialogue is realistic, lively, involving give and take, but
keeping to the point and furthering the development of the dramatic incident. There is
some casual speech ('Yes, O.K. I'm sorry') when it is appropriate, but the Chairperson
of the Governors, in contrast, always speaks with a degree of formality. Altogether,
this is a successful scene.

ANSWER TO QUESTION 3

Television 'soap operas' consist of many short episodes and the writer has caught the
spirit of a quickly changing set. Stage directions are kept to a minimum and the
dialogue is very realistic. Both scenes are very economically constructed, and begin
and end effectively.

COURSEWORK – A STEP FURTHER

As you read plays, or watch them in the theatre or on televsion, be alert to the skills of
the dramatist, and try some of them out for yourself.

The importance of a clear presentation or lay-out, of realism in dialogue and a good
shape to a scene have already been discussed.

You could go on to study how characters are established and react to one another in
plays that you read, and notice that most plays have a fairly limited number of

characters. It can be confusing for the audience if too many people are introduced too quickly.

You may pay particular attention, also, to how scenes begin, end and often reach some point of climax. If your play moves along at a very steady pace all the time, perhaps it would be written better as a story. Experiment with the same situation in two kinds of writing, e.g. *The Governors' Meeting* could also have been written successfully as a report, and *Excuses* as a short story.

R E V I E W   S H E E T

 For each extract, state whether it is dialogue, direct speech or indirect speech.

1 Jane came into the room slowly and sadly. She paused before she said that she was afraid it was bad news. She wouldn't be allowed to come. John replied angrily that it was not fair.

_____

2 Jane came into the room slowly and sadly. She paused before she said 'It's bad news, I'm afraid. I won't be allowed to come.'
    John shouted out 'Oh, that's not fair!'

_____

3 Jane (*sadly*): It's bad news, I'm afraid. I won't be allowed to come.
    John (*angrily*): Oh, that's not fair!

_____

> .Look at these sentences, which involve *direct speech*.
>
>   'Don't shout at your sister!' scolded my mother
>   'Have you seen my cat?' asked the old man.
>   The teacher began, 'Today we will read page twenty seven.'

Write out the following sentences, putting in speech marks, a fullstop, a comma, an exclamation mark or a question mark as required and any other punctuation needed.

1 will you buy me a new pen please asked John

_____

2 don't be late tomorrow Jane shouted to her friend

_____

3 the bus leaves at four o'clock said the driver

_____

4 the shop assistant asked would you like me to wrap that for you

_____

5 what would you like to do tomorrow asked my mother

_____

6 are we having Maths in the next class period asked the boy

_____

7 the woman said I've seen that film before

_____

8 what time will you be home asked my brother

_____

 Interrupted (Broken) Direct Speech

> We will now look at the layout of speech in a slightly more difficult sentence.
> 'Hello,' said Jane as she came through the door, 'has John arrived home yet?'
> You will see that if the speech marks are interrupted then you still separate the direct speech from the rest of the sentence by a comma, exclamation or question mark (except at the end, of course, when you usually need a full stop).
> Notice that you do not continue with a capital letter. This is because the speaker's words have been interrupted but the sentence has not been completed. For example: "Excuse me," she said, "is this seat free?"

Now write out each of these sentences correctly.

1 All passengers for Hong Kong said the announcer should go to gate 16

_____

2 Can you help me said the stranger because I seem to be lost

_____

3 Move over said my friend you're taking up too much space

_____

4 Well done said the captain you've been chosen for the team

_____

5 This film frightens me I said so don't leave me alone please

_____

6 You're very naughty said the woman to the child so you can't have any sweets

_____

7 I love this music said Jane do you

_____

8 Get in said the taxi driver which hotel are you going to

_____

9 Please may I borrow your pen John asked as mine has run out of ink

_____

10 You are very kind I said to have bought me a present

_____

Using a dialogue when writing narrative makes the situation more immediate to the reader. It can help you to revive interest or show detail about a character but as with any technique you need to use it sparingly. If you do use it you must be very careful to punctuate and lay it out correctly.

Remember
1 Each time the speaker changes begin a new line.
2 All words which are spoken must be alongside the name of the speaker, followed by a colon (:).
3 The words spoken must begin with a capital letter and be followed by a piece of punctuation which can be a question mark, an exclamation mark or a full stop.

Rewrite the following passage as *dialogue* and using the correct punctuation (You can include stage directions where appropriate).

Eg: Air Hostess (*briskly*): Excuse me madam, would you like a drink before dinner?

Excuse me madam said the air hostess briskly would you like a drink before dinner Julia looked up from her book and smiled nervously I think I would like an orange juice please the air hostess returned quickly with her drink and Julia took it gratefully she picked at her dinner when it arrived and when the hostess returned to take the dish away she asked anxiously will we land on time I think so madam is it your first time in Singapore yes Im going to play at a concert this evening and if the plane is even a little late Im afraid I will miss the start the air hostess smiled reassuringly at Julia weve made up some of the time we were delayed but Ill see what else I can do she disappeared behind the curtain at the front of the aircraft while Julia again looked worriedly at her watch will everyone please stay in their seats for a moment came an announcement over the tannoy we have an important passenger who needs to disembark quickly Julia thanked the air hostess as she left the aircraft Im sure Ill be on time now Im very grateful for your help that's alright its all part of the service the girl smilingly replied

CHAPTER

PERSUASIVE WRITING

GETTING YOUR FACTS RIGHT

PLAN YOUR ARGUMENT

BE CLEAR IN YOUR OWN MIND

BE TELLING-AND COMPELLING

GETTING STARTED

Some kinds of speech and writing are deliberately presented from one point of view, e.g. political or debating speeches. Others try to offer a balanced treatment, giving equal weight to the views of either side. Sometimes, if you feel very strongly about an issue, this can be a hard thing to do.

This chapter to some extent follows on from Chapters 7 and 11. When you research and write up a topic, you may wish to persuade the reader to agree with your point of view. Similarly, when you write a summary, you may be asked to present it so as to influence a certain kind of reader. **WJEC** Coursework options require two pieces of work 'employing argument or expressing opinion', and most of the Groups require or suggest some coursework of this sort.

ESSENTIAL PRINCIPLES

1 GETTING YOUR FACTS RIGHT

The most important first step is to *get your facts right*. Opinions are more likely to carry weight if your arguments are well informed. Your own views, however sincerely held, will carry little conviction with readers if they can easily demolish what you are saying on the basis of better information.

> *It can be hard to take a balanced view*

Getting your facts right involves knowing about both sides of an issue, and this has the advantage of helping you to put yourself in the place of those you wish to persuade, or present your case to. If you can see all round your subject, you will be able to defend, as well as attack; you will also be able to challenge your audience about what you think may be their mis-held opinions as well as to urge what you wish on your own account. When writing, as well as when talking, it is best not to let your emotions get the better of you. Clarity of thought and argument is usually more persuasive than strong feeling, however sincere.

2 PLAN YOUR ARGUMENT

It is a good idea to *plan your argument* so as to make it as effective as possible. A simple plan for a piece of persuasive writing can be made by outlining the sections to be covered, as in the following example.

a) A strong, or challenging opening.
b) A series of headings, following the stages of the argument, e.g.
   i) 'This discussion is about …'
   ii) 'Some people consider that …'
   iii) 'But others consider that …'
   iv) 'You yourself may feel that both …'
   v) 'However, I would hope to convince you that …'
   vi) 'In conclusion …'
c) Make your own conclusion memorable, reassuring, even a battlecry – whatever seems appropriate.

3 BE CLEAR IN YOUR OWN MIND

Once you have gathered material from which to make a case, and are planning the stages of the argument, try to be *absolutely clear*, avoiding giving any impression that you are in a state of confusion. Try to be simple and forcible, and do not introduce a mass of unnecessary detail.

4 BE TELLING – AND COMPELLING

You will want to hold your readers' or listeners' attention, so avoid dealing entirely in general statements. Try to *enliven* what you say or write with a few well-chosen examples, or an anecdote, e.g. something humorous or dramatic. Most people find that some variety of this kind makes a general argument much easier to follow. A direct appeal is better than an indirect, so avoid using the impersonal 'one'; 'you' is preferable.

USEFUL PRACTICAL APPROACHES

There are some devices of persuasive writing that have been familiar from the time of the Greek civilisation and have often been used since. Of course, persuasive writers and speakers can distort the truth, leaving out vital information and becoming, in short, propagandist. Even so, there are some devices of style in persuasive writing that you could well employ, such as the following:

a) EXAGGERATION

To overstate your case grossly is self-defeating, as the audience will become suspicious. To go amusingly well beyond the facts may, however, help to persuade, e.g.

'For every house they have built, we shall build five hundred!'

An opponent's position can be mocked and undermined by exaggeration, e.g.

'We know that those against us never have any difficulty whatsoever in making ends meet.'

b) FIGURATIVE LANGUAGE

It is best to be sparing with imagery in argument. However, an appropriate extended image can be very telling because it carries the argument forward in a memorable way, e.g.

'Here in England we have a proud heritage. Remember, only a few, a brave band, fought at Agincourt; only a few fought the Battle of Britain. Once again we turn to only a few, as brave and as determined as those noble ancestors to fight and conquer.'

Be telling: be compelling!

c) PERSUADER WORDS

'Certainly', 'surely', 'definitely', 'it goes without saying' – words and phrases such as those give your readers or listeners the feeling that they *must* agree with you, or be unreasonable!

d) REPETITION

Remember, especially when delivering a speech, that things said once are easily forgotten. Effective persuasion consists of making a point, sometimes several times in different ways, e.g.

'They always speak of their generosity to the community. Was it generous of them to close the Community Hall? Was it generous to stop the project to build more low-cost housing for local people? No, friends, we have a different understanding of "generosity".'

e) RHETORICAL QUESTIONS

These appear to be addressed to all members of the audience, but do not require an answer. They can give an audience a sense of being involved all together.

'Will you stand by and let this happen? Will you?'

The reader or listener is not supposed to look up and say 'No, we won't!', but rather to accept the writer's or speaker's position. This is a device of style which should be used sparingly; too much will tip over into parody and the ridiculous.

EXAMINATION QUESTIONS

Here are some questions which give an opportunity for persuasive and argumentative writing. Try an outline plan for one or two before reading the comments in the following section.

1   Write about the advantages and disadvantages of co-education.
2   'The teenager of today is more responsible and more involved in the fate of the world than teenagers of earlier years.' Discuss this proposition.
3   The motor car: a blessing or a curse?
4   How far do you think individuality should be expressed through appearance?
5   Which arguments would you put forward in favour of a national curriculum for primary schools?
6   Plan a speech outlining what you consider should be recognized as pupils' rights.
7   Write a speech as community representative in favour of restricting the traffic flow through the main streets of your town or village.

PUPILS' ANSWERS

ANSWER 1

Here is a pupil's answer to this question.

The advantages and disadvantages of co-education

The question of whether co-education is such a good idea is constantly being asked by many people.

The most important issue that parents would first want to be reassured on if their children were to be sent to a mixed school would be the effect that co-education would have on their son's or daughter's studies.

Members of the teaching profession are often just as worried about the effects that a mixed class would have on the general discipline. Boys, when mixed with girls in class, tend to go in for more answering back than usual and even the best of teachers could sometimes lose control. Girls, on the other hand, tend to be quieter and take a less active part.

The effects that co-education would have on the general standard of work would depend largely on the boy or girl concerned. Assuming that the teacher kept control, then some boys and girls would probably find the competition fiercer, and to keep face, would be likely to work harder – resulting in a general raising of standards. On the other hand, boys and girls with less will-power would be easily distracted from their lessons and might be better off in separate schools.

Many boys and girls often feel awkward when in the company of members of the opposite sex, either from natural shyness or from self-consciousness. For them, compulsory company is very helpful for they do not have to make the move to meet other friends but see them and get to know them every day, and may even be encouraged to take part in school activities, such as plays and operas, with them.

From these few points, it may be seen that the choice between co-education and separate education is a difficult one and that it is not possible to say if one is definitely better than the other.

ANSWER 2

Here is a pupil's answer to this question.

The teenager of today is more responsible and more involved in the fate of the world than teenagers of earlier years.

I think this statement is true, mainly because the problems are much greater than they were years ago. Also the problems that arose yeas ago were not publicized and widespread as they are now. The teenagers of today have realized that things like the atom bomb will be a major problem when they become older, as well as the storage of nuclear waste. They should have a say in the matter as it is they who will have to solve the problem in years to come.

Adults go on about the Ban-the-Bomb enthusiasts and say they're just lay-abouts who think they're big if they support it. In my opinion a minority are, but the majority are sincere in their wishes. The older generation don't realise that the younger generation do take an interest in politics and the future of the world.

Earlier teenagers were aware of the problems of their time but didn't do anything about it. They are probably too scared of the authorities to hold demonstrations and protest marches. The teenagers of today are definitely more involved in the fate of the world, and a lot of them are certainly as responsible as the older generation. All generations, though, have good and bad in them.

Another problem that has made teenagers more responsible is unemployment. They have to consider what sort of future there is for themselves and their children.

ANSWER 3

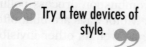 **Try a few devices of style.**

Here is a pupil's outline plan for this question. Read this first, before going on to read the essay itself (see below).

PLAN

Need for cars
1) Form of transport
2) Gives you more time
3) Can be used for work or leisure

Expensive
1) A luxury
2) Tax; insurance
3) Petrol; maintenance
4) Status symbol – Rolls; Jaguar
5) Car clubs – restoring cars
6) Types of cars – sports, saloons

Pollution
1) Fumes – wildlife
2) Noise
3) Motorway – build through countryside

Conclusion
1) Essential to many people
2) Keep industry going
3) Need for balance between nature and the car

The plan is simple but clear. The writer thinks of his arguments under four headings: Need for cars; Expensive; Pollution; and Conclusion. Section one is obviously arguing for the motor car and three is obviously against, and so is section two at the beginning, although it is hard to tell whether points (4) to (6) are for or against. The Conclusion begins by supporting the motor car and ends with a balanced argument. This seems a promising outline plan for an essay which considers both sides of the argument. Now read the essay itself.

The Motor Car: a Blessing or a Curse?

The first motor car was invented one hundred years ago by a Mr Daimler, who was duly helped by Mr Benz. At the time the invention was seen to be something of a folly and was merely felt to be a play thing for the wealthy. Today the story is different; the motor car has become for many people an essential form of transport, which gives comfort and pleasure. In remote areas of the country where buses are infrequent and trains do not run, the car transports people to work and after work provides the transport for leisure outings.

Cars are very expensive to buy, not though as costly as they were before mass production came into being; they come in many forms from sports cars to beach buggies. The sports car enthusiasts often spend countless time and money on their machines; chrome plated engines are just a small luxury for these car lovers. Wives and girlfriends have to take the back seat when it comes to a choice between the annual classic car show or the holiday in Spain. I for one feel this is taking the love of the car just a little too far, but I can see the reason they enjoy their cars so much. Nothing can diminish the thrill and feeling of automatic superiority when behind the wheel of a true aristocrat of cars, such as a Jaguar or Porsche. The car you drive immediately says something about its owner, whether it be true or not. Jaguars and Rolls Royces state the fact that you have money. Porsches that you are successful and in a hurry; these are of course phantasms of the imagination because no one knows for sure what the person behind the wheel is really like. Not too long ago I owned a TR7. I was and still am not wealthy, many thought I was however, the police especially, who took a rather unwelcome fondness towards my car; I eventually sold it. The cost of running and maintaining it was too much and it attracted attention.

To me one of the most neglected issues surrounding the car is its environmental cost. The fumes generated as the waste products of the combustion process pollute our countryside, reducing the wildlife and plant kingdoms. Motorways are built often without due attention to the environment, bringing noise as well as other invisible pollutants.

Despite all the car's disadvantages there are its many advantages. It gives people a freedom which they did not have before and perhaps, most important of all, it provides a great service to industry; something we all benefit from. I do feel though, that a balance has to be set between the environment and the car so we do not lose what many of us have come to take for granted: our countryside.

TUTOR'S OUTLINE ANSWERS

ANSWER 4

Notice that this question begins with the phrase 'How far ...' You will be expected to gauge the extent to which individuality should be expressed through appearance. Here is a topic which almost demands detailed examples. It is difficult to imagine a way of writing successfully and interestingly on it in wholly general terms. On the other hand, there is a danger that you might get too involved in the detailed examples and lose the thread of the argument. Once again, a simple outline plan will avoid this. Spend a few minutes writing one for yourself, taking care to support the main points of argument with good illustrations. The following would be a typical approach:

How far do you think individuality should be expressed through appearance?

1 **People judge by appearances**
a) Appearance makes an impact.
b) Some people like to go to extremes in this respect, e.g. Punks.
c) It is important to make your appearance appropriate for the occasion, though, e.g., weddings, interviews.

2 **Appearance is a way of expressing personality**
a) Most people experiment with different 'looks', especially when they are young.
b) On the other hand, young people tend to choose to look alike, e.g. wearing blue jeans.
c) Sometimes people have to wear a uniform because their role socially is more important than their individuality, e.g. the police.
d) Sometimes whether a uniform should be worn is open to debate, e.g. school uniform.

3 **Conclusion**
a) As far as possible let people have freedom of choice.
b) Remember, though, there is a need for group identity expressed through appearance, too.

This is just one possible plan among many. It does offer a structure and a degree of balance in discussing the issue, though.

ANSWER 5

The matter of a national curriculum for both primary and secondary schools has been much discussed recently, so you would need to do a little research for this question. You could start with what you know, and list what you consider to be basic to the primary curriculum, using your own memories of that stage of education. A well-informed essay would look at some of the current arguments in favour of a more standardized approach to all learning in schools. The arguments against might mention the value of individual teachers passing on what they are enthusiastic about and enjoy teaching. There are also points to be made about equality of opportunity to learn, and the importance of a good grounding in subjects that pupils and society will need more of in the future, e.g. science, or computing. This is a starting point. Try developing a plan along these lines for yourself.

ANSWER 6

In addition to deciding upon your main arguments, you have to think about impressing them on your audience – whether readers or listeners. I'm sure that you will be able to think immediately of a list of possible pupils' rights. Put them down, then check each one to see if it can be reconciled with working in a school community or with the different responsibilities that arise when children are not at home. For example, you may think it should be a right for school children to leave the school premises at lunch times. To deny them this may seem a limitation of their personal freedom. Yet what about the responsibility of the head and teachers for their pupils? How can they be sure that no accidents will occur to unsupervised young people? How would this fit in with their legal responsibilities, etc.?

When you have written your list, think about the likely audience – probably pupils and/or teachers. To persuade, you have to sound as if you believe in the ideas you are putting forward and also show that you are ready to defend against opposing views. Look back at points made earlier in the chapter on how to keep and hold your audience's attention.

ANSWER 7

As this is a written speech, you should devote more attention to wording your arguments very carefully. Such an issue always has people strongly in favour and strongly against. In the first group might be those who wish to preserve the character of the town or village; who live in the main street and would like it to be quieter; who are concerned about the danger to people and buildings from increasingly heavy traffic. Against might be those who say that heavier traffic will bring more trade to the community and perhaps provide public transport too for the convenience of local people. If the traffic is diverted, the town or village may become a backwater – dead, rather than sleepy. Think of a town or village that you know well and relate these arguments, and any others you can think of, to particular circumstances.

TUTOR'S COMMENTS ON PUPILS' ANSWERS

COMMENTS ON ANSWER 1

This answer is well planned and well balanced throughout. It starts with arguments rather against the idea of co-education: parents' concern about standards; the possible adverse effects on boys and on girls; and teachers' worries. The two following paragraphs consider both sides of the case, however: sometimes teachers do lose control; sometimes standards will fall, but, on the other hand, they may be raised in the face of stronger competition, etc. There may be awkwardness for boys and girls at first, but greater familiarity should be beneficial. The final paragraph is a good example of moderation. What is needed in addition are some examples or anecdotes to make one or two of these well-argued points really vivid and memorable. In general, though, this is a competent piece of work.

COMMENTS ON ANSWER 2

The use of the first person pronoun throughout this essay has the effect of catching the reader's attention: here apparently is someone telling you what he or she actually thinks. There are phrases throughout which express strong support for teenagers and, equally important, an awareness of bias against them – that they are considered by some to be boastful 'layabouts' if they take up a cause they believe in. In general the reader is involved, and carried along by the individual 'voice' of this piece of writing. Organization, though, could have been better: the final paragraph, for example, would have fitted in well after the second paragraph, before the discussion is broadened to what adults today think, or what teenagers in the past were like. The sentence 'All generations, though, have good and bad in them', would have made a rather appropriate ending if it had been placed last.

COMMENTS ON ANSWER 3

This is a balanced discussion of the pros and cons of the car, written with good sense and humour. As well as offering a range of points on both sides, the writer introduces some of his own experiences as a car owner, to provide detail. The essay begins well, with a brief historical sketch of early motoring. The temptation to write a lengthy work on the history of the motor car, and by doing so risk a tedious opening, is avoided. The argument moves on from the historical sketch through a discussion of types of cars and problems of ownership to wider issues: e.g. environmental factors. The concluding paragraph is positive and realistic. There are some awkward expressions and a few errors, but this is a very competent discussion.

COURSEWORK –
A STEP FURTHER

Take opportunities to read effective discussions about important contemporary issues and to listen to the wide variety of public speaking styles in the media today. You will learn a good deal about ways of presenting argument: how best to order your points but also how best to have some impact on the receiver of your communication, whether reader or listener. In the latter case, non-verbal communication (NVC, for short) also makes a vital contribution: does the speaker look confident, sincere, honest? Do hand gestures seem vague or suggest the dictatorial? How does the speaker pace his or her utterances – slowly enough for the audience to take in and reflect on what is being argued, or too slowly, tending to drag, boring the audience and losing its interest? In writing, it is vital to keep the interest of your readers if you hope to convince them. Notice devices of style used by writers whose work you admire. Some of these might be experimented with in your own attempts at writing to persuade.

R E V I E W   S H E E T

✎ Write down the 'technique' or 'style' of persuasive writing used in each of the following. (Sometimes more than one 'technique' may be used at the same time!)

1
If they can create 1,000 jobs we will create 10,000.

2
Surely only someone who would willingly mistreat children or animals could possibly hold such a view?

3
Our opponents would, of course, claim that they knew the mind of every reader of this newspaper.

4
No-one in this audience could possibly hold such a view, could they?

5
Was it patriotic to leave the country? Was it patriotic to say such a thing? Was it patriotic to give shelter to an enemy of the people? Was it?

6
As in days of old, when this proud nation defied the might of the invading Spanish Armada, so today we will resist any attempt to invade our land.

✎ In persuasive writing you will often wish to use adjectives with a 'positive' association for things you wish the reader to support, and adjectives with a 'negative' association for things you wish the reader to oppose.

Mark the seventy-five adjectives below with either P for those that normally have a positive connotation or with N for those that normally have a negative connotation.

abhorrent ___	contemptible ___	frustrating ___	putrid ___	striking ___
absorbing ___	crafty ___	hideous ___	pessimistic ___	strong-minded ___
abysmal ___	cunning ___	humane ___	picturesque ___	stubborn ___
alarming ___	decent ___	immoral ___	prejudiced ___	stupendous ___
anguished ___	depraved ___	loathsome ___	promising ___	superb ___
appalling ___	despairing ___	mediocre ___	rational ___	superlative ___
appealing ___	detestable ___	misleading ___	resolute ___	tedious ___
barbaric ___	disgusting ___	moving ___	scrupulous ___	tense ___
base ___	elegant ___	naive ___	selfless ___	touching ___
beneficial ___	enchanting ___	objective ___	sensational ___	touchy ___
biased ___	engrossing ___	obstinate ___	sentimental ___	trying ___
breath-taking ___	evil ___	odious ___	serene ___	unsightly ___
captivating ___	exhilarating ___	offensive ___	shameful ___	wicked ___
congenial ___	fascinating ___	optimistic ___	sinister ___	worthy ___
conscientious ___	foul ___	patronising ___	stimulating ___	wretched ___

✎ Now practise some of the words listed above by choosing an appropriate word to complete the sentences below in any way that seems logical.

1 The view from the top of the mountain is _____ .

2 That people should live in such wretched conditions is _____ .

3 Perhaps it is the most _____ book I have ever read since _____ .

4 Some would call him resolute, but I would call him _____ .

5 Although the story is a little _____ , I found it rather _____ in the end.

6 Some of the symbols which the author uses are very _____ .

7 Despite being very _____ , the village is a rather _____ place to live in.

8 The book is completely _____ ; I could not put it down until I had reached the last page.

9 Not being able to solve our problems is very _____ .

10 He has not written much yet but his work is very _____ .

11. He can be said to be _____ in his analysis since he looks at the facts without bias.

12. It was an _____ performance, losing by ten goals to our opponents.

✎ The word 'should' is often used in persuasive writing to help express strong opinion. Eg. Can it be right that people *should* be treated like this?

Think of a topic that you have strong feelings about – a social problem, perhaps, or the relationships between young and old, rich and poor, men and women. Then continue the sentences below in any appropriate way, using 'should' to emphasise the strength of your feelings.

1 It shocks me that _____ .

2 It is ridiculous that _____ .

3 That _____ astounds me.

4 It is inevitable that _____ .

5 It is remarkable that _____ .

6 Can it be fair that _____ ?

✎ Now *write down* some reasons (or argument/evidence) to support the opinions you have expressed.

1 _____
_____

2 _____
_____

3 _____
_____

4 _____
_____

5 _____
_____

6 _____
_____

DESCRIPTIVE WRITING

GETTING STARTED

In some English Course books published earlier this century there used to be advice on how to set about descriptive writing. The basic idea was what later came to be jokingly referred to as 'the two adjectives to every noun' kind of writing. Even so, the essence of good descriptive writing is to convey to your reader, as vividly as you can, the sensuous aspects of your subject – what he or she would see, smell, taste, touch and hear, and, rather more elusive to put down on paper, its spirit, so that it becomes like a living experience to the reader. All you have at your disposal to achieve this are words. Get into the habit of observing scenes around you closely and trying to capture them in words. The writer, James Joyce, and some others too, used to jot down on envelopes or scraps of paper ideas which occurred to them, rather as an artist uses his sketch book.

ESSENTIAL PRINCIPLES

1 > USING WORDS
WITH
DISCRIMINATION

66 Be observant! 99

The words you choose when you write a description are very important, and should be thought about and selected carefully. It is a common mistake to suppose that you have to clutter your writing with lots of impressive words (worst of all load it down monotonously with 'two adjectives to every noun'). The essential principle is to use words with discrimination, so that they both give a vivid and realistic impression of your subject and help to create the spirit of the thing, as referred to above. You may use words **literally** or **figuratively** (see below for more details of this) but above all use them aptly. Figurative expressions can be very effective in bringing your subject to life, but use them sparingly and try not to 'over write', i.e. use a figure of speech in almost every line, so that the reader finds himself or herself tripping over them, instead of being carried along by them.

2 > LITERAL AND
FIGURATIVE
EXPRESSIONS

Read and think about the following poem written by a fourth year pupil:

THE PIG

Smooth and plump and pink, the pig
With wriggly, curly tail,
Surveys complacently the yard
And the rim of the old tin pail.

'Now tell us, Pig, what are your thoughts?
What is it you can see?'
'I see my yard, my pail, my world –
The world belongs to me.'

'Why, foolish Pig, now don't you know,
Beyond this old stone wall,
There lies a world so very big
You cannot see at all.'

'Don't be absurd,' the pig replied,
'These things just cannot be.
The world is girdled by this wall,
The world belongs to me!'

Why is this simple poem so effective? Surely, because it presents the concentrated point of view of a very limited-minded animal. The pig's world is defined by the boundaries of the wall: it has no words, and no ideas, for what is beyond it.

Now read and contrast this poem, written by the same pupil:

BIRDS

A robin, cheerful companion.
Snaps at caterpillars gaily,
Whistling in his throat so low
You have to strain your ears to hear.
And sparrows, underfed starvelings without fear
Flutter and run, and dart from tree to tree.
And there, so small she's difficult to see,
A tiny lady, a wren hiding shyly.
And in tuneful melody
A single blackbird mounts guard on the fence.
On the lawn, squabbling, a young thrush politician rants;
And a bluetit – tiny impudence _
Swings among the blackcurrants.

This is expressed much less literally: the language is more metaphorical. Both poems communicate very well, though, don't they.

A similar approach can be used in prose descriptions, too. Take a third example:

'The pouncing fire leaps on its prey like an angry lion. It slowly slinks on its paws and then, with a gigantic leap, pours like a shower of sparks on its kill. Its jaws thrust open wide and with a sigh it is gone, sliding amongst the jungle and then, with a sudden spurt of anger, it quivers into life again and rears and destroys.'

The image of the fire is an excellent one by which the writer can explore his subject with an interest, complexity and emotional involvement beyond the potential of any amount of literal detail.

I referred earlier in this chapter to some English Course books of a traditional style. These also often had lists of figurative expressions for the student to learn and, presumably, then imitate. There is a certain danger in this approach. Students can become self-conscious about using figurative language and can so easily overdo it. This is at least an enterprising and adventurous use of vocabulary, but it can have an adverse effect on the reader. It is as if the writer has not fully fused sense and expression: how do you feel about this next example?

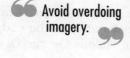
Avoid overdoing imagery.

'Dead! The news stuck like toffee in her mind. It felt heavy and indigestible. Whichever way she spun it out she could not get rid of it. It just stayed stuck!'

I think this makes the point by itself! Remember, though, that those assessing your work are likely to be sympathetic to your experiments with words, and prefer to see you making some mistakes along the way, rather than not venturing into new kinds of expression at all.

Here, then, remembering the warning above, are some examples of *figures of speech* that you could try to use sometimes in your own writing.

3 FIGURES OF COMPARISON

a) SIMILE

A simile is an explicit comparison between two or more things alike in only one respect. The comparison is introduced by 'like' or 'as', e.g.

'She glided cat-like.'

Well-worn or overworked similes in everyday usage are known as **clichés**, e.g. 'as white as a sheet'; 'as red as a beetroot'.

b) METAPHOR

A metaphor is a comparison between two or more things that are alike in some respects. The comparison is usually implied, e.g.

'The fog came on little cat feet'

The comparison is sometimes extended over several lines of expression, as in the following example, written by D. H. Lawrence;

'Naxos thousands of feet below the olive roots,
And now the olive leaves thousands of feet below the lava fire
Peace congealed in black lava on the doorstep.
Within, white-hot lava, never at peace
Till it burst forth blinding, withering the earth;
To set again into rock,
Grey-black rock.
Call it Peace?'

In this case it is called an **extended metaphor**.

There are well worn cliché metaphors, too. When several of them are combined in one utterance they become almost meaningless and sometimes amusing, e.g..

'We are the captains of our fate and must pull ourselves up by our bootlaces, to avoid the sea of troubles ahead.'

c) PERSONIFICATION

This is a metaphor in which human characteristics are attributed to something inanimate, e.g.

'Winter whipped the trees bare.'

On a larger scale, the **fable** and **allegory** are both forms of metaphor.

d) FABLE

A fable is a short narrative, where animals usually represent some trait of human beings for a moral purpose. Often the moral is written separately at the end, e.g. Aesop's *Fables* from the sixth century B.C. A more recent fable is George Orwell's *Animal Farm*.

e) ALLEGORY

An allegory is a story with two levels of meaning: one literal and another more generally understood, e.g. Bunyan's *The Pilgrim's Progress*.

a) ANTITHESIS

This is a comparison in which one idea is set against another, e.g.

Better to live happy and die poor, than live rich and die wretched.'

b) PARADOX

A paradox is a statement which seems to be self-contradictory, but which actually asserts something true, e.g.

'The freezing ice burnt her hand.'

a) ALLITERATION

This is the figure of speech in which the sounds of consonants occurring in words close together are the same, or similar, e.g.

'The cold, cruel, keen northern wind.'

b) ASSONANCE

In assonance the sounds of vowels or syllables in words close together are the same, or similar, e.g.

'She heard a crisp sound, as if of ice splitting and hissing.'

c) ONOMATOPOEIA

This is the figure of speech in which the sound of a word imitates a well-known sound, often in nature, e.g.

'Miaow'.

EXAMINATION QUESTIONS

All the Groups are likely to give candidates an opportunity to write a 'set piece' description (either in a written paper, or as coursework), and you will probably include stretches of description in your other creative writing. For descriptive writing in response to a stimulus, see the next chapter.

Here is a list of typical questions. (Some of them relate to passages, set by the Groups on GCSE papers, which have been discussed in earlier chapters. Page references have been given where appropriate, so that you can turn back.)

QUESTION 1

Write descriptively about an old and perhaps ruined castle or church.

QUESTION 2

Think of something you would really like to own (it might be a piece of equipment of clothing or even a toy) and write a description of it, explaining in detail what it is, where it can be bought and why you want it. **(ULEAC)**

QUESTION 3

Imagine that you are the vet in the passage written by Jacqui Durrell. Describe your experiences of a typical visit to her home based on what you have read in the passage from *Intimate Relations*. (see page 112) **(SEG)**

QUESTION 4

Write a description of a place you know and love well. **(NEAB)**

QUESTION 5

'A Wet Day by the Sea.' **(MEG)**

QUESTION 6

'A Walk in Autumn.'

QUESTION 7

'Clouds.'

QUESTION 8

Describe a crowded beach. As you watch, a thunderstorm breaks and the holidaymakers run for shelter. Describe the events as they happen and conclude by describing the deserted beach. **(WJEC)**

QUESTION 9

The joys and miseries of a winter's afternoon on the school field. **(WJEC)**

QUESTION 10

What is it like where you live? You may like to write about the kind of people who live near you, perhaps describing some of the well-known characters and/or some of the places that you think make your neighbourhood lively and interesting or dismal and boring. **(NEAB)**

OUTLINE AND PUPILS' ANSWERS

There are two kinds of descriptive writing required by these questions: free writing, and writing related to a passage you are given. Remember that in the second case (Questions 1, 2, 3 and 4 above) you must write within the limitations of the details in the passage, unless you are specifically told that you may expand on them.

ANSWER 6

Here is a pupil's *outline* for an essay 'A Walk in Autumn':

It is Autumn
Rough winds
Cold weather becoming wintery
Trees are bare
Old houses are dominant and rickety
Autumn fireplaces burn wood, creating smoke
Three people walk down the lane. A solitary gentleman and two women.
The surrounding lands are dying.
The lane is well worn, probably by horse and cart
The twist in the road encloses the village
The gentleman is going home for his tea
The two ladies are out for an Autumn walk in the fresh, cool air
The sky is filling with clouds as the blue clear skies of Summer fade away
The clouds ride the skies
There are no animals to be seen as they are probably hibernating
The valley to the left looks cold and secluded
Snow is soon to fall.

As you see, it is a list of quick impressions, moving from general ideas which characterize the weather and the appearance of the countryside at this season, to setting the scene in a particular village, where three people are out walking. The mood changes, towards the end, with hints that winter is coming: '… the blue clear skies of Summer fade away'; 'There are no animals to be seen as they are probably hibernating' and 'Snow is soon to fall'.

Now read the essay right through:

The figure of a gentleman, briskly walks home from his day of work at his workplace. He is on his way home to his wife who will have prepared tea and biscuits to warm him from the cooling air of Autumn.

The rough winds blow the leaves from the trees and bushes as he passes them by. The trees are now looking bare and shodden as the Autumn gusts create a wintery feel to the air. The surrounding land appears to be dying as leaves turn to brown and die, falling gently to the ground.

The sky now begins to fill with Autumn clouds as the blue, clear, quiet skies of Summer fade away. The clouds are dark and glide briskly through the skies as they bring new weather to the scene.

The village lane appears well worn over the years by horse and cart as they would have crashed through the village. The meander in the road encloses the village houses as the lane disappears up the hill into the distance.

Two ladies are taking a walk up the lane in this cold evening scene. They are well wrapped up in cloaks and they are talking with one another. The cool air fills their lungs as they breathe in. They too are walking home like the gentleman.

The village houses appear old and well used. They have high chimney stacks releasing the smoke created by the burning warmth of the fire below. Smoke rolls from the stacks into the overcast evening sky. The dormant rickety old house at the front of the lane stands like a loner, away from the crowd of the other village houses. It appears empty and still, as if it has not been used for many years and shall soon crumble to a small waste.

There are no animals to be seen. They are probably now hibernating as the months of Winter rapidly build their wake of freezing chills.

The winds now blow and snow is imminent as the barren signs of Winter approach. The trees rustle and crack their branches together in the wind.

The valley behind the village to the left of the scene looks cold and secluded from the rest of the land. Fog is building up, soon to cover the village in a blanket of cool air.

ANSWER 7

Here is a pupil's essay with the title 'The Cloud'. It is chiefly descriptive writing but it is also a story, as you'll see.

The Cloud

Over the countryside a thundercloud formed. Heavy and grey, with an unholy line of light at its rim, it drifted across the setting sun, casting a sudden shadow. As the sun disappeared it grew, and passing over towns in the night gained a murky, yellowish-grey hue that only showed clearly the next morning. It was a cloud like smog; but it wasn't smog.

In the morning the sky was grey and overcast. The cloud drifted over towns to the countryside once more. As the rain began to fall, drops fell from the yellow cloud – large and impure, leaving a brown mark on whatever they touched. Most of the rain from the cloud fell into or drained into a moorland stream, that trickled its way and poured its poisoned waters into a river. The rain stopped falling. The river ran on its way. Imperceptibly at first, its waters became gradually slower and instead of being crystal clear it was now a poisonous brown. Sluggishly it slid through the countryside, past ploughed, brown fields, past grassy, muddy fields where cows came down to drink. The cows who drank from the brown river did not live long, but died the next morning, gasping for air and kicking feebly. No weeds grew in the ploughed fields, and when the planting season came the birds that pecked at the seeds died, quickly.

The river flowed on, carrying its poison with it. The sun, that had once brought sparkles to the clear surface, now only glinted dully in the water making it seem more miserable than before. During a day the leaves in the willow trees turned from green to brown. The rushes in the water turned brown as well and seemed to decay gradually.

A child was paddling in the river's edge and stumbled, falling into the water. The river was shallow at that point and he should have been able to regain his balance. But, strangely, once the brown water had covered him he did not come to the surface again. His body was washed up some miles further down the river. The same happened to a boy, who, climbing in a willow tree, felt the branch crumble beneath him where previously it had been steady as a rock, and he fell downwards into the river.

The river flowed on. Soon it left the countryside and came to a town. On one side it still had a grassy look but for some reason the grass withered and died, leaving only bare earth. Children fishing from the bank were disappointed when hour after hour yielded no fish, not even a tadpole. Anglers had no more success.

A child playing near the river bank scratched himself; a bit of mud from the river entered the scratch, and though the child washed it again and again he fell ill – some sort of tetanus, the doctor said – and the child died.

Where the river widened at one point it was usual for boats to be taken out. This had been done for several years – but only now did the paint flake off and a kind of wood rot come into the bottoms of the boats so that they became unusable.

The river flowed on, bringing death wherever it came. It left the town and crawled through the country again till it slid into the sea and scattered there.

Above the coastline a ragged wisp of yellow cloud appeared, that grew, towards sunset, and drifted away with the wind.

ANSWER 8

A piece of work for this question should be built around the contrasts indicated. You could begin with the crowded beach and end with it deserted. It would be worth while thinking about that first: what details would you observe on the beach on a Summer's day. The sudden storm should be a dramatic happening causing panic and a total change in the behaviour of the sun-bathers. You could conclude by observing the beach, swept by the rain and left to the gulls, soaring overhead. The wording of the question helps you to give a shape to your work, doesn't it.

ANSWER 9

Here you have a choice: the joys *or* the miseries … This title gives an opportunity for strong involvement, perhaps of enthusiasm for your favourite game, or wry humour, as you recall those foggy afternoons when you couldn't see the other players, let alone the ball! Giving a satisfying shape to your work could be a problem here. It would be easy to wander from detail to detail and not really know how to end. Some planning *before* you start is recommended, then. You could, for instance, follow a pattern of contrasts, similar to that in Question 8. Imagine the warmth of the changing rooms and the grim (or enticing) look of the misty field through the window; the numb fingers and toes gradually becoming warm through exercise and, finally, the welcoming sight of the open school door and the gust of warmth blowing out from the central heating!

ANSWER 10

This question, too, invites the use of contrast: you may choose to pick out the lively and interesting or dismal and boring aspects of the place where you live. This is only a suggestion, though, put in to help you get started, as are ideas about the local people or places. A short, honest consideration of the place where you live is the best way to start. Having jotted down a list of things you definitely must write about, think next about how to prevent your essay becoming list-like. Here is a chance to give some attractive anecdotes about local characters, or memories you associate with a particular place. A personal view is asked for, so this should be a very individual account.

A TUTOR'S COMMENTS

These are comments on the above two pieces of work by pupils.

COMMENTS ON ANSWER TO QUESTION 6

In his final version, the writer changed his initial plan slightly. The opening has more impact, with the human interest of the gentleman hurrying home to his tea. The ominous mood has been kept and is built up through a series of details – the 'dying' land, the darkening clouds bringing new weather then the threat of 'freezing chills'. The ending, though, is a little flat and seems incomplete. Notice how well the writer has used contrasts, both to intensify the mood of the piece and to structure it, to some extent. One contrast is drawn between the bleak weather and the warmth of home: the gentleman hurries to tea and biscuits which will 'warm' him from the cooling air of Autumn. The ladies hurry home to village houses where chimneys smoke from 'the burning warmth of the fire below'. One empty house stands apart. That no longer has a human connection and seems likely to return to waste ground soon. Even the animals are sheltering, well away from 'freezing chills'.

The range of vocabulary is not very extensive but describes the scene quite well. There is appeal to four of the senses: sight, in the pictorial aspects of the scene; smell, in the smoke and warm tea; taste is involved there, too, perhaps, and touch in the suggestion of the 'rickety' and 'crumbling' house. The weather is effectively evoked: Autumn 'cooling', 'rough', 'gusts create a Wintery feel'. Clouds are 'dark and glide briskly' unlike the 'blue, clear, quiet skies of Summer' – three simple words which make a good picture.

There is even an attempt at figurative language: a 'meander' is really a bend in a river, crossing a plain. Here, it is applied to the road. The house is 'dormant', i.e. wrapt in a long sleep, and has another human characteristic: it is isolated 'like a loner away from the crowds'. Winter, too, is personified, having 'mouths' which blow 'freezing chills'. The trees have animation – they themselves, rather than the wind, 'rustle and crack their branches'. Finally the fog is said to be about 'to cover the village in a blanket of cool air'. All these images are well integrated into the writing: you probably didn't notice them all on your first reading. Altogether this is rather a successful short description of an Autumn scene.

COMMENTS ON ANSWERS TO QUESTION 7

Although this reads at first as if it is simply descriptive the writer introduces ominous hints about the Cloud, with such words and phrases as 'unholy', 'murky' 'sudden shadow', and the first paragraph ends with the worrying sentence 'It was a cloud like smog; but it wasn't smog.' This suggests a double threat: something dangerous – and unknown.

By the second and third paragraphs the Cloud is openly stated to be poisonous, affecting the river and the vegetation that comes into contact with it. Soon afterwards, a child is affected too. While these events are unwinding, attention is being paid to the appearance of the river: 'The sun, that had once brought sparkles to the clear surface, now only glinted dully in the water' and 'The rushes in the water turned brown as well and seemed to decay'.

Progress of the story is maintained by the river's course; it flows next through the town, with similar results. Perhaps a chance was missed here to give details which would differ more from those given earlier – the child playing is almost a repetition of the earlier incident. A chilling detail is slipped in, though, with the description of the boats and the corrosive effect of the polluted waters upon them 'only now did the paint flake off and a kind of wood rot come into the bottoms of the boats so that they became unusable.' Moving towards the end of the essay, the writer increases the scale of the threat: 'The river flowed on, bringing death wherever it came.' The quiet 'ragged wisp' of cloud drifting away, suggests that the menace will be diffused even more widely.

This very restrained piece of descriptive writing is extremely effective.

COURSEWORK – A STEP FURTHER

In a radio talk called 'Capturing Animals', the poet laureate, Ted Hughes, gave some excellent advice on writing descriptively. He recommended close observation and perception of what you want to describe: 'Just look at it, touch it, smell it, listen to it, turn yourself into it', and then choose words which will bring it to life, until, in short, you will have 'captured a spirit'. This advice could hardly be bettered.

R E V I E W   S H E E T

Figures of speech (or figurative language) help to make our writing more vivid and effective when describing things.

Write down the name given to each of the following *figures of comparison*. Then write a sentence of your own using a different example for each figure of comparison.

1   'The urchin hissed and spat like an angry cat'

Figure of speech: _____

Own example: _____

2   'The snow crept in silently under the door'

Figure of speech: _____

Own example: _____

3   'In the graveyard I laid her to rest in a noiseless nest'.

Figure of speech: _____

Own example: _____

Write down the name given to each of the following *figures of sound effect*. Then write a sentence of your own using a different example each time.

1   '*C*ontentedly *c*ruise the *c*ontinent'

Figure of speech: _____

Own example: _____

2   'Our echoes *roll* from *soul* to *soul*'

Figure of speech: _____

Own example: _____

3   'He listened to the *murmur* of his heart'

Figure of speech: _____

Own example: _____

Good descriptive writing engages the *senses*. Which senses does the poet appeal to in this verse?

> I cannot see what flows are at my feet,
>   Nor what soft incense hangs upon the boughs,
> But in embalmed darkness guess each sweet
>   Wherewith the seasonable month endows
> The grass, the thicket and the fruit tree wild;
>   White hawthorn and the pastoral eglantine;
> Fast fading violets covered up in leaves;
>   And mid-May's eldest child,
> The coming musk-rose, full of dewy wine,
>   The murmerous haunt of flies on the summer eves.

(Keats: 'Ode to a Nightingale')

_____

_____

_____

_____

Which of the five senses of sight, sound, touch, smell and feel are involved in each of these examples? Write down the sense and then write out a sentence of your own with a description involving that sense

rough carpet;   sense – _____

Own example: _____

crash of doors;   sense – _____

Own example: _____

dazzling colours;   sense – _____

Own example: _____

scent of lilacs;   sense – _____

Own example: _____

bitter, sweet flavour;   sense – _____

Own example: _____

✎ Returning to *similes* and *metaphors* as figures of comparison, write down which of these is a simile and which a metaphor.

1   He's as dull as yesterday's news. _____

2   She looked like a freshly opened rose. _____

3   She was a freshly opened rose. _____

4   He's as interesting as a bowl of rice. _____

5   The waves thundered ashore. _____

Now write *three similes* of your own.

1   _____

2   _____

3   _____

Now write *three metaphors* of your own.

1   _____

2   _____

3   _____

✎ Use *each* of the following words in writing a short paragraph describing a person. You might write about a real or an imaginary person.

ingenious	eccentric	distinctive	recognisable
enthusiastic	slightly clumsy	careworn	shabby

_____

_____

_____

_____

_____

_____

_____

_____

RESPONDING TO A STIMULUS

RELEVANCE
QUESTIONS
OUTLINE ANSWERS
PUPIL'S ANSWERS

GETTING STARTED

Earlier, in Chapter 10, the way you might respond to the stimulus of something you had read and enjoyed or felt strongly about was discussed. Other kinds of stimuli, however, are also likely to be part of your work; for instance, looking at pictures and illustrations, watching television programmes, and listening to music. All these are recognized as being good starting points for talking or writing, e.g. the **ULEAC** syllabus for coursework includes 'personal response to such stimuli as pictures, music, poetry and prose'.

The stimulus may be suggested to you by your teacher or tutor, in which case you will probably be guided in writing a response.

If you are taking a written paper, you may be set a task based on a photograph or picture, e.g. a composition based on a photograph (**MEG**); a photograph to be written about in any way you wish (**NEAB**); or, write imaginatively in response to *one* of two pictures (**WJEC**).

Finally, it should be noted that responses to a stimulus also occur as *oral* coursework: **ULEAC, MEG, SEG, WJEC**.

ESSENTIAL PRINCIPLES

1 > RELEVANCE

66 Find a good starting point 99

The chief matter of importance in responding to a given stimulus is to be reasonably relevant. Unless specifically told otherwise (and it is unlikely that you will be), you must not talk or write about it for a few seconds and then move on to spend most of the time allocated on other things. The rule is to be certain that someone reading or listening to your response could see a clear connection between what you write or say and the original stimulus. Also, avoid being too original or unusual; e.g. when given a photograph of a tramp examining an old boot, a pupil wrote about a weekend job in a shoe shop!

EXAMINATION QUESTIONS

The following is a selection of questions of the kind you might find on an examination paper, or that might be suggested to you by your teacher or tutor for coursework.

QUESTION 1

Look at the photograph below. Write about it in any way you wish.   **(NEAB)**

Fig. 16.1 *BBC Hulton Picture Library*

QUESTION 2

Write imaginatively in response to *one* of the pictures (Fig. 16.2 or Fig. 16.3). **(WJEC)**

Fig.16.2 *BBC Hulton Picture Library*

Fig.16.3 *BBC Hulton Picture Library*

QUESTION 3

Write a story, a description, or other composition suggested by *either* Fig. 16.4 *or* Fig. 16.5. (Your writing should be about the subject of the picture, or take some central suggestion from it.)

Fig 16.4

Fig 16.5

QUESTION 4

Use the picture supplied with this paper as a basis for your writing. (MEG)

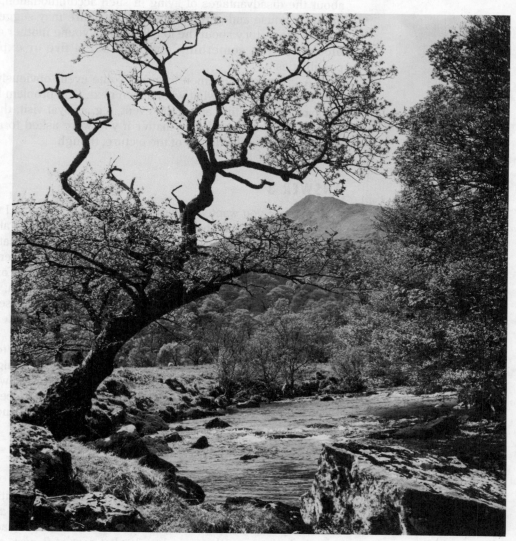

Fig 16.6 *Barnaby's Picture Library*

QUESTION 5

Listen to a recording of the opening of *The Flying Dutchman* by Wagner or Handel's *Water Music*, and write a story or a description based on your response.

QUESTION 6

Compare reading a play with seeing it on television or in the theatre.

OUTLINE ANSWERS

ANSWER 1

A photograph of children playing is an attractive stimulus. It could lead to memories of the games you played as a child, a description of the children in the picture or perhaps a story, featuring them as characters. Children and games should be a central concern of the writing.

ANSWER 2

i) A tower block suggest quite a range of kinds of writing. You may decide to write about the disadvantages of living in such accommodation, compared with the home having a house and garden. Town architecture may suggest itself as a topic, or you could write a story about the loneliness of a young mother and her children in a tower block, or even something dramatic like a fire or explosion. There are many possibilities.

ii) A group of policemen awaiting some event obviously leads to wondering why they are waiting, and what will happen next. One problem here could be that you get so involved in writing about the event, e.g. a royal visit, that you forget all about the policemen. That would only matter if you were asked to make a clear link between your writing and the details of the picture, though.

ANSWER 3

i) Suppose you wanted to write about this photograph. I think it suggests a story of some kind. The small boy seems to be setting off alone along the breakwater, on an apparently deserted beach. The shadow may suggest that it is late afternoon. What might happen next? To write so that the photograph is central to your concerns, you should keep his adventures of a kind likely to happen. For example, he goes too far along the beach; later, his worried parents search for him; some people say they have seen him – every clue as to his whereabouts is eagerly seized upon; meanwhile, the small boy is sitting by a rock pool in a cave, perfectly content. This is just one possible approach.

(ii) This photograph, of an old inn with a mountain towering behind it, has no suggestion of period. You could write a story of smuggling in the last century, or set your scene in the present day: the inn looks isolated, and would be a good hide-out for someone. Perhaps it has a more innocent story: you spent a very enjoyable family holiday there. Whatever you choose to write on, the inn and its lonely situation should be highlighted.

ANSWER 4

A picture of a natural scene seems to invite descriptive writing, though not necessarily. You might imagine a group of characters who were just about to enter the scene, or who had just left. Try thinking about the location of the place shown; the season of the year it depicts: are the trees bare?; what sort of flowers are in bloom? etc. Look for clues in the picture to help to make your writing more realistic.

ANSWER 5

Responding to a piece of music poses problems because it is subjective. Although many may agree as to the effect of certain musical instruments – e.g. heavy base drumming sounds ominous, slow violins sound peaceful – probably no two people would write similarly in response to listening to music. The pieces suggested in the question are what is termed 'programme music', i.e. they have titles which tell you something of what the music was meant to represent. That is a helpful clue, though you would not be tied to such an approach. The first piece is lively, dynamic music, perhaps suggesting a storm at sea or some other violent action. The second seems more stately and calm, though equally dramatic, suggesting perhaps a march, or something progressing steadily until a climax is reached. Those are my responses; yours could be very different. Whatever you write about, remember that your reader may not know the piece of music, and that your story or description should be able to stand by itself as a piece of satisfying communication.

PUPILS' ANSWERS

ANSWER 6

Here is a piece by another sixteen-year-old, after watching G. B. Shaw's *Pygmalion* on television, and comparing that with her own reading of the play.

Eliza Doolittle from the play 'Pygmalion'

Before Eliza became a duchess she was a poor flower girl. When we first met her she was sitting on a plinth of the column, sorting her flowers. She was about eighteen-twenty but not any older. She wore a little sailor hat made of black straw which was very dirty and hardly been brushed. Her hair needed washing badly, the colour was hardly natural, she wore a black coat which went down to her knee. She had a brown skirt with a coarse apron and her boots were not fit to wear. By the time Professor Higgins finished with her she was just as good as a duchess, maybe even better. She wore fine and expensive clothes and jewellery, she looked much cleaner and the main thing was she could speak proper English, just like a duchess.

An important incident at a tea party was although she could speak better English, she didn't know what to say like she said 'somebody pinched it', and 'what I say is, them as pinched it done her in'. Another one is when she went to the garden party she passed as a duchess but, when they came back Pickering and Higgins didn't thank her or even congratulate her for her appearance at the garden party.

Eliza Doolittle reminds me of a film on television which was called 'My fair lady'. The girl was exactly like Eliza and she even talked like her and the story was the same, because both the teachers were teaching the pupils to speak English properly.

Eliza doesn't get on with professor Higgins very well, she always gets into arguments with him. Eliza gets on quite well with Pickering because I think Pickering understands Eliza better than Higgins. Higgins treats Eliza as a common flower girl and as if she is worth nothing. Mr Doolittle doesn't like Eliza very much and she doesn't like him; they don't get on very well.

I think Eliza is a clever girl because she learnt her lessons quick and well. Eliza is a kind girl because she goes to her father's wedding although he was wicked to her she said 'Oh well, Just to show there's no ill feelings'.

I think that the play was very good because it was all about Eliza learning to speak English properly. The story was also very good. Twiggy and the rest played their parts very well. I enjoyed the play very much.

TUTOR'S COMMENTS ON PUPILS' ANSWERS

COMMENTS ON ANSWER 6

The writer achieves quite a good balance here. She tells us quite a lot about the plot, but does give some of her own responses as well, e.g. 'Eliza gets on well with Pickering because I think Pickering understands Eliza better than Higgins. Higgins treats Eliza as a common flower girl and as if she is worth nothing.'

She conveys a keen sense of enjoyment of both reading and watching the play. It might have been better, perhaps, if she had discussed some of the ways that a television version is different from the text of the play, because a different medium is used, e.g. close-ups can emphasise details that we would not necessarily notice much when we read: cuts may be made to the text, or, as in the case of the film version of *Pygmalion*, a happy ending substituted because that has more box-office appeal. One version ends with Eliza Doolittle approaching Professor Higgins and saying dreamily,

'I washed my hands and face before I came.' The camera produces a close-up shot with soft focus, to create a mood of romance. We are left to conclude that the next development will be marriage and a happy-ever-after relationship, which was hardly what G. B. Shaw had in mind! There are errors of expression, though not enough to impede communication seriously.

COURSEWORK – A STEP FURTHER

Look out for pictures in the newspapers, especially any that are striking and seem to tell a story. Imagine how you could write about them in different ways. Another interesting thing to do with pictures is to get a set and try sequencing them in a different order: how does the story differ, for example, if the picture of the isolated inn comes last, instead of first? A set of pictures can help you to plan your piece of writing, because it offers you several stages along which to progress.

R E V I E W   S H E E T

✎ In describing what you see in a picture or photograph, the appropriate use of *precise* adjectives and adverbs will be helpful. Try to avoid *general* words such as 'good', 'bad', 'nice', 'beautiful' and 'lovely'.

Replace these general words in the following sentences with more precise descriptive words of your own. Sometimes you may have to change other words in the sentence as well. Write out each answer.

1 There are some beautiful paintings at the art gallery.

2 She is always very nice to her grandparents.

3 You can eat very nice food there.

4 It is a very beautiful little village.

5 It would be a very good idea to make swimming lessons compulsory for all children.

6 There are some very good programmes on television as well as some very bad ones.

7 I think that he is foolish rather than bad.

8 We spent a lovely day there.

9 You will meet nice people where you travel in the world.

10 The most beautiful music I have ever heard was composed by Mozart.

11 I read a lovely book last week.

12 Promoting such a person would be bad for the company.

✎ In writing imaginatively about a piece of stimulus material it is also important to avoid 'weak' words, such as 'get'.

Now replace 'get' or 'got' in each of these sentences with a stronger and more interesting word or words. Sometimes you may have to change other words in the sentence as well. Write out each answer.

1 No one can get to the top without hard work.

2 It is possible to get by quite happily without much money.

3 She started to get suspicious when she saw them together at lunchtime one day.

4 We managed to get him to do what we wanted.

5 It is important to get the roof repaired as soon as possible.

6 He got a large dog for a birthday present.

7 We got some interesting souvenirs in the market.

_____

8 When I opened the door I got a nasty shock.

_____

9 It is hard to get jokes in a foreign language.

_____

10 We seem to be getting nowhere at the moment.

_____

11 Her parents are always getting at her.

_____

12 It is time they got down to some serious work.

_____

Look at the list of compound adjectives (two parts) below. Divide the adjectives into those that describe body appearance (A), those that refer to clothing (C) and those that describe personal character (P). Write down the correct letter next to each word.

big-headed ___	broad-shouldered ___	brown-eyed ___
close-fitting ___	drip-dry ___	duty-conscious ___
easy-going ___	even-tempered ___	flat-footed ___
God-fearing ___	good-looking ___	good-natured ___
hand-made ___	kind-hearted ___	long-legged ___
long-sleeved ___	loud-mouthed ___	open-minded ___
open-necked ___	open-toed ___	right-handed ___
rosy-cheeked ___	self-conscious ___	self-controlled ___
sharp-eyed ___	short-sighted ___	slim-hipped ___
slow-witted ___	snub-nosed ___	soft-spoken ___
straight-haired ___	stuck-up ___	sun-tanned ___
thin-lipped ___	tight-waisted ___	two-faced ___

Write a paragraph describing a _persons character_ using at least _five_ of the adjectives you have marked with the letter (P).

_____

_____

_____

_____

_____

_____

_____

Repeat the above, describing someones _appearance_ using _five_ of the adjectives beginning with the letter (A).

_____

_____

_____

_____

_____

_____

_____

_____

_____

PERSONAL WRITING

SELECT WHAT IS IMPORTANT

BE REALISTIC

WRITING ABOUT AN EVERYDAY EXPERIENCE

COURSEWORK

GETTING STARTED

Personal writing, or writing based on your own experience, is probably the easiest to get started with as it has been said that 'there is one book in each of us'. Even so, given a free choice, it can be hard to choose one thing from many possibilities. It is a good idea, then, to keep a list of things you would like to write about, when they occur to you; ideas can come along when least expected. All sorts of things experienced can make successful pieces of writing – a conversation overheard in the supermarket, a family argument, an occasion when you were suddenly filled with strong emotion and felt that this was a very significant moment in your life, and so on.

Perhaps because describing it comes naturally, extra care is needed in communicating what happens in real life to a reader: some shaping will usually be needed. The advantage of writing from experience is that the piece often has a great deal of impact and interest because of your involvement in what you are saying.

ESSENTIAL PRINCIPLES

1 ▶ SELECT WHAT IS IMPORTANT

The *first* important thing to do is to think about the experience you have chosen and **select what is important to you**. That will give it immediate shape. Sometimes, if it has been in your mind for a long time, it will already have taken on the shape from your recalling the experience again and again.

2 ▶ BE REALISTIC

Secondly, do not drift into far-fetched or imaginative extensions of what happened. **Keep the piece as realistic and as vivid as possible**. Ways of doing this include describing how you acted and what you said and felt, as honestly as you can, and reporting exactly how other people who were involved reacted. Remember, we are very close up to our own experiences and must make them extra clear to readers who have not shared them – extra explanations may be necessary.

3 ▶ WRITING ABOUT AN EVERYDAY EXPERIENCE

You can begin straight away by writing about something that happens as part of your everyday experience. At first thought, something personal like this may seem unlikely to be very interesting to other people; but this is not necessarily so. Your personal experiences could well be very interesting to someone not familiar with the way that you lead your life, especially if you can describe them with skill and detachment.

As an experiment, try writing a short account of your family at meal-times. When you have written it, put it aside for a few days, then critically re-read what you have written and ask yourself the following questions:

- How have I presented myself?
- How have I presented members of my family as characters?
- What have I left out?
- Have I started and ended in a satisfactory way?

❝ Three rules for writing from experience ❞

Such an exercise can be very instructive: you should learn something about the differences between life and written accounts of it, and also of your own ability to select and describe incidents, and portray character in personal writing.

Here is a pupil's attempt at this exercise. She chose to write about Saturday lunch-time wen she came home from her weekend job for a meal with her family, and tended to see them in a new light because she had been away from them for a while.

The Family at Dinner – Saturday

I stalk into the house via the open front door, throw down my coat and proceed to climb, with unladylike eagerness, up the stairs to enquire as to what is for dinner. I have one hour in which to cram enough fuel into my stomach to last me for another two hours' work in the shop, and I make sure that I make the most of the time allotted for this enjoyable necessity.

Mum is usually bent over the steaming cooker preparing some delicious meal and Dad, at this time, is usually pottering about in the garden. When the cry 'Grub!' goes up, we all instantaneously leave whatever we have been attending to and gallop for all we are worth to the kitchen, where the meal is on the table. My sister is the fondest of her food and naturally is always the first there. The conversation following is typical.

Dad: 'Been busy?'
Me: 'Yes.'
Mum: We saw you in there …'
Me: 'Oh.' (*Various assorted sounds of eating and clanking.*)
Sister: 'We went up to get some wood.'
Silence. Two minutes' pause.
Me: 'What for?'
Dad: 'Cupboards.'
Four minutes' pause.
Me: 'This is lovely. I'm starving.'
Mum: 'There's no more.'

Sister: 'Ooooh!' (*disappointment*). *Two minutes's silence.*

Me: 'I've got piles to do.'

Dad: 'You can help wash up.'

Me: 'I've got too much to do.'

Dad: 'Never mind about that. You could have done it last night. You help your Mother.'

Me: 'But ...'

Mum: 'You haven't helped me for a long time.'

Me: 'But ...'

Dad: 'She can help as well' (*referring to my sister, who offers no excuse but a disturbing scowl*).

We finish eating and we sit for a couple of seconds and, as usual, my sly sister sidles out of her chair and makes a dash for the toilet.

Me: 'I knew she'd do that, Mum. It isn't fair!'

Mum: 'She'll be out in a minute.'

Dad: 'Can't you help on your own for a change?'

Me: 'I did it on my own last time.' (*Whimpering protest.*)

Dad: 'Look, Sally, are you going to help your Mother or not?'

Me: (*Muffled protest*).

Mum gets up and puts the dishes in the bowl and starts running the hot water. My sister suddenly appears, and with a horrified look because the dish-washing has not yet started, disappears into the hall once more. This time, she is caught in the act of escaping by her father, who whisks her off to the kitchen and presents her with a tea cloth.

By this time there is nothing left of my lunch-hour in which to do any chores, so I am 'let-off' with a warning that I'll be doing it next time!

You can see that the writer is very self-aware at the start: she 'stalks' into the house and shows 'unladylike eagerness' for her food. Next, she sketches a typical Saturday lunch-hour scene with Mum bent over the cooker and Dad pottering about in the garden. Her sister is first introduced as 'fondest of her food' and 'naturally ... first there', when food is on the table. This may strike you as slightly critical, and it soon emerges that there is indeed rivalry between the sisters.

The move into dialogue in the central stretch is strikingly realistic; the reader seems to be allowed to overhear the family's conversation. The piece ends with a little drama: a sly sister not managing to get out of helping with the washing up but the writer's good excuse accepted – with a warning This concludes the piece in a satisfying way.

When these comments were made to the writer, she was very surprised. She thought she had just written it as it had happened, not thought about the impression the piece would make, or tried to shape it at all.

EXAMINATION QUESTIONS

You will probably wish to include one or more pieces of personal writing in your coursework, and most written papers, except those concerned with factual material, will give some opportunity for this. Here are some examples from the Group's specimen papers.

QUESTION 1

Tell a story about the time when you were embarrassed when you discovered something about yourself or your relationships with someone. (Here are some suggestions which you may use, if you wish. You may write about your own private thoughts and feelings, or about how other people did not understand you or made you feel worse because they mocked you.) (**NEAB**)

QUESTION 2

You have been called unexpectedly to a person in authority over you, at school or work. You do not know why you have been sent for. Write about your feelings before and during the interview. (**ULEAC**)

QUESTION 3

Write a story beginning with the following words: 'Looking back, I now realise it was a stupid thing to do.' (**ULEAC**)

QUESTION 4

My Mum or My Dad. (**WJEC**)

QUESTION 5

'I have never felt so ashamed in my life!' Write about a personal experience – perhaps a joke that misfired or a time when you unthinkingly hurt a loved one – which ended with your feeling very guilty and ashamed. (**WJEC**)

QUESTION 6

Write about an occasion when, for the first time, you succeeded in doing something which many other people find quite easy. (**MEG**)

QUESTION 7

A question of loyalty. (**MEG**)

QUESTION 8

Write an account of a visit you made with your parents to the seaside. You may write in any way you like but you might like to try writing about a time when you were younger and particularly enjoyed new challenges such as swimming, climbing on the rocks, or going out in a boat; *or* you might like to write round the idea of being lost, or cut off by the tide. The account can be real or imaginery. (**MEG**)

4 > COURSEWORK

Here is a selection of titles you might like to write about for coursework. Try making your own list, too.

- My life from two to fifteen years.
- A frightening experience.
- The world around me.
- How I would like to change my life.
- My first day at school.
- Harassment.
- My first journey abroad.
- Sisters! or Brothers!

PUPIL'S ANSWER TO QUESTION 1

ANSWER 1

Here is an account of a misunderstanding based on something that happened to two friends at school. It would make an appropriate piece of writing for this question. Read it through and think about how the writer has given her work shape. Then consider what we learn about her feelings, and Angie's feelings. How do we learn this: through action, speech, or in some other way? Which details make the account seem real and vivid?

Misunderstanding

It was three fifty five in the afternoon. I was waiting for Angie outside in the playground. I was getting impatient and restless as I had already waited twenty-five minutes. Me and the rest of my fifth year class thought Angie was slow witted and dumb. We thought she didn't know anything about her schoolwork, but I di'dt know why I was the closest to Angie, although I didn't like her very much.

Angie was very innocent and she looked it too. She would never answer anyone back or ever argue, she even hesitated to answer questions in class. Most of the time she kept quiet and hardly gave her opinion towards anything or anyone, except once, when we were having our Biology lesson. It was about the way the muscles in the body worked. Angie told Miss James, the teacher, that in her previous school she had done this project. Miss James suggested that Angie should tell the rest of the class about her experience.

At first she was very nervous and wished that she hadn't told Miss James and because she did, she had to face about twenty four people and explain about the way the muscles in the body worked. Miss James quietened the class down. Angie stood up in front of the class and started explaining, I could hear giggles at the back of the class. Some girls were laughing at Angie because of the way she talked. All her words were getting jumbled up as she was very nervous. I felt embarrassed because she was my friend. After about six minutes of explaining Miss James asked Angie to sit down. She came and sat next to me. Eventually the pips went. I was glad it was our last lesson and we could go home.

Angie and I were going down stairs to the exit when Angie remembered that she didn't get her Mock exam grade to say whether she was doing 'O' level or CSE. She told me to go down and wait for her while she went to see Mr Smith the teacher to ask about her grade. I could have easily told her that she failed because she wasn't in the school long enough to do all the coursework required for the exam. I thought that I would let her get the shock for herself. I went down and was waiting. It wasn't long until me and the other people in our class were proved wrong.

Angie came down with a surprised look on her face, but she also was very happy. She came running down the ground floor corridor and when she saw me she burst out with the news that she came second in the class with eighty seven per cent. I asked her who came first thinking she would say my name, but to my disappointment it was Louise, brain box of our class. I asked Angie how many marks I got. She replied sixty two per cent. At that moment I felt so jealous that I could have killed Angie. I felt so ashamed that Angie had only been in the year for the last five months and she managed to pass the exam with a better grade than mine. Angie, seeing the look on my face, wanted to comfort me because to her I was her only friend. She said 'Never mind, Chris at least you passed and beat some people in our class. Sixty two per cent is quite good. If you work hard I'm sure Mr Smith would enter you in for the 'O' level exam.' I felt good when Angie said that to me. I thought to myself that although I didn't like Angie in the past, she saw me as her very close friend. At the end it seemed that I was the stupid one for misunderstanding Angie.

Comments on this piece of work can be found on page 217.

OUTLINE ANSWERS

ANSWER 2

A piece of writing based on this idea seems likely to fall into two parts: the feelings, possibly of apprehension, that you have before the interview and the encounter itself. Events will be presented from your point of view and so may be very one-sided. Unlike the balance often required in argumentative writing, one side of the truth in personal writing can be a good thing, as it can offer a definite point of view. Suppose, for instance, that you were to be told that you had been chosen to represent the school on a visit to a pupils' conference abroad. Imagine how surprised and excited you would be and, legitimately, how these feelings would swamp the piece. The pleased and proud attitude of the headteacher would have its place, but would be of lesser importance.

ANSWER 3

You are invited to write a story. This may not be direct personal experience, but you will almost certainly be able to think of occasions in your life when you have said this, or something like it, to yourself. Spend a short time thinking of incidents that would be an exploration and analysis of your own behaviour, looking back afterwards. There is likely to be a contrast between how you felt when you entered into the experience and how you felt later, and, possibly, some realization that you had matured as a result of it all.

ANSWER 4

A portrait in words is asked for here. As you have to concentrate on one member of your family, you will need to sustain your comments for some time. It may seem obvious that you could write almost for ever about your Mum or Dad, because you know them so well, but a few moments spent thinking about what details you want to include of, perhaps, appearance, early life, likes and dislikes, relationship with you, hobbies and interests, job, friendships and so on will be time well spent. As with other topics where a lot of detail is included, you may find that you have a tendency to write in a list-like way, so reserve a little time in your planning for thinking about how best to arrange your ideas, and how to begin and end effectively.

ANSWER 5

This question, like Question 3, asks you to look back at a past experience – this time one of embarrassment or shame but involving someone close to you. Similar procedures should be followed to those outlined in the notes to Question 3. Notice, though, that you are told how to end this time: with feelings of guilt and regret.

ANSWER 6

This is an interesting question. I suppose there may be some people who have never had this experience, but they must be few and far between! Most of you will have had the uncomfortable experience of being slow to learn something, whether it was tying your shoe-laces, coping with a subject at school, or, later, learning to drive. The feelings of inadequacy, loss of self-respect and even, in some extreme cases, of desperation and of hopelessness which such an experience can cause may be painful to recall but are likely to make a powerful piece of writing if you can communicate them honestly and clearly. Try to avoid generalizing too much about the experience. Go through the stages of learning, as far as you can remember them, and your reactions each time you failed. Perhaps the experience turned out well in the end, in which case you can conclude with the disproportionate joy you felt when you eventually succeeded.

ANSWER 7

This could be a story without any particular personal slant. It would be a good title for personal writing, however. Loyalty to friends, family, beliefs, or a cause that matters to us is a basic human response and, again, one often very strongly held. If you can think of something you had to defend because you really believed in it and can write about it, then by communicating the same strength of feeling you may be surprised at how good a piece of writing you produce. As usual, though, to achieve a successful piece of work it is essential to have good planning, careful selection of incident, honest recall of how you felt and what happened, and an overall satisfying shape to the work.

ANSWER 8

This piece of writing may be real or imaginary. In either case, it should be based on your own experience. The first option suggests that you might like to recall a seaside experience from the past, when you were younger and faced some challenge. Likely challenges are offered but you do not have to write about those. This is the sort of topic where vivid recall of the detail of the experience will help to bring it to life for the reader. If you were to choose to write about rock-climbing you could try to remember what the rocks looked like; the physical experience of trying to get a foot-hold on slippery, jagged or narrow surfaces; the emotional experience you might have had – fear as you suddenly found that there was nowhere safe ahead to move to, or pleasure at reaching the top. These are only a few possibilities: your own experiences will be much richer.

The second option suggests something definitely dramatic: lost, or cut off by the tide. Something like this may actually have happened to you. If so, your task will be easier because you can draw on your memory of what it was like. If not, try to think yourself into the likely events, and your corresponding feelings, remembering to plan and shape your work, and trying, above all, to write realistically once again.

A TUTOR'S COMMENTS

COMMENTS ON PUPIL'S ANSWER TO QUESTION 1

The opening paragraph of *Misunderstanding* tells us a great deal quickly. The first sentence, 'It was three fifty five in the afternoon', sets the scene, and by the end of the paragraph we know what is essential to know about Angie and her relationship with the writer. After that the writer lets the natural course of events – e.g. during the Biology lesson – take over. Angie's ordeal is dealt with in one paragraph; the second part of the incident turns the tables. Chris feels inferior and inadequate, and Angie takes the role of comforter. The final two sentences conclude the episode neatly, and sum up what Chris feels she has learnt from it: 'When Angie said that to me, I thought to myself that although I didn't like Angie in the past she saw me as her very close friend. At the end it seemed that I was the stupid one for misunderstanding Angie.'

Most of the acount is circumstantial – what happens in school on that afternoon – but there is variety, with some dialogue and quite a lot about the feelings of each girl: 'Some girls were laughing at Angie because of the way she talked. All her words were getting jumbled up as she was very nervous. I felt embarrassed because she was my friend.' But later, in contrast 'Angie came down with a surprised look on her face, but also she was very happy. She came running down the ground floor corridor and when she saw me she burst out with the news that she came second in the class....' there are very vivid touches, in addition to what has already been mentioned – the way Angie's words were getting 'jumbled up as she was very nervous' (how like life!), or how she came 'running down the ground floor corridor' and 'burst out' with her happy news. There are some faults of expression, but altogether this is a well-shaped, honest and attractive piece of personal writing.

COURSEWORK –
A STEP FURTHER

Fluency and skill in writing about personal experiences comes, as do most things, partly through practice. You should try to acquire gradually a good sense of what is both interesting and important to you and likely to be of wider interest and significance, as well as increasing your ability to communicate effectively. One way of doing this is to write regularly, e.g. keep a diary, even try writing poems, or short descriptive sketches of episodes in your life that you want to explore and remember. One writer who did this spoke of producing verbal 'snapshots'! It is something you could try for yourself.

R E V I E W   S H E E T

In personal writing, on some occasions you might sum up your experience or that of someone else by using a proverb.

In each of the proverbs below one word is missing. What is it?

1 Birds of a _____ flock together.

2 It's the last _____ that breaks the camel's back.

3 You can take a horse to water but you can't make him _____ .

4 Absence makes the heart grow _____ .

5 All that glitters is not _____ .

6 It's no use _____ over spilt milk.

7 A bird in the hand is worth _____ in the bush.

8 The grass is always _____ on the other side of the fence.

9 Every cloud has a _____ lining.

10 It's an ill wind that blows _____ any good.

11 What's sauce for the _____ is sauce for the gander.

12 One man's meat is another man's _____ .

Which of the proverbs above is being explained in each case below. Write the correct number alongside each explanation.

a) Being sure of one thing is better than vague hopes of more things. [ ]

b) You can't assume that something is good simply because it looks good. [ ]

c) You love someone more when you are missing them. [ ]

d) People tend to mix with others who are similar to themselves. [ ]

e) You can usually find something positive in any seemingly bad situation. [ ]

f) There is usually someone who benefits from every bad situation. [ ]

g) There's no point in making a lot of fuss about something that cannot
   now be changed. [ ]

h) When a person has a lot of burdens it may be something quite small that finishes
   him or her off. [ ]

i) What one person loves, another hates. [ ]

j) What someone else has always looks more interesting than what you
   have yourself. [ ]

k) If something is good enough for one person then it's good enough for another. [ ]

l) You can't force someone to do something that you want them to do however much
   encouragement you may give them. [ ]

In personal writing, as in description, the use of 'strong' and precise adjectives or adverbs, rather than 'weak' and general ones, is important.

Look at the following sentences and replace the 'general' words such as 'good', 'bad', 'nice', 'beautiful' and 'lovely' with more precise and effective words.

1 'One man one vote' certainly sounds like a good way to elect a government.

_____

2 Terrorism is a very bad crime.

_____

3 The opportunity to import allows our country to enjoy a lot of nice things produced in other countries.

4 Travelling is much nicer than it was in our grandparents' day.

5 If one had no knowledge whatsoever of mathematics everyday shopping would probably involve many bad experiences.

6 The beautiful pictures which you see on your television screen are created in quite a complex manner.

7 Some lovely tourist spots are being gradually destroyed by erosion.

8 It would be good if we could find a cure for the common cold.

9 A dictionary is a very good companion to have with you on holidays abroad.

10 The beautiful stone used in building in the north of the country is quarried in the locality.

11 There are some lovely ceremonies in some of the more remote villages in my country.

12 I should love to be able to paint nice paintings.

Using effective *verbs* is also important in personal writing.

Look at the sentences below about each of the topics and replace all the uses of 'get' with more effective verbs.

1 Many incompetent people get a seat in parliament.

2 I think that terrorists should get capital punishment.

3 We get much of our meat from New Zealand.

4 How did our grandparents get by without all the things that we now enjoy?

5 Without any knowledge of mathematics you would regularly get cheated in shops business transactions.

6 How does the telephone get our messages to us?

7 Our coastline is getting quite seriously eroded in some places.

8 Some diseases have already been got rid of.

18

A SAMPLE COURSEWORK FOLDER

PERSONAL WRITING

NARRATIVE WRITING

SHORT PLAY

TWO LETTERS

IMAGINATIVE WRITING-RESPONSE TO A PICTURE

GETTING STARTED

The following sample folder has *five* pieces of work, involving personal, narrative and dramatic writing, letter writing and imaginative writing. Seeing such a folder will give you some idea of what a range of assignment work might look like. You could try to make your *own* estimate of the material presented before looking at the Examiner Comments which follow.

Here is the front cover of the Coursework Folder which will help you to see what is covered in this chapter.

Written Expression	
Unit 1 2 3 4 5	
Title/Question	*Nature of Task*
Unit 1 *Personal Writing*	Writing from personal experience
THE CHALLENGE	
Unit 2 *Narrative*	Write a short story
DOG	
Unit 3 *Dramatic*	Write a short play, based on a school situation
THE GOVERNORS' MEETING	
Unit 4 *Letters*	Writing formal and semi-formal letters
LETTER TO MR & MRS KEATING	
LETTER TO MR SAMUELS	
Unit 5 *Imaginative Writing*	Writing in response to a picture
A FRIGHTENING EXPERIENCE	

ESSENTIAL PRINCIPLES

THE CHALLENGE

I got up stretching and yawning. I felt terribly sick and worried. I had to do it. I couldn't back out now, I thought to myself. I slowly got dressed and went downstairs to have a wash and brush my teeth. When I had finished washing, I went into the kitchen and sat down at the table. My cornflakes were already set out on the table. I saw something white out of the corner of my eye. I got up and walked over to the draining board. There was a note. I picked it up and read it:

'Michael,
I've had to rush out early today and I'll be back a bit later than usual, so don't stay in on my account. Go out and play with your friends and I will see you when I get back.
    Lots of love,
    Mum.'

Why couldn't she have forced me to stay in for once? I thought. Well, I could tell my friends that I had to stay in, and then they would want to see the proof, or they would call me 'chicken'. So that idea went down the drain. I was so scared and frightened about going ahead with my challenge. Why did I say 'yes' in the first place? I asked myself over and over again in my mind. I put down the note and sat down again. I poured lashings of milk over my cornflakes with a sprinkling of sugar. I ate as slowly as possible, and when I finally did finish I washed up my bowl and spoon and put them on the draining board to dry. I sat down once again with my head in my hands. I had to think of something. I just couldn't bear to hear them all calling me a chicken.

As the day wore on I managed to convince myself that I was going to do it, that I was going to win, even if it killed me. My thoughts were interrupted by a knock at the door. My heart seemed to beat faster like the beating of a drum. Thoughts of who it could be were going through my mind as Gary, Peter and John had come rather early, if it was them. I thought maybe it could be the milkman, but no – Mum had paid him yesterday. As I walked towards the front door I was nearly convinced that it must be one of Mum's friends. But as I opened it I knew that my fears were realised, for there, standing at the door, were Gary, Peter and John. My heartbeat was faster than ever and the same old sickly feeling came flooding back into my body.

'You ready, then? asked Peter, with a big grin across his face.

'Not chickening out, are you?' said Gary, grasping hold of his sports bag.

'No, I'm just coming. But you're early, aren't you?' I asked, scratching the itch in the back of my neck.

'Well, we're just making sure we don't have to get a replacement, you know!' snapped Peter, as if he was almost implying that I was going to cry off.

'Well, you don't!' I snapped back. 'I'll just get my stuff together now.'

I shut the door and went upstairs. I got together all my swimming gear and bunged it in a plastic carrier bag. As I reached the street door I felt very apprehensive but I couldn't back out, I kept telling myself.

'Come on, Michael!' I heard them shouting outside. I opened the door and stepped out onto the street. We caught the bus and made our way down to the beach. When we reached the beach there were crowds of people sitting and lying all over the sand. I looked beyond the crowds and noticed a sign 'ALL BOYS TAKING PART IN THE COMPETITION LINE UP HERE.' Standing by the sign there was a man dressed in a dark blue tracksuit, and a blue cap with a whistle around his neck. That must be the coach, I thought. We made our way down to the spot where the race was taking place.

'Changing rooms over there,' he said, pointing to a few huts. We went inside them and changed from our clothes to our swimming trunks. I waved across the sand and made my way down to the water's edge, where everyone was ready and waiting for the big competition to start.

'Right! Listen, boys,' shouted the coach. 'The first one to reach the black rock is the winner.' Everybody was lined up against the edge of the water.

'Are you ready? On your marks, get set (there was a pause), GO!' He blew his whistle and everyone jumped in. I swam as fast as I could. I was in the lead, but for how long? Within ten minutes I was very tired. As I started to struggle, I could feel my legs and arms getting weaker and weaker. But I had to go on now that I had got this far. Just a few more yards, I kept saying to myself. Just a few more yards. By now I was slowing down and tiring out but all the other boys were way behind me. I could see that they too were tiring. A few of them had dropped out altogether. I was not doing a doggy paddle and breast stroke, whereas before I was doing front crawl. I was getting weaker and weaker. Only a few more strokes. I had to do it. I could faintly hear the crowds on the beach shouting: 'Come on, Michael!' By now I was coughing and choking. One more stroke – I had done it! I could just about hear the crowds on the beach cheering and shouting. I had won!

2 NARRATIVE WRITING

DOG

'Get out of here, you disgusting dog!' The rubbish bin was all over the floor and there were tins and the remains of last night's dinner scattered everywhere.

'Marian!' a voice called out from the living room. 'What's happened?'

'The dog has had the rubbish out all over the floor!' she shouted back, picking up all the rubbish.

'Where is the little runt?' John, her husband got up out of the chair and picked up a belt from the sideboard.

'Come here, dog. You're going to get it now!'

the dog was cowering under the table, and John dragged him out by the scruff of his neck and whipped him right across the muzzle with the belt. The dog yelped in pain, but John persisted in beating him.

'You've had it now, boy.' He beat him again and again. He dragged him out of the room and straight out of the front door.

'Now keep away from this house and take your bloody rotten fleas with you.'

He went inside and slammed the door behind him. The dog stood yelping on the pavement, throbbing with pain, and blood oozed out of his wounds. As he limped off down the street he was whining and crying in pain. He limped on about a mile before he came to a lake. He drank as much water as he could and cleaned his wounds with his paw.

He travelled for days until one late afternoon he woke up to find himself surrounded by two children pitying him. He could hear them speaking and his first instinct was to crawl away from them, but he could feel a warmth and a kind of feeling between them. He stood up and walked over to them, wagging his tail with great effort.

'Look at him; he looks as though he hasn't been fed for a week,' one of the children said, stroking his sore back. The dog felt pain as she touched him gently, but he was able to bear it, as he could feel she meant well.

'Let's take him home to Mum,' the other one said. They reached the huge gates of the house where the two young girls lived and they both rushed off inside the house.

'Mum! Mum! Look what we have found. We've found a dog.' They jumped up and down with excitement. The dog walked into the kitchen and cowered down under the table as the children's mother came closer to him.

'Hello, boy. You look as if you need a good feed.'

'Where did you find him, Jennifer?' she asked. The younger of the two replied, 'We found him sleeping in the Park.'

'Well, he certainly looks ill. Was he with anyone?' she asked.

'No, Mum. He was on his own.'

The mother of the children bathed his wounds and put some food down on the tiled floor. Within seconds the dog had wolfed down every scrap of meat.

'Oh, look at him. He must have been very badly beaten. If only he could talk. If only he could tell us who did this to him. He's such a beautiful dog. People who ill-treat their dogs should be horse-whipped.' She bent over to stroke the dog.

'He's an alsatian, you know.'

'Oh. Mum can we keep him, please?' pleaded the elder of the two.

'Oh yes, of course, but if the owners contact us we will have to give him back.'

A few days passed, then a few weeks. As the dog got stronger he filled out and became fit and healthy again, just like an alsatian should be. His beautiful brown and black coat shone again and looked a whole lot better than the day they first found him. They treated him well and the dog loved them very much. But he still had the memory of his former owners who beat him and starved him deep in his brain. His immediate instinct was to get his revenge.

One night, the family had all gone to bed and everything was quiet in the house. The dog stood up, shook himself and trotted off out of the back yard and onto the pavement. He trotted on down the street, and turned the corner.

The next morning the family came down into the kitchen where the dog was curled up in his basket, sound asleep.

'Hello, boy. How are you this morning?' they said. The dog got up quickly and ran to greet them at the kitchen door. He was wagging his tail frantically. He looked very pleased to see them and also a look of satisfaction was all over his face. The morning papers had just been delivered and Jennifer came rushing back with them in her hands. She gave them to her mother who was sitting on a chair drinking a cup of coffee. There was a sudden look of horror on her face as she read the front page.

'Oh my god!' she said. 'Look at the state of her!' She was reading the headlines: 'COUPLE SAVAGED BY MYSTERY ANIMAL.'

'Mrs Marian Jones and her husband, John Jones. They were mauled to death, attacked by some animal in the night, probably by a wolf. Lucky that we have a dog to protect us all.'

The dog curled up in his basket. He knew exactly what had happened.

3 ▷ SHORT PLAY

THE GOVERNORS' MEETING

This play is set in the office of the Headmistress, Mrs Catherine Williams. Five people are attending this meeting: Mrs Margaret Keating (the mother of the pupil being discussed), John Andrews (best friend of Ken Samuels, the teach who was attacked), Walter Richmond (friend of Margaret Keating's husband) and Elizabeth Walker (Chairperson of School Governors).

Walker: Would you like to come in, ladies and gentlemen? (They all go into the room.)

Williams: Take a seat, please.

(They all sit around a large table.)

Walker: First I must say thank you for attending this meeting. Now, we are all here to discuss the incident involving Jennifer Keating and Mr Ken Samuels, the Humanities teacher. I have made out five copies of the report. Would you all please take one.

(They all take one and read it.)

Keating: This isn't fair at all! This is not what happened! He's lying! This report is all lies!

Williams: Calm down, Mrs Keating. Perhaps you would like to give your account of the incident.

Keating: Well, Jennifer was talking quietly to a class mate when she was told to shut up in the most rude way. Anyway she refused because of the way he spoke to her. She was then asked to leave the room and she refused still. So he took her by the arm and pulled her out of the chair to lead her out of the classroom and she pulled away and he fell over and hit the floor. That's what happened. No big deal! You see, Mr Samuels should be sacked for dragging my daughter about, not my daughter expelled for just defending herself.

Williams: Well, Mrs Keating, if that's the case, then it makes no difference. You see, she still refused to do as she was asked, so she still would be punished.

Keating: Yes, but why should she do anything anyone tells

her to do? I'm her mother, I tell her what to do, no-one else!

Walker: Mrs Keating, you are not being very co-operative at all! While Jennifer is in school she is under our authority and we have every right to tell her when she is in the wrong.

Andrews: Mrs Keating, imagine if you can, that you are looking after a friend's daughter. Now this little girl happens to be helping herself to your dinner for the night. Tell me, Mrs Keating, would you think that you have no right to tell this little girl what is wrong to do and what is right to do or would you tell her that it is wrong to take something not belonging to her, and take it away?

Keating: I'd kill the little cow if she pinched my dinner!

Andrews: Well, there you are, so what makes you think that only you can tell people what to do and nobody else is permitted to, especially with your daughter?

Keating: Yes, all right. I was being a bit stupid, wasn't I? But that's still no reason to expel my daughter.

Williams: Well, Mrs Keating, we will decide that at the end of this meeting.

Walker: Let's get on with the meeting shall we? Now, going by Mr Samuels' report, Jennifer was talking and chewing when the rules clearly say that chewing is strictly forbidden. So that's one rule broken. Another is, one way or another, Jennifer Keating did actually assault Mr Ken Samuels.

Richmond: Yes, but only because he assaulted her!

Williams: Ah, but Jennifer gave him reason to.

Richmond: I see. If it was the other way round then Jennifer would probably still get the blame.

Walker: Mr Richmond. It doesn't matter what you would like to think, the truth is she did assault Mr Samuels so there are no ifs and buts about it.

Richmond: Yes, OK. I'm sorry.

Walker: Now, another broken rule was swearing, and swearing is also strictly forbidden and we will not have our pupils abusing the teachers no matter what!

Williams: Well I'm sorry but the only possible thing we can do is to suspend Jennifer for a little longer, in order to be fair to both sides. It is not a serious enough case for Jennifer to be expelled. Mr Samuels was hurt but it wasn't intended that way. So I have decided that she should be given a clear warning and told not to do it again. If she can abide by these rules then I am willing to have her carry on at this school. Is everyone agreed?

Keating: Yes, that sounds fair to me. I'm sure she won't do it again.

Walker: Well, we shall have Jennifer back in two weeks from today. (Everyone mumbles, some with relief and some with disagreement. They all get up and leave the room.)

4 > TWO LETTERS | LETTER TO MR AND MRS KEATING

Dear Mr and Mrs Keating,
  Following the governors' meeting on Tuesday, I am writing to convey to you the decision taken about Jennifer after discussion of the incident that took place last week in school.
  It was agreed that Jennifer should send a written apology to the teacher concerned and be suspended from school for two weeks, starting on Monday. We expect to see her back on Monday, 19 March.

                                        Yours sincerely,

                                        Elizabeth Walker
                                        Chairperson of Governors

LETTER TO MR SAMUELS, THE TEACHER WHO LODGED THE COMPLAINT

Dear Mr Samuels,
  I am writing to inform you that Jennifer Keating is to carry on school after a two-week break. We have come to this decision because, although she was being very tiresome, it is clear that she did not intend to hurt you.
  I understand that she is very sorry, and she will be asked to offer an apology which we hope you will accept. She will be returning to school on 19 March, in two weeks' time.

                                        Yours truly,

                                        Elizabeth Walker
                                        Chairperson of Governors

5 > IMAGINATIVE WRITING – RESPONSE TO PICTURE

A FRIGHTENING EXPERIENCE

A young boy, by the name of Max Maddison, was walking along the street all alone, frightened and worried, after running away from his foster parents. He was a young boy of ten, with dark skin and black hair, wearing jeans and a jacket made of denim. As he walked along the gloomy street he passed many different people. Some were black, some white; some not quite black and not quite white. It was very strange to him, as he had not been allowed out of his foster-home alone after his real parents had neglected him when he was only five months old.
  'Hello, son,' a voice called out from behind him. 'Who are you, then?'
  Max looked at the man, very frightened. He peered up at his brown complexion. He was carrying a jacket across his shoulder and Max noticed a gold watch on his wrist, and he wished he had something like that.
  'What's the matter, son I only asked who you are? I mean, it's not every day I see a young boy like you walking around the streets all alone.'
  Max became even more frightened. He leaned against a

lamp-post and stared up into the strange man's face.

'Would you like to come home with me, then? I have a very cosy house. You can stay tonight if you want to.'

Max was so young, so naive that he didn't know that this man that had picked him up could mean serious trouble. He did not know whether to turn to the nearest police station and be taken home again, to be locked up behind four walls, or he could go with this complete stranger and be safe out of this street full of other people. He did not know. But this man was a stranger to Max.

'Well, then. Do you want to come with me, or not?' the man said again.

Max just managed to force a few words out: 'No, I don't want to, thank you.'

He slid along the lamp-post, and took off down the street, around the corner and down an empty alley-way. He walked slowly and got his breath back. He felt very lonely and sad. At least at home he had a nice warm room with plenty of central heating to keep him warm. For the first time since he had run away he wished he was back in his welcoming room. He walked down the High Street and looked into the show window. He thought of his foster-parents being worried sick that he had run away. Max knew that he had to return home. There was no way he could survive out in the dirty, gloomy and smelly streets. He made his way home. The flat door was half open and half shut when he arrived. Perhaps they hadn't even noticed that Max had run away. He pushed the door to behind him. He was very scared.

He walked into the living room and saw his foster-parents sitting on the sofa, watching television. They noticed him standing there and Max's heart beat faster than ever.

'Hello, Max. There's a good programme on television. Come and watch it, if you want.'

Max looked very surprise, but he didn't mind that they didn't know. He sat down to watch television.

'Mum, can I have a watch?'

EXAMINER'S COMMENTS

Considered as a whole, this folder would certainly be assessed at a good C grade or above. There might be some concern about the balance between creative and transactional pieces (the two letters are the only sample of the latter). In other respects, though, the student has presented a good range of imaginative writing. The piece of personal writing is convincing, well-shaped and accurately expressed. The short story 'Dog' handles the emotions of all concerned effectively and with restraint. The ending is particularly successful in this way. The short play not only develops the situation clearly, it is well-planned, with clashes of feeling and resolutions of disagreement among the speakers, and the dialogue is good. The letters are written in an appropriate tone, are quite well expressed and sensibly paragraphed. The lay-out is correct, apart from the missing addresses. The final story is delicate in its understatement of the implications of the situation. The child's confusion is sensitively handled, and the ending does not try to do too much: mixed with the childlike wish for an impressive possession, which might have led him to make a wrong decision, is a drawing nearer to his foster-parents. It offers hope for a better life for Max.

Overall, this folder of work shows a standard of achievement that any candidate for GCSE/Key Stage 4 English could be pleased with.

CHECKING AND CORRECTING

CHECKING WRITTEN ANSWERS IN THE EXAMINATION ROOM

CHECKING COURSEWORK

PUNCTUATION

SPELLING

GETTING STARTED

This chapter aims to give you advice about going over your work when it is finished, looking at it critically and correcting any errors you may have made. As it comes last it will remind you of matters considered earlier in the book and serve as a form of revision of some of them for you.

Your techniques for checking work will vary considerably, depending on the kind of task you are involved in, and whether you are taking a written paper or doing coursework. Certainly, you will be able to spend much less time revising an answer in a written paper than a piece of coursework.

Remember that all published work that you read has not just been written down and printed. It has probably gone through several drafts and revisions before reaching its final form. This is likely to be true, too, of radio talks or other prerecorded performances: they are usually edited before transmission. Much of the work you do for the examination should be seen as 'work in progress', your progress along the road to becoming a more accomplished writer or talker. Even so, you are presenting some of what your produce for assessment, and will want it to be the best you can do at that stage. What follows should help you to achieve this.

The amount of time you have available largely determines the checking you are able to do. Let us consider basic aspects in two sets of circumstances.

1 **Checking written answers in the examination room**
and
2 **Checking coursework.**

Always leave yourself five to ten minutes for checking over your paper. There are several basic points to look for here. Check that you have

a) **followed the instructions**
b) **written relevantly**
c) **written accurately.**

ESSENTIAL PRINCIPLES

a) HAVE I FOLLOWED THE INSTRUCTIONS?

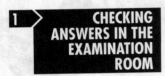

CHECKING ANSWERS IN THE EXAMINATION ROOM

It is obviously very important to read all the general instructions (or **rubrics**), as well as the working of questions in an examination very carefully.

Many people understandably do not feel very calm in an examination room, and nervous haste can lead to errors and, in the long run, loss of time. It is far better to read, then re-read the whole question (or even paper) carefully before you begin. Remember a major mistake, such as misunderstanding the general instructions or how to tackle a particular question, often cannot be corrected.

Make sure that you read all pages of a paper: you would be surprised how many pupils in examinations forget to read over the page, it if happens to finish with the end of a paragraph.

The most common ways of *not* following the instructions are

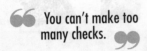

> You can't make too many checks.

> Five don'ts for the examination room.

i) **answering too many questions**
ii) **leaving out important aspects of a question**
iii) **using an inappropriate tone or style**
iv) **ignoring word limits**
v) **ignoring the marks awarded for a question.**

i) Answering too many questions

Think how frustrating it must be to discover, when you are checking, that you have written three essays, when only one was asked for! If you do find yourself in this position, do not despair. Most probably your longest or best essay will be assessed. One candidate tore her paper into quarters when she realised that she had written more answers than she was asked for, and left the examination hall in tears. The invigilator taped her script together again, sent it in with the rest, and she passed the examination. Take care not to make the same mistake yourself: you might not be so fortunate! If, however, you do something of this sort, and realised it at the end, it is probably best simply to leave it to the examiner to consider the situation. He or she will mark the paper, within the requirements of the mark scheme, in the way most favourable to you.

ii) Leaving out important aspects of a question

This mistake usually comes about because examinees skim-read, or read carelessly in nervous haste. For example, you might be asked to write a speech at a public enquiry discussing a certain proposal, and read 'opposing' instead of 'discussing': or, for another question, not notice that a report supporting *or* opposing is required and not one offering a balanced discussion of the issue. Again, you might be asked to write a newspaper article with a headline and sub-headings, and forget the sub-headings. Hasty attempts to put right this sort of mistake in your final five or ten minutes usually make matters worse, although in the case of sub-headings, you could insert them in the margin at the appropriate point.

iii) Using an inappropriate tone or style

Sometimes the audience to which you direct your writing is specified and this immediately should indicate to you something about style. A report on fellow pupils' views about curriculum problems will be rather different if written up for a meeting of the school governors or for the school notice-board; a letter to the manager of a travel firm will be more formal and restrained than one to a personal friend, and so on. If you fail to take in the kind of audience you are meant to be addressing you lose marks for writing in an unsuitable tone or style.

iv) Ignoring word limits

The most common error here, of course, is writing too much on one question and running short of time for the rest, or even failing to answer part of the paper, because of bad timing.

The best adivce is *not* to exceed a word limit. In a short piece, where conciseness is an important factor, you may well have work disregarded after the word limit has been reached. In a larger piece, such as a five hundred word essay, the more you write the more errors you make, so you will be losing marks for yourself. Every examiner knows that an extremely long essay, written in examination conditions, is very often a weak essay. Not only will there be problems of accuracy but it will almost certainly be rambling, expansive and dull. Avoid these problems by respecting the word limit: it is there to help you. But if, when you are checking, you find that you have exceeded it, you could quickly re-read your piece of work to see if you can make any cuts, *without damaging the overall style and shape of the work.*

v) Ignoring the marks awarded for a question

The marks awarded for a question is another indication of how much time you should spend on it. To take the example of a comprehension exercise where you have five marks for the first two questions, ten marks for the next two, and twenty marks for the final one, you should spend about four times as long on the last question as on the first. And if you are pressed for time, it will probably be best to begin with the last question. Again, when you are checking at the end of the exam, you should clearly devote most time to improving your answer to the last question.

b) HAVE I WRITTEN RELEVANTLY?

Stress has been put on the importance of relevance more than once in this book. In written papers, where candidates are all being assessed on the same range of tasks, it is a serious weakness to stand out as not fulfilling the necessary requirements, but instead, doing something either quite different, or only roughly related to the task in hand. It is good advice not to try to be widly original or experimental in an examination. By all means, if you have what seems like a very good idea for an answer and are keen to try it out, do so, but not before asking yourself firmly: 'Am I really answering the question or am I indulging a personal enthusiasm which is taking me away from the question?' As has already been stated (see Chapter 16) ingenious interpretations of topics, or writing on something you have prepared beforehand and so must attach to a topic, are all best avoided. This advice has been given before, but it is worth repeating. An experienced teacher and examiner always said the following to her pupils in the final lesson before a written examination: 'I have three pieces of advice to give if you hope to succeed in the examination – be relevant, BE RELEVANT and BE RELEVANT!'

If you find, when checking your paper, that you haven't been strictly relevant you may sometimes be able to do something about it. Suppose, for example, that you had written an essay with the title 'Junk Food'. You had started quite relevantly in the first paragraph, explaining that you enjoyed eating junk food, but that it was never provided at home. You then wrote three or four paragraphs describing the wonderful traditional meals cooked for you by your mother, which you also loved eating, and had finished with an account of a recent particularly splendid meal. A moment's reflection then told you that you had wandered from the point and, in a way, reasonably, because you rarely had the chance to get any junk food. You could, in such a case, quickly make a few insertions. In the central stretch of the essay, you could slip in occasional remarks, such as *'far from spending Saturdays eating hamburgers . . .* we always have grilled fish . . .', etc., or add something along the lines of 'When Sunday lunch comes I find on my plate roast beef baked potatoes, Yorkshire pudding and cauliflower, *not Kentucky Fried Chicken'.* In conclusion, you could add *'I do really enjoy eating junk food, on the rare occasions that I have the opportunity to get some . . .'* This would not be ideal, but it would signal to the marker your intentions to bear the title in mind in the writing.

c) HAVE I WRITTEN ACCURATELY?

Obviously, in written papers, whatever the audience you appear to be addressing in your work, the actual reader will be the examiner and he or she will be comparing your work with that of others. Part of his or her concern will be with how well you are acquainted, not only with the grammatical structures and vocabulary of the English language, but also with what may be called 'the conventions of written English': correct spelling and punctuation. He or she will also much prefer you to write legibly. It is doubtful if you will have time at the end of an examination to work on the grammar of your answers, but you may be able to improve the punctuation and spelling, especially if you are allowed to use a dictionary.

Before leaving the examination you should make some final checks.

First, look at the cover of your answer book. Are your name, examination number and Centre number clear and correct? Have you listed the numbers of questions and parts of questions you have chosen, in the order you have answered them?

Next, check that you have numbered each question, or part of a question, clearly within the answer book. Also, cross through all rough work or false starts – anything you do not want to be assessed.

Finally, make sure that any supplementary sheets are firmly attached to your answer book!

66 Finally . . . 99

2 > **CHECKING COURSEWORK**

A piece of coursework will often exist in draft for some time before it is submitted for assessment, and so there may be opportunities for your teacher, and perhaps some of your friends, to look at it critically and give you the benefit of their advice. There are three main forms of evaluation:

a) **Teacher evaluation**
b) **Pupil evaluation**
c) **Self-evaluation**.

If you take advantage of all three, you should get a good deal of advice about how best to present your work.

a) TEACHER EVALUATION

Sometimes your teacher or tutor may find time to discuss a piece of coursework in school or college with you. Ideally your teacher's personal comments should help you a good deal. Also, try to go back over several of your pieces of work and build up a picture of your strengths and weaknesses, as they emerge from these comments. Teachers and tutors often complain that pupils seem to make no real use of the comments they spend so much time making on their work. As explained in Chapter 2, GCSE assessment is based on criteria, so remarks and marks on your work for the examination will be telling you how you measure up to the set criteria, as well as offering you personal encouragement and response.

b) PUPIL EVALUATION

Have you tried working with a friend, or in a small group, exchanging ideas about each others' work? You can discuss errors you have made (especially of spelling or punctuation), any parts of the work where you have not been quite clear, ways of developing good ideas that you have had, and possibly different ways of setting out or presenting the work.

c) SELF EVALUATION

66 Do you evaluate your work? 99

Your own checking is best done some time after finishing the piece of work, if possible, since you will then be able to look at it as editor, rather than creator. If the work is of some length, or incorporates different pieces of material, make sure it is properly arranged and easy to read. Now is the time to do any necessary pruning.

If your piece of coursework has been done under supervised or controlled conditions – and usually each folder should have at least one piece of this kind included in it – then you will have to depend upon yourself for the accuracy and presentation of the work. Most of your work, though, will probably be produced as part of normal classwork or homework.

When the work has reached the final draft stage, it is time to do some 'proof reading' or sometimes have an editorial conference with teacher, tutor or friends, as part of normal classwork. It is a good idea to get used to a set of symbols which will show eactly what needs to be done to correct the work. Below you will find detailed advice on how to do this. Remember that you should include the draft work, with the corrections made, and a note about the help given, along with your final piece for assessment in the examination folder.

USEFUL PRACTICAL APPROACHES

In the end, punctuation and spelling are probably the things most easy to improve in a piece of written work, so here are some final remarks on these matters.

1 > PUNCTUATION

66 **Don't forget the full stops!** 99

It is helpful to think of punctuation as marks to help the reader to follow more easily the sense of what is written. In the eighteenth and early nineteenth centuries punctuation marks were much more frequent in a piece of writing than they are today. The growth of modern business practice, among other developments, has led to much lighter punctuation. Even so, candidates in examinations sometimes write several pages without a single comma or full stop! That can mean that a reader has to go over stretches of the text again, to be sure of what is intended.

Punctuation can be used differently, according to what you are writing. It can pace your work most effectively. Consider the following examples:

a) As he entered the dark wood he suddenly felt tense: he could almost hear the silence. Then, suddenly, there was a sharp crack. Crash! The bough of a tree smashed through the thick canopy of leaves, somewhere to his right. He turned quickly. There was only a slight patter, as leaves settled on leaves.

b) 'But you did see the thief, didn't you!' she shouted, accusingly.
'Well . . . I can't be sure. It was so gloomy in the room. There was someone there, in the far corner, I believe.'

c) The grass was springy and fresh and Jack threw himself down on it and lay absent-mindedly, pulling at a blade of rye grass, gazing up at the clear, blue distant sky.

I think you will agree that each depends on punctuation to achieve very different effects. The first is dramatic and needs careful pacing to build up suspense gradually. The second is also dramatic, but more urgent: punctuation here suggests how the voice would emphasise particular words in speech, or in reading this aloud. The third is slow-paced. Only a comma or two is needed to indicate slight pauses.

Occasionally you may like to try working in a pair or as part of a group at an editorial discussion of draft work.

As you read through the piece you should indicate any mistakes you find by a mark in the text. Some of the marks used for this purpose are in the *central* column of the table below. At the same time, you also make an explanatory mark in the margin, level with the mark in the text – for these, see the *right-hand* column in the table. For example, if you think the writer should have started a new paragraph, you make the appropriate mark in the text and write 'n.p.' in the margin.

Table 20.1 gives a version of some of the symbols used by publishing houses for proof reading authors' work.

As you discuss the piece with others you may find sometimes that there is disagreement about, for instance, whether a comma is really needed, or a capital letter, in a particular case. Talking over these points will help you to learn more about the need for certain punctuation marks, as well as increase your own level of accuracy.

66 **Try a little proof-reading.** 99

Here is an example of a piece of a pupil's work corrected, using the marks given in the above table.

Moving House

It was dreadful weather when we moved house of course but as mum said that was only to be expected. The removal men came early they kept tramping through the house, bringing in mud from the garden. They went to and fro, lugging huge packing

Meaning of mark	Mark in text	Mark in margin
Word or letter left out	∧	∧ plus word or letter
Full stop left out	∧	⊙
Comma left out	∧	∱
Question mark left out	∧	?
Quotation marks left out	∧	⁹⁄
Apostrophe left out	∧	⁹⁄
Change to capitals	≡	cap
Begin a new paragraph	⊏	n.p.
Run two paragraphs together	⌐⌐	run on
Figures or abbreviations to be spelt out	encircle words or figures to be altered	spell out
Take out	/	∂⁄

Table 20.1

cases as if they were nothing at all. One labelled Glass – with care was half thrown into the back of the van. Mum said she felt relieved when the van finally drive off. The men seemed very cheerful because half of their work was over but we felt miserable to leave our old house. As the van turned the corner I took a last look at out big apple tree the one where I use to swing on a tyre when I was little. I felt sadder and sadder all the way to the new house. It was only about ⑤ miles away, but it was in a totally different area. When we got to the new house, it looked horrible through the rain the garden was terribly overgown and the convolvulus was even creeping in at the window. Why did we have to come here, mum? I asked, but she just stared glumly through the car window. It really was an awful first impression.

2 ⟩ SPELLING

Good spelling habits.

If you follow the advice given in Chapter 4 about improving spelling for yourself you should not be too worried about it. Some students, though, have chronic spelling problems that are not easily overcome. If you feel that this a weak area for you, get a friend, or your teacher or tutor, to indicate which words are wrong in your work, but *not to write in the correct spellings*. It is more valuable for you to find out the correct version for yourself using, as appropriate, a dictionary, writing it down to see if your visual memory tells you that it 'looks right', applying an appropriate rule (if there is one), and (though this is least rewarding, since English is not a regularly phonetic language) 'sounding out' the word. The last is at least usually a check that you have the right consonants and number of syllables.

Don't let weak spelling loom too large in your thoughts. It should not be so very worrying, for example, if you try a word you do not often use, e.g. 'charismatic' or 'environmental', and get it wrong. The spellings to concentrate on first are those of commonly recurring words, and of words that you use frequently in a particular piece of work. If you can get those right, what you are trying to communicate will be clear to the reader, for the most part.

Although the advice given in this book is intended mainly to help you to prepare for the GCSE/Key Stage 4 examination in English, it may also extend your range of speaking, listening, reading and writing experiences. When the examination is over you should continue to enjoy doing some of these. If you do, you will also continue to improve your skills.

INDEX